Mann's Magic Mountain
World Literature and Closer Reading

OXFORD MODERN LANGUAGES AND LITERATURE MONOGRAPHS

Mann's Magic Mountain

World Literature and Closer Reading

KAROLINA WATROBA

OXFORD
UNIVERSITY PRESS

OXFORD
UNIVERSITY PRESS

Great Clarendon Street, Oxford, OX2 6DP,
United Kingdom

Oxford University Press is a department of the University of Oxford.
It furthers the University's objective of excellence in research, scholarship,
and education by publishing worldwide. Oxford is a registered trade mark of
Oxford University Press in the UK and in certain other countries

First Edition published in 2022

Impression: 1

Published in the United States of America by Oxford University Press
198 Madison Avenue, New York, NY 10016, United States of America

British Library Cataloguing in Publication Data
Data available

Library of Congress Control Number: 2022936455

ISBN 978-0-19-287179-4

DOI: 10.1093/oso/9780192871794.001.0001

Printed and bound in the UK by
Clays Ltd, Elcograf S.p.A.

Acknowledgements

Given my methodological outlook, it is not surprising that I can only ever think and write well with readers in mind. Ben Morgan was an extremely receptive first reader of my work—a fantastic doctoral supervisor, generous with his time, interested in even the most niche texts that I wanted to write about, and enthusiastic about my ideas from the start, but also ready to ask big, challenging questions about them in every supervision. Two other particularly important readers for this project were the two anonymous reviewers at Oxford University Press: I am very grateful to them for their close and careful engagement with my manuscript and their generous and sympathetic responses to it. I am indebted to the entire team at OUP too for seeing this project through to completion.

I would also like to thank my doctoral examiners—Ben Hutchinson and Ritchie Robertson—for their helpfully wide-ranging and thought-provoking questions and comments in the viva. Rey Conquer, Rita Felski, Kevin Hilliard, Rachael Hodge, Maciej Jaworski, Motohiro Kojima, Joanna Neilly, Jim Reed, Marina Soroka, Kasia Szymanska, and Gemma Tidman read drafts of various sections of the manuscript and responded with useful tips, valuable observations, and generous encouragement.

I am grateful for the opportunity to present and discuss parts of this project at the following conferences and seminars: 'The New Reception Studies' panel at the annual meeting of the ACLA in 2017, the 'Recycling the Canon' panel at the AGS conference in 2017, the colloquium for early career researchers organized by the Deutsche Thomas Mann-Gesellschaft at Deutsches Literaturarchiv Marbach in 2017, the 'Worlding Murakami' panel at the '40 Years with Murakami Haruki' conference in 2018, 'The Postlingual Turn' panel at the annual meeting of the ACLA in 2018, the colloquium 'The Representation of Central European Hotels, Spas and Resorts' at the Prokhorov Centre in 2018, the Ida Herz Lecture at the English Goethe Society in 2020, the conference 'Uses of Literature' at the University of Southern Denmark in 2021, as well as numerous more and less formal academic gatherings in Oxford. Some sections of this book were first published, in a revised form, in *The Publications of the English Goethe Society* and *The Point*, as indicated in relevant footnotes. I would like to thank the publishers and editors for allowing me to reuse this material here.

All Souls College was an exceptionally supportive environment in which to turn my doctoral thesis into a book, and I would not have been able to begin this project at all without graduate funding from the Ertegun Scholarship, the Clarendon Scholarship, and Merton College. One Ertegun friend, Conor

Brennan, proof-read the entire manuscript at an early stage. He caught some embarrassing typos, made enthusiastic comments whenever he thought I wrote something particularly good, and generously shared his 'Sprachgefühl' with me, tirelessly offering advice on the vicissitudes of English grammar and style.

Kacper Kowalczyk had to hear more about Thomas Mann and his readers than anybody else, and could probably write a whole book on the topic himself by now. But instead he lovingly supported me as I wrote mine. Thank you!

Contents

Contents

Introduction

1. Somehow Beside the Point?

Thomas Mann's novel *Der Zauberberg*, known in the English-speaking world as *The Magic Mountain*, tells the story of Hans Castorp, a young German man who voluntarily spends seven years in a tuberculosis sanatorium in Davos in the Swiss Alps, having initially come to visit his sick cousin.[1] To his surprise, he enjoys his stay there immensely. It gives him the time to think, talk, read, listen, love, learn, and unlearn: most of his days are dedicated to digesting food and ideas. When Mann's 1000-page-long novel was published in 1924, it quickly became a popular bestseller as well as a critical success in Germany. It was soon translated into numerous other languages and established Mann's international reputation, leading to his award of the Nobel Prize in Literature five years later. In time, *The Magic Mountain* has come to be seen as one of the masterpieces of European modernism and a powerful symbol of traditional learning and encyclopaedic erudition.

Outside Hans's sanatorium, the Berghof, the world is in crisis: the First World War is about to break out. But rather than leaving the sanatorium to pursue a career as a marine engineer, Hans turns to the edifice of human culture and different branches of learning, from philosophy to biology, and beyond. What good does it bring him? We are faced here with the foundational question that students and scholars of the humanities always come back to: what is the use of culture and learning in an age of crisis? *The Magic Mountain* is a novel about the uses of culture, but it is also a cultural text itself, one that Mann wrote in an attempt to think through the rising tensions in the Weimar Republic. In our age which, like many before it, often seems like one long, never-ending crisis, my study—*Mann's Magic Mountain: World Literature and Closer Reading*—seeks to understand how and why readers have used Mann's text over the years: how and why people read *The Magic Mountain*.

One might think that every study of *The Magic Mountain*, or of any literary text for that matter, is a study of its reading; very few are, however. Studies are written by academic readers who surprisingly often do not present themselves as readers

---

[1] Quotations from the novel in the text are taken from the following edition: Thomas Mann, *Der Zauberberg*, ed. Michael Neumann, GKFA (Frankfurt am Main: Fischer, 2002). All translations are mine unless otherwise stated. English translations from *Der Zauberberg* are taken from the following edition: Thomas Mann, *The Magic Mountain*, trans. John E. Woods (London: Everyman, 2005).

Mann's Magic Mountain: World Literature and Closer Reading. Karolina Watroba, Oxford University Press.
© Karolina Watroba 2022. DOI: 10.1093/oso/9780192871794.003.0001

at all. Exegetists, scholars, theorists, writers, teachers, yes—but not readers. In fact, many literary studies come across as attempts to erase the act of reading with its surges of emotion, moments of boredom, distraction, and interruption, difficulties, confusions, and uncertainties. The everyday activity of reading is replaced with 'a reading'—an academic interpretation.

If academic readers reflect on this erasure at all, they are likely to see it as justified by the valuable contribution their scholarship makes to how we understand the work in question. But who exactly are the 'we' here? Academic scholarship does not tend to be read by non-academic readers; it is mostly read by other academic readers, who are a small fraction of all readers—an exception, not the rule. Literature is not written for academic readers and is not read exclusively by them, yet most academic accounts of literary texts seem to tacitly assume as much. This is puzzling, given that one of the most powerful justifications for the academic study of literature is that the entire human species cares enormously about telling and being told stories.

Of course, I am not the only reader to marvel at the fact that academic readers rarely have meaningful conversations with non-academic readers, even though both groups are passionate about books, and, as I will argue later, 'there is a common reader in every professional critic'.[2] But before moving on to discuss some recent (and not so recent) academic approaches to this problem, which will form a theoretical background to my study of *The Magic Mountain*, I would like to introduce the most memorable articulation of the disconnect between academic and non-academic readers that I came across while working on this book. It is a passage from Elif Batuman's debut novel, *The Idiot* (2017), a finalist for the Pulitzer Prize for Fiction.

The protagonist Selin—a first-year undergraduate at Harvard—decides to attend a Russian literature seminar because Leo Tolstoy's *Anna Karenina* (1878) is one of her favourite books. But to her disappointment,

> everything the professors said seemed to be somehow beside the point. You wanted to know why Anna had to die, and instead they told you that nineteenth-century Russian landowners felt conflicted about whether they were really a part of Europe. The implication was that it was somehow naïve to want to talk about anything interesting, or to think that you would ever know anything important. I wasn't interested in society, or ancient people's money troubles. I wanted to know what books really meant. That was how my mother and I had always talked about literature. 'I need you to read this, too', she would say, handing me a *New Yorker* story in which an unhappily married man had to get a rabies shot, 'so you can tell me what it really means'.[3]

[2] Terry Eagleton, 'Not Just Anybody', *London Review of Books*, 39.1 (2017), 35–37, p. 35.
[3] Elif Batuman, *The Idiot* (New York: Penguin, 2018), p. 16.

What is so compelling about this passage—apart from Batuman's deadpan wit and penchant for the absurd, coupled with the lucidity of her language—is that her protagonist's plight in the novel is in fact not at all dissimilar from nineteenth-century Russian landowners' conflicting feelings 'about whether they were really a part of Europe'. Throughout *The Idiot*, Selin—a child of Turkish immigrants who grew up in the United States—is forced to navigate seemingly irreconcilable sets of cultural allegiances, too. Selin's problem with her literature professors, then, is not that their response to *Anna Karenina* is irrelevant to her interest in the novel. It is rather that her professors frame their motivation for studying Tolstoy's book differently, and consequently talk about *Anna Karenina* in terms that are meaningless to Selin, making her feel naïve and inept.

How could readers like Selin and her mother have meaningful conversations about the books they love with literature professors? It surely is an important question—and yet it does not often attract attention in literary scholarship, let alone guide the method of academic literary analysis. In this study of *The Magic Mountain*, I set myself the task of considering it more seriously. In this section of the Introduction I explain my motivations more fully, in Section 2 I discuss my methodology, and in Section 3 I sketch out my argument, chapter by chapter. For now, however, I will stay with Batuman's writing a little longer, for reasons that will soon become apparent.

As illustrated by the passage from *The Idiot*, the most common setting in which academic and non-academic readers meet is the undergraduate literature classroom, where professors try to mould 'naïve' readers into academic readers, either through explicit instruction or by modelling intellectual habits that students are expected to pick up. In portraying Selin's immersion in this process at Harvard, Batuman channels her own experiences: she too went to Harvard and studied literature there in the 1990s. Her first book—*The Possessed: Adventures with Russian Books and the People Who Read Them* (2010), a collection of interconnected essays previously published in *The New Yorker* and other magazines—recounts the next few years of her life, which she spent studying for a PhD in Comparative Literature at Stanford.

This was a time when it might have seemed that Batuman had been successfully transformed into an academic reader: in 2007, she submitted her doctoral dissertation, which bore the suitably cryptic title 'The Windmill and the Giant: Double-Entry Bookkeeping in the Novel'. But in *The Possessed*, she retraces her steps and comes out as a non-academic reader. In a series of suggestive, whimsical essays, Batuman revisits the texts she studied during her doctoral degree as objects of passion and obsession rather than dispassionate analysis, and recounts her classes, research trips, and conferences she attended and helped organize, reflecting on the intellectual habits of academic readers with affection as well as a healthy dose of irony.

In the first paragraph of the introduction to *The Possessed*, Batuman asks: 'How does someone with no real academic aspirations end up spending seven years in suburban California studying the form of the Russian novel?'[4] An attentive reader of my own introduction might notice that the time span specified here is the same as the time that Hans Castorp spent in his Swiss sanatorium, a parallel that is not lost on Batuman either. This is the first paragraph of *The Possessed* in full:

> In Thomas Mann's *Magic Mountain*, a young man named Hans Castorp arrives at a Swiss sanatorium to visit his tubercular cousin for three weeks. Although Castorp himself does not have tuberculosis, he somehow ends up staying in that sanatorium for seven years. The plot of *The Magic Mountain* mirrors the history of its composition: Mann set out to write a short story, but ended up producing a 1,200-page novel. Despite the novel's complexity, its central question is very simple: How does someone who doesn't actually have tuberculosis end up spending seven years at a tuberculosis sanatorium? I often ask myself a similar question: How does someone with no real academic aspirations end up spending seven years in suburban California studying the form of the Russian novel?[5]

Elif Batuman features so prominently in the introduction to my own study because her work offers a particularly stimulating perspective on straddling the boundary between academic and non-academic reading and writing. In the different genres of her work—the elegant academic prose of her Stanford dissertation, the playful collection of essays that revisit her field of research from the perspective of a recovering academic, and the novel which fictionalizes her experience as an undergraduate student of literature—Batuman explores the potential of novelistic form to capture 'the protagonist's struggle to transform his arbitrary, fragmented, given experience into a narrative as meaningful as his favourite books'.[6] In this way, Batuman's writing articulates both real-life and fictional readers' attachments to literature, which are the subject of this book, too. How fitting that the novel selected by Batuman as the narrative lens through which to view her negotiation of the boundaries between academic and non-academic reading and writing is none other than *The Magic Mountain*.

Batuman's reference to Mann's novel can serve as a great introduction to the subject of this book too, that is, the cultural uses to which readers put books—*The Magic Mountain* being my main case study—and what these uses can tell us about the books themselves. In the words of Rita Felski, a critic whose work I turn to next, 'to propose that the meaning of literature lies in its uses is to open up for investigation a vast terrain of practices, expectations, emotions, hopes, dreams,

---

[4] Elif Batuman, *The Possessed: Adventures with Russian Books and the People Who Read Them* (New York: Farrar, Straus and Giroux, 2010), p. 4.
[5] Ibid.   [6] Ibid., p. 94.

and interpretations'.[7] In this first approximation of the uses to which *The Magic Mountain* can be and has been put, including by myself, we get a glimpse of the theme that runs throughout this book: Mann's 'Magic Mountain' as a space in which to explore the attractions and dangers of a life devoted to the self-indulgent cultivation of intellect. (Selin, the protagonist of *The Idiot*, reads *The Magic Mountain* too—in Hungary, where she works as an English teacher over the summer. 'I found a lot to relate to in *The Magic Mountain*', she notes; 'particularly how they ate breakfast twice a day.'[8] It is a useful reminder that Mann's novel is not quite about the ethereal life of the mind, but rather about various kinds of pleasure, ranging from the intellectual to the culinary.)

Some literary scholars who feel more at home in the world of academia than Elif Batuman have also written engagingly about bridging the gap between academic and non-academic readers. Rita Felski's work, quoted above, is a particularly influential recent example. I have already gestured towards her critical vocabulary when I talked about the cultural uses of books. In 2008—while Batuman was honing her voice as a non-academic reader with academic credentials—Felski took over as the general editor of *New Literary History* (an influential journal founded in 1969, aiming to 'inquire into the theoretical bases of practical criticism and, in doing so, re-examine the relation between past works and present critical and theoretical needs'[9]), and published a book called *Uses of Literature* in the Blackwell Manifestos series.

The front cover of Felski's book bears the endorsement of Gerald Graff, president of the Modern Language Association at the time. 'Rita Felski demonstrates the impossible', it says, namely 'that recent literary theorists and common readers not only have something to say to each other, but actually need one another'. Graff's distinction between 'literary theorists' and 'common readers' corresponds to my distinction between academic and non-academic readers. Other critics talk about 'lay', 'amateur', or 'general' readers as opposed to 'professional' readers. I find these terms imprecise and unnecessarily judgemental. The distinction between academic and non-academic is more effective at articulating the most important difference between these two groups of readers: their position within or outside academia with its peculiar institutionalized reading practices. The fact that Graff describes a set of suggestions for a meaningful conversation between academic and non-academic readers as an 'impossible' feat shows just how profound the disconnect between these two groups of readers has become.

Felski's argument, which she further developed in *The Limits of Critique* (2015), is that the default mode of engagement with literature in contemporary academia—whether in Freudian, Lacanian, Marxist, feminist, queer, or

---

[7] Rita Felski, *Uses of Literature* (Oxford: Blackwell, 2008) , p. 8.   [8] Batuman, *The Idiot*, p. 359.
[9] Ralph Cohen, 'The First Decade: Some Editorial Remarks', *New Literary History*, 10 (1979), 417–21, p. 417.

postcolonial criticism, or most other recent schools of criticism—is to approach literary texts suspiciously, as objects to be dissected and subsumed under a theoretical paradigm that can explain them away.[10] She is drawing here on Paul Ricoeur's famous description of Nietzsche, Marx, and Freud as 'les maîtres du soupçon'—'the masters of suspicion'.

What I term 'academic reading' largely overlaps with what Felski terms 'critique', especially given that in *Uses of Literature* she argues that even the critics who shrug at the omnipresence of 'ideological' literary theory, such as Marxism or feminism, are unable to engage with non-academic readers' approaches to literature. In a passage that resonates with Selin's experiences in *The Idiot*, Felski writes:

> faced with the disconcerting realization that people often turn to books for knowledge or entertainment, [critics] can only lament the naïveté of those unable or unwilling to read literature 'as literature'. To read in such a way, it turns out, means assenting to a view of art as impervious to comprehension, assimilation, or real-world consequence, perennially guarded by a forbidding 'do not touch' sign, its value adjudicated by a culture of connoisseurship and a seminar-room sensibility anxious to ward off the grubby handprints and smears of everyday life.[11]

Felski's 'seminar-room sensibility' corresponds to Batuman's portrayal of the Russian literature seminar, where Selin grasps instinctively that her professors (Felski's 'critics') find it 'naïve to want to talk about anything interesting, or to think that you would ever know anything important'—which is how she and her mother talk about books. Felski paints a similar picture of a hierarchical relationship between 'disconcerted' critics who 'can only lament [those readers'] naïveté' and non-academic readers who 'turn to books for knowledge or entertainment'. Selin and Batuman, with their desire to relate their own experiences to narratives of their favourite novels, threaten to leave their 'grubby handprints and smears of everyday life' on the critics' cherished books—or perhaps Books, written with a capital 'B' to reflect a 'theological' reverence at play here, as Felski puts it.[12]

How to expand the scope of academic reading to better reflect the everyday experience of reading? It is important to clarify here that neither Felski nor I wish to simply 'critique critique', as it were; we both agree that it has given rise to many fascinating readings of literary texts and theories of what literature is and what it does in the world. Felski's ambition, described here in *Critique and Postcritique*, a volume that she edited with Elizabeth S. Anker in 2017, is rather to 'shed fresh

[10] See Rita Felski, *The Limits of Critique* (Chicago: The University of Chicago Press, 2015).
[11] Felski, *Uses of Literature*, p. 5.   [12] See ibid., p. 4.

light on what have become ubiquitous ways of reading'[13] and 'reimagine the aims and practices of literary and cultural studies'.[14] Both this volume and *The Limits of Critique* focus more on the former than the latter goal, and offer fewer practical examples of what an alternative to critique could be than in Felski's earlier *Uses of Literature*, where she describes the experience of reading through the lens of four 'modes of textual engagement'[15]—recognition, enchantment, knowledge, and shock. Her most recent book, *Hooked: Art and Attachment* (2020), further develops this alternative approach to the academic study of both 'high art' and 'popular culture' by analysing three 'attachment devices that connect audiences to works of art: identification, attunement, and interpretation', as the back-cover blurb has it.[16]

Like many other scholars over the past couple of decades, Felski sees phenomenology and affect theory as two particularly powerful tools to create a new language for literary scholarship. 'Phenomenology' is a term adopted from philosophy, where it describes 'structures of consciousness as experienced from the first-person point of view'.[17] 'Affect' is a term adopted from psychology, where it describes 'emotion or subjectively experienced feeling'.[18] In many literary studies that employ these terms, though, it is unclear why one could not just use the more straightforward '(description of) experience' and 'feeling'/'emotion', respectively. Often when coming across a formulation like 'the phenomenology of affective states' in literary scholarship, I wonder what is gained by using such a phrase rather than asking more straightforwardly 'how it feels to experience emotions'. It is paradoxical that branches of literary scholarship that set out to better capture the everyday experience of reading and to 'call into question the mistrust of ordinary language and thought endemic to critique'[19] end up adopting more jargon, that is specialized language whose benefits are at best not clear and at worst non-existent. If our goal is to build bridges between academic and non-academic readers and we believe that 'suspicion of the commonplace and everyday risks entrenching the notion that critical thinking is the unique provenance of intellectuals—enclosing it within the rarefied space of the academy',[20] we should attend more seriously to the impact of linguistic and rhetorical choices we make in our writing. As literary scholars, we surely are very well equipped to do so.

---

[13] Elizabeth S. Anker and Rita Felski, 'Introduction', in *Critique and Postcritique*, ed. Elizabeth S. Anker and Rita Felski (Durham, NC: Duke University Press, 2017), pp. 1–28, p. 1.
[14] Ibid., p. 2.   [15] Felski, *Uses of Literature*, p. 14.
[16] Rita Felski, *Hooked: Art and Attachment* (Chicago: The University of Chicago Press, 2020).
[17] David Woodruff Smith, 'Phenomenology', in *The Stanford Encyclopedia of Philosophy*, ed. Edward N. Zalta <https://plato.stanford.edu/archives/sum2018/entries/phenomenology> [accessed 18 March 2019].
[18] Andrew M. Colman, *Oxford Dictionary of Psychology* (Oxford: Oxford University Press, 2015), p. 16.
[19] Anker and Felski, *Critique and Postcritique*, p. 14.   [20] Ibid.

In the Introduction to *Critique and Postcritique*, Felski and Anker persuasively rebut various ideological objections to their formulation of the critic's task, but they do not address the question of practical challenges to it. One such practical challenge lies in the fact that even though Blackwell Manifestos 'set out to engage and challenge the broadest range of readers, from undergraduates to postgraduates, university teachers and general readers',[21] *Uses of Literature* (published in that series) was highly unlikely to reach this kind of wide audience. This is because the stated goal of the series is undermined by its position in the book market: Felski's 150-page paperback, at £25, is in line with the price of academic publications purchased mostly by university libraries rather than that of non-fiction titles commonly available in bookshops. This is an external challenge faced by academics who want to follow in Felski's footsteps. But there is also a related internal challenge that needs to be addressed. To best explain its nature, I will revisit the circumstances under which I first read *Uses of Literature* and *The Limits of Critique*.

I first came across Rita Felski's work at around the time that I read David Lodge's *Campus Trilogy*. During the day, I would sit in my office and study *The Limits of Critique*; in the evening, I would come back home and flick open *Small World: An Academic Romance*, the second instalment of Lodge's trilogy. Published in 1984, when Lodge was a professor of English literature at Birmingham University, and set in 1979, *Small World* follows the adventures of several faculty members and graduate students from different universities as they keep running into each other at various academic conferences around the world over the course of several months. As the novel's subtitle indicates, its narrative structure is modelled on the genre of the romance, understood as a series of episodes in which the satisfaction of sexual desire is repeatedly deferred, and full of witty allusions to specific traditional romances, including Spenser's *The Faerie Queene* and Ariosto's *Orlando Furioso*. (At one point, one of the academic protagonists encourages an airport clerk to have a go at *Orlando Furioso* rather than resorting to her favourite Harlequin romances.) The novel's grand finale takes place at the MLA convention in New York, the 'megaconference'[22] organized annually by the Modern Language Association of North America (the organization of which Gerald Graff was president in 2008). Forty years on, Lodge's description of its annual convention in *Small World* is still eerily familiar.

The most talked-about event at the MLA in *Small World* is the forum on 'The Function of Criticism' which comprises five talks. Four of them can easily be subsumed under Felski's category of 'critique': a French professor argues for the merits of structuralist narratology, a German professor extols the methods of reader-response theory (in its most 'scientific spirit',[23] therefore dealing with

---

[21] Felski, *Uses of Literature*, p. ii.
[22] David Lodge, *Small World* (London: Vintage, 2011), p. 313.   [23] Ibid., p. 318.

'implied' or 'ideal' rather than real-life readers), an Italian professor offers an impassioned plea for Marxist criticism, and an American professor gives a provocative talk on deconstruction. But the very first speaker, an old-school British professor called Philip Swallow, describes a very different approach to literature:

> He said the function of criticism was to assist in the function of literature itself, which Dr Johnson had famously defined as enabling us better to enjoy life, or better to endure it. The great writers were men and women of exceptional wisdom, insight, and understanding. Their novels, plays and poems were inexhaustible reservoirs of values, ideas, images, which, when properly understood and appreciated, allowed us to live more fully, more finely, more intensely. But literary conventions changed, history changed, language changed, and these treasures too easily became locked away in libraries, covered with dust, neglected and forgotten. It was the job of the critic to unlock the drawers, blow away the dust, bring out the treasures into the light of day. Of course, he needed certain specialist skills to do this: a knowledge of history, a knowledge of philology, of generic convention and textual editing. But above all, he needed enthusiasm, the love of books. It was by the demonstration of this enthusiasm in action that the critic forged a bridge between the great writers and the general reader.[24]

Even though Felski makes the occasional gesture of distancing herself from the dogmas of literary studies before the rise of theory in the 1960s, many aspects of Swallow's conception of the function of criticism are surprisingly similar to hers. She would not endorse his normative talk of 'the great writers'—in *Uses of Literature* she discusses Henrik Ibsen alongside Hayao Miyazaki (a Japanese anime master) and Bertolt Brecht alongside Gayl Jones (a controversial African American novelist)—and her conception of literature's value is more capacious than Swallow's: she believes it can shock as well as reassure us. But there is a lot that Felski and Swallow have in common. They both take literature seriously as a source of knowledge and enjoyment, and as an instrument of self-intensification (all these concepts play an important role in *Uses of Literature*); they both value the curatorial function of literary scholarship as a valid form of expertise, distinct from but not inferior to critique; neither of them shies away from the powerful language of love; both use the metaphor of 'forging a bridge' to express the ideal of literary scholarship as an activity that connects literature to life, rather than separating them. There seems to be a lot that could endear Swallow to Felski.

But however likeable and quirky, Swallow—who represents the school of counter-theory widespread in Britain in the 1970s—is fearful of, even hostile to, any intellectual project that challenges his 'love of books'. In Lodge's novel, literary

[24] Ibid., p. 317.

theorists present their ideas as a rigorous and ambitious antidote to Swallow's spurious and complacent approach to the study of literature. As Siegfried Mews writes, Swallow comes across as 'a quaint dilettante' in comparison with other academics portrayed in Lodge's campus trilogy.[25] As Felski acknowledges, the exciting promise of theory—of critique—was the recognition that what we read and how we read are shaped by implicit theories about value, meaning, and understanding, and the call to make these theories explicit, to acknowledge their multiplicity, and to study their differences. This is the process in which Swallow stubbornly refuses to participate and in which the other academics in *Small World* revel. But there is a decisive twist: these highly specialized, 'hard-nosed profes- sional star[s]'[26]—the French narratologist, the American deconstructionist, and so on—are themselves satirized as smug and self-righteous. In other words, Lodge's novel does not glorify Swallow's approach to literature, but it does not blindly endorse his colleagues, the theorists, either. It simply shows that these different attitudes towards 'the function of criticism', with their respective attractions and shortcomings, coexist in academia.

What is the upshot of my discussion of *Small World*? Lodge's novel shows that the full spectrum of views on the function of literary criticism recently discussed by Felski has been in play since at least the 1970s. What is more, it registers the advantages and the disadvantages of *both* critique *and* its opposite, which in the context of his novel might be termed 'pre-critique'. Reading Lodge alongside Felski is a forceful reminder of an alternative history of engagement with literature in modern Western scholarship that predates the rise of theory, and which theory set out to correct. If Felski's alternative to critique is to be successful, it must address the shortcomings of Swallow's approach to literature. 'Post-critique' can only get us so far; if critique did not manage to solve the problems of 'pre-critique', just being mindful of critique's shortcomings will not be enough either.

So what is the solution to this problem? The first step is to notice what the texts by Batuman, Lodge, and Felski discussed so far have in common. In Lodge's *Small World*, Swallow advocates 'forg[ing] a bridge between the great writers and the general reader'. But he never actually talks to a single 'general reader', and his 'love of books' and of reading is exposed as a self-indulgent obsession rather than a public mission with a humanist agenda. (In *Changing Places*, where we first meet Swallow, we find out that 'in odd moments when nobler examples of the written word were not to hand he read attentively the backs of cornflakes packets'.[27] In *Nice Work*, the third and final instalment of Lodge's trilogy, a precariously employed English professor in Swallow's department works on Elizabeth Gaskell's industrial novel *North and South* but finds it excruciatingly

---

[25] Siegfried Mews, 'The Professor's Novel: David Lodge's *Small World*', *MLN*, 104 (1989), 713–26, p. 716.
[26] Ibid.   [27] David Lodge, *Changing Places* (London: Vintage, 2011), p. 11.

uncomfortable to talk to anybody who actually works in the industrial sector.) Selin, the protagonist of *The Idiot*, is made to feel stupid and naïve in a seminar on *Anna Karenina*, even though it is her favourite novel. In *The Possessed*, Batuman stages her own dilemmas as a passionate reader who does not feel fully at home in academia.

On the cover of Felski's *Uses of Literature*, Graff tells us that 'literary theorists and common readers [...] need one another', but the book was not in fact marketed to those 'common readers' at all, and in her other books Felski mostly addresses other academics like herself too. Despite her 'commitment to non-expert readers and ordinary life'[28] and her aim of 'narrow[ing] the gap between academic criticism and nonprofessional ways of reading',[29] in *Uses of Literature* and *The Limits of Critique* Felski only occasionally draws on reading experiences other than her own or those of other academics—something that she has in common with other critics who have recently called for the creation of more space to discuss non-academic experiences of reading in literary scholarship.[30]

In his characteristically animated review of *The Limits of Critique* in the *London Review of Books*, Terry Eagleton—who, as he disarmingly acknowledges, has 'been known to indulge in the practice [him]self'[31]—finds Felski's take on critique compelling and timely, and reiterates his commitment to literary scholarship that grips the attention of non-academic readers. But, he observes humorously yet aptly:

> it has always been an embarrassment to literary scholars that reading, along with talking about what you read, is something that a lot of non-scholarly people do as well. This is not the case with brain surgeons or analytic philosophers, whose professional status is untroubled by the awareness that ordinary men and women may be practising such pursuits in their front parlours.[32]

To repeat once more a question that I have already asked several times in this introductory chapter: how can academic readers have meaningful conversations with non-academic readers? The solution is obvious, and yet it has proven surprisingly difficult to implement. We need to listen to what other readers have to say about the books we study. In the next section, I discuss how to go about it.

---

[28] Heather Love, 'Critique Is Ordinary', *PMLA*, 132.2 (2017), 364–70, p. 367.   [29] Ibid., p. 368.
[30] See, for example, Philip Davis, *Reading and the Reader* (Oxford: Oxford University Press, 2013), and Evelyne Ender and Deidre Shauna Lynch, eds., 'Cultures of Reading' [special issue], *PMLA*, 134.1 (2019).
[31] Eagleton, 'Not Just Anybody', p. 35.   [32] Ibid., p. 37.

2. World Literature and Closer Reading

World literature and closer reading, the two concepts in this book's subtitle, have been particularly useful in puzzling over this problem. The first has been at the centre of comparative literary scholarship for about twenty years, since the publication of David Damrosch's *What Is World Literature?* in 2003,[33] and goes back much further, at least to Goethe's famous reflections on 'Weltliteratur' some two hundred years ago.[34] The various uses of this concept have two things in common. First, they displace the category of the nation as the most appropriate container for literary production, even though most literature departments have historically been organized around it. As Damrosch points out in his more recent book, *Comparing the Literatures: Literary Studies in a Global World* (2020):

> [National literature departments] have typically organized their studies in terms of a literary history divided into broad periods, subdivided into movements within periods. Each period and movement would have its particular canon of major and minor figures, who with few exceptions would have written in the national language, contributing to its refinement and to the prestige of the nation itself. Comparatists have often had an uneasy relation to national literatures conceived in these terms, whether through an ideological opposition to nationalism or through their impatience with the parochialism of national traditions seen as essentially self-contained entities.[35]

A world literature lens allows us to sidestep these limitations of national literary histories by building the corpus of study in a dramatically different way, through an emphasis on the circulation of literature around the world, seen as a process that does not take us away from 'what books really mean', as Selin might say, but very much into the heart of the matter. This is the second methodological insight that various successful uses of the concept of world literature have in common.

Circulation of texts can be studied in various ways. One prominent example of such methodologies is 'distant reading', in Franco Moretti's term[36]—a combination of surveys of large-scale literary histories and digital methods that can, for instance, map the publication of various editions and translations of a certain text. Another important example is book history, which pays special attention to the institutions and networks that fuel and sustain the movement of books, or

---

[33] David Damrosch, *What Is World Literature?* (Princeton, NJ: Princeton University Press, 2003).

[34] See Peter Goßens, *Weltliteratur. Modelle transnationaler Literaturwahrnehmung im 19. Jahrhundert* (Stuttgart: Metzler, 2011).

[35] David Damrosch, *Comparing the Literatures: Literary Studies in a Global World* (Princeton, NJ: Princeton University Press, 2020), p. 207.

[36] Franco Moretti, 'Conjectures on World Literature', *New Left Review*, 1 (2000), 54–68.

'bibliomigrancy', as B. Venkat Mani called it.[37] But there are other possibilities, too. We can tell the histories of texts by tracking their readings by individual, specific readers who left behind traces of their engagement with books. Such a 'midlevel' or 'midscale' perspective, as Rita Felski recently pointed out, often gets 'short shrift in the recurring spats between formalists and historicists' but is nevertheless 'key to clarifying why literature and art are worth attending to'.[38]

I propose to call such an approach 'closer reading', a term I encountered as the title of Laura Baudot's recent essay in *The Point*.[39] Her 'Closer Reading', subtitled 'Teaching Fiction at Work', recounts her experiences teaching literature to a range of professionals working at a big corporation, and its effects on her teaching methods in the undergraduate classroom at Oberlin, where she is a professor of English. The phrase 'closer reading' is not glossed further in the essay, and in fact does not appear outside of the title at all; it does not seem to have been used elsewhere either. But, as I will explain in a moment, the phrase immediately struck me. These two concepts—world literature and closer reading—offer inroads into the vast, messy terrain of reading habits, and they can help navigate my specific case study—various readings of *The Magic Mountain*.

How is the concept of world literature helpful here? To start with, *The Magic Mountain* is usually studied as a classic of German—or European, or Western—literature. Such an approach unhelpfully reduces its actual cultural reach. Mann's novel has also been influential—to varying extents—in places like Eastern Europe, Australia, Latin America, East Asia, the Middle East, and Central Africa. But even more importantly, once we stop expecting from *The Magic Mountain* qualities that we have been primed to expect from conservative literary canons, tied to constructs such as national culture or Western civilization, we may begin to notice other features of the text more easily. Read as a classic of European culture, *The Magic Mountain* is likely to be examined for characteristics such as seriousness, impenetrable complexity, difficulty. The necessity of deep study to get anything out of it will be assumed; mediation through educational institutions such as universities will be deemed the most appropriate. This way of reading has its unquestionable merits and rewards, and has produced many insightful studies of Mann's novel. My goal is not to discredit or abandon such readings, which may be termed academic, since they almost always take place as part of academic study and research: it is rather to point out that other readings are possible—and valuable—too. Read as a text that circulates around the world, *The Magic Mountain* can more easily be appreciated as a playful novel that pays attention to and is part of everyday life. Approaching Mann's novel as world literature can

---

[37] B. Venkat Mani, *Recoding World Literature: Libraries, Print Culture, and Germany's Pact with Books* (New York: Fordham University Press, 2017).

[38] Felski, *Hooked*, p. 144.

[39] Laura Baudot, 'Closer Reading', *The Point*, 19 (2019) <https://thepointmag.com/examined-life/closer-reading/> [accessed 1 May 2021].

bring to light readings that do not adhere to the rigorous protocols of literary scholarship but can nevertheless yield new, stimulating insights. A re-examination of the text itself through the lens of such readings will show that it can accommodate or even model unorthodox responses like these, that the text is in fact keenly interested in the role that books play in their readers' lives.

In other words, reading *The Magic Mountain* as a work of world literature allows us to mobilize more diverse resources for its study. Some are relatively well established by now, though arguably still not fully integrated into the mainstream of literary scholarship, at least not the scholarship on Mann's novel: the circulation of books, understood as both physical objects and the stories they tell; their life in translation; how they are often, to use Rebecca Walkowitz's term, 'born translated' themselves;[40] how their authors position themselves as international celebrities; and how books reflect, evoke, and help create complex networks of cultural, social, and political relations around the world. Liberated from a focus on one nation, one literary culture, a homogeneous linguistic context—all concepts which are themselves problematic, as scholars have been demonstrating over the last few decades—we can start noticing new possible research angles.

For example, two recent monographs on Thomas Mann have made use of a world-oriented optic to radically alter our view of his work. Tobias Boes's *Thomas Mann's War: Literature, Politics, and the World Republic of Letters* (2019) analyses Mann's international career from the 1920s until his death in 1955, often by studying archival materials and ideological aspects of the global circulation of his books, to show his savvy approach to questions of commercial and intellectual popularity, even celebrity.[41] Todd Kontje's *Thomas Mann's World: Empire, Race, and the Jewish Question* (2011) persuasively shows how Mann's 'deeply autobiographical fiction expressed not only the concerns of the German nation, as he liked to claim, but also of the world in an era of imperial conquest and global conflict'.[42] Veronika Fuechtner's forthcoming book on Thomas Mann's Brazilian-German mother Julia Mann, *née* da Silva Bruhns, similarly promises to 'radically alter the way we read not only Mann's writing but also his place within German literature, ultimately undermining the notion of canonical German literature and its unspoken assumption of racial and cultural homogeneity'.[43]

---

[40] Rebecca Walkowitz, *Born Translated: The Contemporary Novel in an Age of World Literature* (New York: Columbia University Press, 2015).

[41] Tobias Boes, *Thomas Mann's War: Literature, Politics, and the World Republic of Letters* (Ithaca, NY: Cornell University Press, 2019).

[42] Todd Kontje, *Thomas Mann's World: Empire, Race, and the Jewish Question* (Ann Arbor, MI: University of Michigan Press, 2011), dustjacket blurb.

[43] Veronika Fuechtner, 'The Magician's Mother: A Story of Coffee, Race, and German Culture', presented at The American Academy in Berlin, 14 February 2020 <https://www.americanacademy.de/videoaudio/the-magicians-mother-a-story-of-coffee-race-and-german-culture/> [accessed 1 May 2021].

Looking at such specific examples of the concept of world literature being put to good use is one way of responding to its common critiques. Gayatri Spivak, Emily Apter, and Ottmar Ette—all prominent critics of world literature studies as practised by Damrosch and others—detect a neo-colonial or hegemonic under-current in contemporary attempts to study culture on a global scale.[44] To conceive of a category that has such a broad scope as world literature, they argue, it is necessary to occupy a privileged position from which a broad view is possible, and which bestows authority on the observer. These claims are, of course, true with regard to any broad theoretical category. The stated aim of most world literature theories, though, is to counter the biases that have made most of the world's literature almost invisible, chief among them the propagation of conservative Western literary canons. Seen in this light, the fact that those very theories are now being developed largely by American scholars at American universities becomes deeply problematic. Moreover, as Damrosch acknowledges, 'it is the privilege of critics writing within a hegemonic power to mock "the nationalistic heresy" [...]. Among colonized or otherwise dominated populations, literature has long been a prime force for fostering national identity and rallying opposition to imperial or hegemonic powers, and [...] literary nation-building has often had a significant comparative and international dimension.'[45]

The most successful uses of the concept of world literature, however, are sensitive to these differences between national contexts and do not seek to make generalizing claims in pursuit of illusory universal truths about the totality of human culture. Rather, they painstakingly trace the lives of specific books in the world, cautiously working around the reigning paradigms of literary history, be it monolingual national literature or literary period, so they can dramatically reveal new networks of cultural connections. Some fifteen years ago Wai Chee Dimock asked: 'What would literary history look like if the field were divided, not into discrete periods, and not into discrete bodies of national literatures? What other organizing principles might come into play?'[46] The most refreshing scholarship inspired by the concept of world literature consists in case studies that develop such new organizing principles by describing how individual books exist in the world. This approach does not preclude illuminating generalizations (of which a national literature and literary period are perhaps the most prominent examples) but is not hampered by them. It most certainly does not require us to ignore the role played by social forces and political pressures either; if anything, it allows us to describe them in more fine-grained detail. It does not necessarily (and this

[44] See Gayatri Chakravorty Spivak, *Death of a Discipline* (New York: Columbia University Press, 2003), Emily Apter, *Against World Literature* (London: Verso, 2013), and Ottmar Ette, *WeltFraktale. Wege durch die Literaturen der Welt* (Stuttgart: Metzler, 2017).
[45] Damrosch, *Comparing the Literatures*, p. 208.
[46] Wai Chee Dimock, 'Genre as World System: Epic and Novel on Four Continents', *Narrative*, 14.1 (2006), 85–101, p. 85.

anxiety is perhaps the most widespread) spell the end of close reading: it is not, or at least not exclusively, about sociological surveys of huge data sets seeking to establish impersonal patterns of how literature works.

In her essay, 'What Was "Close Reading"? A Century of Method in Literary Studies', Barbara Herrnstein Smith shows how 'the practices of close reading have operated in literary studies not as one method among others'—such as structuralism, feminism, deconstruction, and many more—'but as virtually definitive of the field'; 'their ongoing performance may be the one constant in a field notorious for its succession of new "approaches"', she writes.[47] Close reading, then, is a practice fundamental to the study of literature, which involves paying close attention to the unfolding of meaning through the medium of language and literary form. Rather than giving a similar definition, however, the first sentence in the entry on 'close reading' in the *Oxford Research Encyclopedia of Literature* highlights another aspect of the practice: 'close reading describes a set of procedures and methods that distinguishes the scholarly apprehension of textual material from the more prosaic reading practices of everyday life'.[48] Indeed, close reading is not just an approach to texts, but also—or even more importantly—a mark of professional identity. The contrast between 'the scholarly apprehension of textual material' and 'the more prosaic reading practices of everyday life' brings us squarely back to the disconnect between academic and non-academic reading that I outlined at the beginning of this chapter.

As I argued there, this disconnect is a problem because it erects an unhelpful barrier between different kinds of readers, which in turn thwarts our understanding of what reading is all about. 'Close reading directs us to the words on the page; yet critics may want to raise their eyes from the page and ask how these words connect to a larger world,' writes Felski in *Hooked*.[49] This is why I was so struck by the term 'closer reading' in the title of Laura Baudot's article about her experience as a professor venturing to talk about literature to readers outside the university walls. It sounded to me both like a bold answer to Moretti's distant reading, which has been causing such a stir for the past twenty years, and the next logical step after close reading. Closer reading is not an attempt to displace close reading, an extremely valuable practice which I have recourse to often throughout this book. At the same time, I share Felski's conviction 'that the social meanings of artworks are not encrypted in their depths—perceptible only to those trained in professional techniques of interpretation. Rather [...] any such meanings can be activated or actualised only by their differing audiences: calling for a rethinking of the fundamentals of aesthetic experience.'[50] In my usage, the comparative

---

[47] Barbara Herrnstein Smith, 'What Was "Close Reading"? A Century of Method in Literary Studies', *the minnesota review*, 87 (2016), 57–75, pp. 57–58.

[48] Mark Byron, 'Close Reading', in *Oxford Research Encyclopedia of Literature*, 25 March 2011 <https://doi.org/10.1093/acrefore/9780190201098.013.1014> [accessed 1 May 2021].

[49] Felski, *Hooked*, p. 19.   [50] Ibid., p. xiv.

suffix '-er' is meant to imbue the familiar phrase with the reality of reading that scholars have long attempted to bracket out. It invites an explicit reflection on the value of various reading practices and the deeply personal and emotional investments that make them worthwhile for readers.

Ultimately, academic and non-academic readings are not opposites; the distinction is more provocation than accurate description. It is meant as an invitation to notice the disconnect between what counts as a valuable reading within academia and outside it, and a rallying call for a more capacious understanding of which modes of reading can produce valuable insights about the meaning of books. As Felski notes, when it comes to 'what counts as evidence of people's reactions to movies or music or novels', 'no source can be definitive or unimpeachable', which means that we need to draw on 'a variety of examples: memoirs, works of fiction, critical essays, reflections on [our] own attachments, audience ethnographies, and online reviews'.[51] In my study of *The Magic Mountain*, I use most of those types of sources and more, following the lessons of reception studies.

In one shape or another, the study of reading has been part and parcel of literary scholarship for decades, and is associated nowadays by most scholars with 'Rezeptionsästhetik', or reader-response theory. Hans Robert Jauss and Wolfgang Iser, who founded the Konstanz School of 'Rezeptionsästhetik' in the late 1960s, made the most substantial German contribution to the development of literary theory in the twentieth century, and their theories were later developed in the United States under the name of reader-response theory, whose most prominent representative is Stanley Fish.[52] The most basic postulate of 'Rezeptionsästhetik' and reader-response theory is, to use Jane Tompkins's compelling metaphor, that meaning 'is not something one extracts from a poem, like a nut from its shell, but an experience one has in the course of reading'.[53] In other words, the study of reception does not do away with an interest in a literary text's meaning to focus instead on some vague idea of subjective opinions about it that this or that reader might happen to have; it is rather that scholars of reception can produce more compelling accounts of meaning by focusing on how readers arrive at it, and why it might differ from reader to reader.

But, as I indicated when introducing the German professor from Lodge's *Small World*, these theories deal predominantly with abstract models populated by

[51] Ibid., p. 38.
[52] For foundational texts of this tradition, see Hans Robert Jauss, *Literaturgeschichte als Provokation* (Frankfurt am Main: Suhrkamp, 1970), Wolfgang Iser, *Die Appellstruktur der Texte: Unbestimmtheit als Wirkungsbedingung literarischer Prosa* (Konstanz: Universitätsverlag, 1970), and Stanley Fish, *Is There a Text in This Class? The Authority of Interpretive Communities* (Cambridge, MA: Harvard University Press, 1980).
[53] Jane P. Tompkins, 'Introduction', in *Reader-Response Criticism: From Formalism to Post-Structuralism*, ed. Jane P. Tompkins (Baltimore, MD: Johns Hopkins University Press, 1980), pp. ix–xxvi, p. xvi.

'implied' and 'ideal' rather than real-life readers—that is, with theoretical concepts rather than evidence of everyday reading practices outside the university. As Ika Willis's book *Reception*, published in Routledge's New Critical Idiom series in 2018, powerfully demonstrates, though, reading and readers have also been investigated for decades in various other quarters of literary studies and related disciplines—even if few connections have so far been made between these different branches of scholarship, ranging from Biblical studies and classics to book history and cultural studies. In particular, the division of methods and approaches to 'high' and 'popular' culture is still very entrenched, but giving it up can be liberating—and productive. Jonathan Rose distinguishes between reception history's interest in 'professional intellectuals'—'literary and social critics, academics, clergymen'—and audience history's focus on 'the common reader—defined as any reader who did not read books for a living'.[54] As Felski points out, 'It is not that research on lay audiences is lacking—many such accounts have piled up over the years—and yet they've made barely a dent in prevailing views about what it means to be a sophisticated reader or discerning appreciator of art.'[55] In this book I aim to bridge this gap.

Willis is the first scholar to clearly and systematically capture the complex, multifarious field of scholarly engagement with reading, and show how all the available approaches to it are deeply interrelated. (Willis uses the terms 'reception' and 'reading' nearly interchangeably, and ultimately favours the term 'reception' because it is more capacious and does not privilege literature over other branches of art. I prefer 'reading' because it is more widely used in ordinary language and makes clearer the active nature of the experience.) She observes that reception is usually studied only in part, but that we will not be able to fully understand the activity of reading unless we relate all these disparate parts to each other.

In what follows, I list various types of evidence, and critical methods that build on them, that can be helpful in exploring the reception of *The Magic Mountain* specifically, in the many senses of the term 'reception' that Willis outlines. I include 'text-to-text' and 'text-to-reader' reception, to use her terms, as well as approaches that ask what it even means to read, and what institutional and sociocultural factors impact it powerfully. I point to studies of other texts where no comparable study of Mann's novel has yet been undertaken. I then give some examples of how I use these different types of evidence and critical methods in my study.

---

[54] Jonathan Rose, 'Rereading the English Common Reader: A Preface to a History of Audiences', *Journal of the History of Ideas*, 53.1 (1992), 47–70, p. 51.

[55] Felski, *Hooked*, p. 4.

Reviews and Famous Readers' Accounts
of Their Reading Experience

The most widely used sources of information about the reception of literary texts in literary scholarship are contemporary reviews; in the case of *The Magic Mountain*, there has hardly been any research beyond them.[56] Hugh Ridley, Michael Neumann, and Meike Schlutt discuss a selection of contemporary reviews of the novel in Germany and beyond.[57] Neumann also includes comments by some contemporary readers who are generally perceived as the most interesting intellectuals of the Weimar Republic, such as Walter Benjamin and Martin Heidegger. In 1975, to commemorate the hundredth anniversary of Mann's birth, Marcel Reich-Ranicki invited eighteen writers and thinkers to answer the question 'was bedeutet Ihnen Thomas Mann?' ('what does Thomas Mann mean to you?'). Their responses were first published in the *Frankfurter Allgemeine Zeitung* (*FAZ*) and ten years later revisited and compiled into a slim book.[58] Other similar examples include Susan Sontag's and Roland Barthes's personal accounts of their experiences reading *The Magic Mountain*.[59] In general, though, literary critics tend to pay much less attention to reviews and reading accounts that are not contemporary with the publication of the text. This approach rests on assumptions about the value and meaning of literary texts that my study sets out to challenge, such as that a work can only be properly understood in the specific chronological—as well as geographical, linguistic, and sociocultural—context of its conception.[60]

[56] Hermann Kurzke, *Thomas Mann: Epoche, Werk, Wirkung* (Munich: Beck, 2010), p. 307. Even Holger Pils, *Thomas Manns 'geneigte Leser': die Publikationsgeschichte und populäre Rezeption der 'Bekenntnisse des Hochstaplers Felix Krull', 1911–1955* (Heidelberg: Universitätsverlag Winter, 2012), the most substantial reception study of any of Mann's novels, focuses mostly on press reviews.

[57] See Hugh Ridley, *The Problematic Bourgeois: Twentieth-Century Criticism on Thomas Mann's 'Buddenbrooks' and 'The Magic Mountain'* (Columbia, SC: Camden House, 1994), Michael Neumann, *Thomas Mann, 'Der Zauberberg': Kommentar*, GKFA (Frankfurt am Main: Fischer, 2002), pp. 103–26, and Meike Schlutt, *Der repräsentative Außenseiter: Thomas Mann und sein Werk im Spiegel der deutschen Presse 1898 bis 1933* (Frankfurt am Main: Peter Lang, 2002). See also Klaus Schröter, ed., *Thomas Mann im Urteil seiner Zeit: Dokumente 1891–1955* (Frankfurt am Main: Klostermann, 2000).

[58] See Marcel Reich-Ranicki, ed., *Was halten Sie von Thomas Mann?* (Frankfurt am Main: Fischer, 1988). See also Charles Neider, ed., *The Stature of Thomas Mann* (New York: New Directions, 1947), Heinz L. Arnold, ed., *Text und Kritik: Sonderband Thomas Mann* (Munich: Edition Text + Kritik, 1976), and Hans Jürgen Balmes, Jörg Bong, and Helmut Mayer, eds., 'Thomas Mann' [special issue], *Neue Rundschau*, 116.2 (2005).

[59] See Susan Sontag, 'Pilgrimage', in *A Companion to Thomas Mann's 'The Magic Mountain'*, ed. Stephen D. Dowden (Columbia, SC: Camden House, 1999), pp. 221–39, and Kate Briggs, *This Little Art* (London: Fitzcarraldo, 2017), where she discusses Barthes's life-long engagement with *The Magic Mountain*.

[60] For a well-articulated challenge to this wide-spread attitude, see Felski, *Uses of Literature*, pp. 10–11.

Ordinary Readers' Accounts of Their Reading Experience

Even less attention is usually paid to comments by readers who have no claim to fame comparable to Benjamin or Barthes. One reason why the aesthetic experiences of ordinary readers are less widely discussed in academic criticism is that written accounts of them are harder to come by. In some cases, including that of Thomas Mann, authors received fan mail; there are also examples of marginalia in readers' copies of books.[61] In 1984, Janice Radway demonstrated how scholars could go beyond these relatively rare and haphazard pieces of evidence in her pioneering ethnographic study *Reading the Romance*.[62] She constructed a theory of the genre of the romance based on extensive interviews with a closely knit group of female readers in a small American town and participatory observation of their book club meetings. Radway's next book, *A Feeling for Books*,[63] explored the Book of the Month Club—a quintessential US institution, which featured several of Mann's novels (but not *The Magic Mountain*), significantly impacting his sales in America.[64] With the rise of the internet, we have gained unprecedented access to a wealth of material, including blogs and reviews on websites such as Goodreads and Amazon. This gives us an opportunity to get an insight into written records of reading experiences by readers with different levels of education, as well as of different linguistic backgrounds, nationalities, ethnicities, races, genders, ages, and health levels (which can be particularly interesting in the case of *The Magic Mountain*, an iconic novel about illness).

Not Reading

An intriguing reversal of this type of research is the study of readers who fail to engage with a given book. Inspired by Pierre Bayard's claim in *How to Talk about Books You Haven't Read* that 'a book is less a book than it is the whole discussion about it',[65] and drawing on archival research, Priyasha Mukhopadhyay's work on book history in colonial South Asia explores the reading habits of 'unlikely readers': 'bored soldiers, savvy peasants, impatient office clerks, and aspirational

---

[61] For a compelling recent example of study of marginalia, see Andrew M. Stauffer, 'An Image in Lava: Annotation, Sentiment, and the Traces of Nineteenth-Century Reading', *PMLA*, 134.1 (2019), 81–98.

[62] See Janice Radway, *Reading the Romance* (Chapel Hill, NC: University of North Carolina Press, 1991).

[63] See Janice Radway, *A Feeling for Books* (Chapel Hill, NC: University of North Carolina Press, 1997).

[64] See David Horton, *Thomas Mann in English: A Study in Literary Translation* (New York: Bloomsbury, 2016), p. 3.

[65] Pierre Bayard, *How to Talk about Books You Haven't Read*, trans. Jeffrey Mehlman (New York: Bloomsbury, 2007), p. 150.

women'. These readers 'had always been marginal to reading publics, and yet derived their understanding of what it meant to inhabit empire through close and even intimate relationships' with the printed word—which, however, 'routinely went unread'.[66] Mukhopadhyay's research shows how much we can learn about books if we pay attention to the reasons why some people refuse or otherwise fail to read them. This approach acknowledges the fact that readers are usually informed by widely held ideas about a particular book without ever having read it. In the case of *The Magic Mountain*, readers might, for example, develop an idea of the novel based on its academic reputation, or even from references in annual press reports on the World Economic Forum held in Davos.

Material Book History

Records held by S. Fischer Verlag and Mann's overseas publishers, including Alfred A. Knopf in the USA, as well as by public and private libraries, can also illuminate the relationship between *The Magic Mountain* and its readers. This includes sales figures, advertising campaigns, prices, and physical properties of various editions of the novel (is it hardback or paperback? published in one or two volumes? with high- or low-quality materials? what is the cover design?), loan records in libraries, as well as annotations and glosses in various personal and library copies. Invigorated by Robert Darnton's influential article 'First Steps Toward a History of Reading' from 1986,[67] literary historians have developed ingenious approaches to extrapolating information from such data, and linking it productively with other sources, such as reviews, letters, and diary entries, to provide both quantitative and qualitative (or macro- and micro-level) insights into the reading habits of all sorts of readers. For example, as I will discuss in Chapter 1, Wilhelm Haefs, Björn Weyand, Catherine Turner, and Tobias Boes have recently studied marketing strategies that were used to sell *The Magic Mountain* in Germany and the United States in the interwar period.[68]

---

[66] Private correspondence. See also Priyasha Mukhopadhyay, 'On Not Reading *The Soldier's Pocketbook for Field Service*', *Journal of Victorian Culture*, 22.1 (2017), 40–56.

[67] See Robert Darnton, 'First Steps Toward a History of Reading', *Australian Journal of French Studies*, 23 (1986), 5–30.

[68] See Catherine Turner, *Marketing Modernism Between the Two World Wars* (Amherst, MA: University of Massachusetts Press, 2003), pp. 81–110; Wilhelm Haefs, 'Geist, Geld und Buch. Thomas Manns Aufstieg zum Erfolgsautor im S. Fischer Verlag in der Weimarer Republik', in *Die Erfindung des Schriftstellers Thomas Mann*, ed. Michael Ansel, Hans-Edwin Friedrich, and Gerhard Lauer (Berlin: De Gruyter, 2009), pp. 123–59; Björn Weyand, *Poetik der Marke: Konsumkultur und literarische Verfahren 1900–2000* (Berlin: De Gruyter, 2013); Tobias Boes, 'Thomas Mann, World Author: Representation and Autonomy in the World Republic of Letters', *Seminar: A Journal of Germanic Studies*, 51 (2015), 132–47.

Translation Studies

The Magic Mountain began its life in translation even before it was first published in German: the Hungarian and Swedish translators started working on the novel's first sections while Mann was still finishing the final chapter.[69] The book was then translated into several European languages in the late 1920s, and has since been translated and re-translated into around thirty different languages, ranging from Chinese, Japanese, and Korean to Yiddish and Hebrew.[70] The twenty-first century alone saw the first Arabic translation (2010), as well as new Spanish, Portuguese, Italian, and French translations (2005, 2009, 2010, and 2016, respectively). Susan Bernofsky's new translation into English is forthcoming.[71] That many readers encounter *The Magic Mountain* in translation rather than in the original German, though, is not taken into account in most academic studies of it. David Horton's comparative reading of translations of *The Magic Mountain* by Helen Lowe-Porter (1927) and John E. Woods (1995) gives an idea of the impact of different translations on the reading experience.[72] Kate Briggs's book-length essay on literary translation focuses on translators themselves being readers, and among the most careful, meticulous, and highly attuned readers at that. With this in mind, she reconstructs a personal account of Lowe-Porter's work on Mann's novel, which she carried out in Oxford while her husband worked as a lecturer at the university.[73] More comparative translation-oriented approaches to canonical novels can be very illuminating too. 'Prismatic Jane Eyre', a research project currently underway at Oxford, brings together more than thirty scholars of different languages, whose 'collaborative experiment looks closely at Brontë's novel as it is translated into multiple languages, understanding this process as transformation and growth rather than as loss', and develops methods for 'comparative close reading [...] in a global context'.[74] In this way, 'Prismatic Jane Eyre' attempts to wrest the tools of digital humanities from the proponents of distant reading, often seen as a threat to the practice of close reading, and instead focuses on new reading experiences that are enabled by *Jane Eyre*'s journeys in translation.

---

[69] See Thomas Mann, *Selbstkommentare: 'Der Zauberberg'*, ed. Hans Wysling and Marianne Eich-Fischer (Frankfurt am Main: Fischer, 1993), p. 40.

[70] Georg Potempa, ed., *Thomas Mann-Bibliographie: Übersetzungen/Interviews* (Morsum/Sylt: Cicero Presse, 1997) lists all translations up to the late 1990s.

[71] See Susan Bernofsky, 'Fresh Air', *The Berlin Journal*, 34 (2020), 58–59.

[72] See Horton, *Thomas Mann in English*, pp. 83–121.   [73] See Briggs, *This Little Art*.

[74] Matthew Reynolds, 'Prismatic Translation' <http://www.occt.ox.ac.uk/research/prismatic-translation> [accessed 22 March 2019].

'Implied' or 'Ideal' Readers

Rather than considering accounts of real-life readers, or openly relying on their own reading experiences, literary scholars often discuss so-called 'implied' or 'ideal' readers. Both these terms are used to denote 'a hypothetical reader'—one 'towards whom the text is directed' in that it is he or she who 'would be best equipped [...] to get the most out of a particular text'—'equipped in terms of knowledge, sympathies and prejudices, strategies of reading, previous experience of reading', expectations, and so on.[75] But this normative conception of an abstract reader implied by the text can be extremely limiting when one considers its actual, real-life readers. Hermann Kurzke begins his authoritative monograph, *Thomas Mann: Epoche, Werk, Wirkung* by describing 'der beste Thomas-Mann-Leser'[76]— a blend of an 'ideal' reader and Mann's real-life readership—which makes him reach rather short-sighted conclusions about who can productively read Mann in the twenty-first century:

> Der beste Thomas-Mann-Leser ist immer noch ein Bildungsbürger auf Abwegen, der sich nicht mehr mit den Interessen seiner Klasse identifiziert, aber auch keine andere Heimat findet. Bürgerliche Bildung und Erziehung ist schon deshalb eine schwer ersetzbare Voraussetzung fruchtbarer Thomas-Mann-Lektüre, weil man [...] die Konventionen kennen muss, wenn man ihre ironische Verfremdung wahrnehmen will. Hier hat es große Verluste gegeben, die nur schwer durch das Surrogat schulischer und akademischer Nachhilfe ausgeglichen werden können.

> The best reader of Thomas Mann is still a traditionally educated middle-class man gone astray, one who no longer identifies with the interests of his class but who has not found any other spiritual home either. If nothing else, traditional middle-class 'Bildung' is a nearly indispensable prerequisite for a fruitful reading of Thomas Mann because one [...] needs to be familiar with the various conventions to properly appreciate their ironic subversion. Great losses have been sustained in this respect, losses that can hardly be offset by the surrogate of instruction in schools and at universities.[77]

Judging by this, the only readers these days who can truly appreciate and enjoy Thomas Mann are, it would seem, German academics who specialize in his work. All readers outside Germany are doomed from the start, since they will not have had a chance to experience first-hand the characteristically German model of 'Bildung', namely, cultural education imbued with moral ideas about the forma-tion of the character and the integration of the individual into society. But even

---

[75] Andrew Bennett, ed., *Readers and Reading* (Abingdon: Routledge, 2013), p. 236.
[76] Kurzke, *Thomas Mann: Epoche, Werk, Wirkung*, pp. 14–15.   [77] Ibid., p. 15.

among German readers, only those of a certain class stand a chance—those
from good bourgeois families, whose forefathers resembled Mann's own proto-
plasts, but who have grown critical of their milieu. The world is changing,
though, and with every generation the traditions of early twentieth-century
'Bildungsbürgertum' are fading away, making it nearly impossible to educate
young Germans on such matters at school or even at university. The implication
is that, in the end, the only men left standing (for it is 'der beste Thomas-Mann-
Leser' not 'Leserin' that Kurzke considers here) are those belonging to an older
generation of German literature professors whose research is devoted to Thomas
Mann. As my study of various readers of *The Magic Mountain* demonstrates,
Kurzke's assessment is deeply reductive. It is not the case that non-academic
readers who know little about Schopenhauer, Nietzsche, Wagner, Novalis, the
tradition of the 'Bildungsroman', or Thomas Mann's evolving political views never
read *The Magic Mountain*, or read it without any degree of sophistication. On the
contrary: looking at how non-academic readers approach Mann's novel and come
to enjoy it demonstrates the vast scope of possible readerly responses to the novel
and shows that academic readings are but a tiny fraction of them. Taking stock of
the variety of responses to the novel can help us create a productive exchange
between different sorts of readers and readings, and help us better understand
Mann's novel and its enduring cultural appeal—an appeal of which readers locked
in the ivory tower of academia seem almost entirely unaware.

Fictional Depictions of Reading

Another way of countering Kurzke's model of how best to read Thomas Mann is
to look at scenes of reading (or reception, to use Ika Willis's broader term) in *The
Magic Mountain* itself, as well as at scenes of reading *The Magic Mountain* in later
texts. I will discuss both in turn. Hans Castorp spends a lot of time in the
sanatorium reading books and responding to other works of art. He discards his
English textbook on ocean steamships in favour of handbooks on biology and
anatomy and looks down on other patients who pass around a French guide to
flirtation; he watches an early black-and-white film in the cinema; listens to his
favourite classical music on the gramophone; marvels at a medieval Pietà sculpture; attends lectures on psychoanalysis; hears about various strands of European
philosophy from Settembrini and Naphta, and so on.[78] To borrow Hermann
J. Weigand's phrase from his early study of *The Magic Mountain*, whenever
Hans reads, sees, or hears something interesting, 'the knowledge he absorbs ceases
to be mere knowledge. It becomes completely integrated with the emotional core

---

[78] See Massimo Bonifazio, '"Non si leggeva poco...". Considerazioni su Hans Castorp lettore',
Bollettino dell'Associazione italiana di germanistica, iv (2011), 83–95.

of his personality. It becomes part of his living tissue.'[79] Decades later, Anthony Heilbut put it somewhat more irreverently: 'although [Hans is] capable of great bouts of research, his purpose is never scholarly. His discoveries shrivel into little nuggets of detail, retained only if they are emotionally useful'; Mann's 'sporadically inquisitive hero was made for the Internet'.[80] Hans's encounters or—to use the novel's own idiom—'experiments' with culture in *The Magic Mountain* can be read as models for our own experimental encounters with Mann's novel.

There are also numerous characters in later novels, short stories, and films who are portrayed reading Mann's novel. The first such scene I came across appears in a short story published in 1927, just three years after *The Magic Mountain*, and written by none other than Vladimir Nabokov, at that point a young Russian immigrant living in Berlin. The story is called 'Podlets' (literally 'The Scoundrel', but known in English as 'An Affair of Honor') and its protagonist feverishly reads about Settembrini and Naphta's duel in *The Magic Mountain* in the middle of the night, awaiting his own duel with a man pointedly named Berg, who is having an affair with his wife.[81] Nabokov's protagonist could hardly be more different from Elif Batuman's Selin, who, in a novel published exactly ninety years after 'An Affair of Honor', reads *The Magic Mountain* on her summer trip to Europe and relates to how the characters in the novel 'ate breakfast twice a day' more than anything else. As these two very different examples illustrate, reading Mann's novel through the lens of its uses in later texts can drastically and imaginatively expand our conception of what it is about *The Magic Mountain* that can strike a chord with its readers—understood as both later writers, and the literary characters that they create.

Cognitive Literary Studies

Those who worry that analysing literary depictions of fictional characters reading *The Magic Mountain* takes us further away from the everyday activity of reading and deeper into the realm of fiction might turn to cognitive literary studies, a discipline which sets out to explore the very mechanisms underlying our ability and inclination to read fiction. In the last couple of decades, psychologists and cognitive scientists have started carrying out laboratory experiments on readers, such as brain scans to measure brain activity during reading. Keith Oatley's *Such Stuff as Dreams: The Psychology of Fiction* (2011) and Terence Cave's *Thinking with Literature: Towards a Cognitive Criticism* (2016) are two influential examples

---

[79] Hermann J. Weigand, *'The Magic Mountain': A Study of Thomas Mann's Novel 'Der Zauberberg'* (Chapel Hill, NC: University of North Carolina Press, 1964), p. 142.
[80] Anthony Heilbut, *Thomas Mann: Eros & Literature* (London: Macmillan, 1996), pp. 408 and 398.
[81] Vladimir Nabokov, 'An Affair of Honor', in *Nabokov's Quartet*, trans. Dmitri Nabokov (London: Panther, 1969), pp. 11–49.

of overviews of the field written by a psychologist and a literary scholar, respectively, focusing on a number of cognitive mechanisms that underlie readers' experiences of literature. These include building mental models of spaces and situations, activating mirror neurons, identifying with characters as a tool to develop empathy, sustaining attention, and so on. The attraction of cognitive literary studies is that they promise to provide rigorous scientific tools to capture the biological underpinnings of our reading experiences. The explanatory power of such approaches has been limited so far, however. In an attempt to provide an objective and generalizable description of how and why we read, cognitive literary studies often impoverish the rich personal involvements with books that individual readers are able to forge. That said, the rapidly developing technologies available for such experiments coupled with an increasingly sophisticated design of the experiments themselves might yield more interesting results in the future.

Reception in Literature and Art

Texts inspire other texts in various ways. At one end of the spectrum are the adaptations that retell a story in a new medium. *The Magic Mountain* has been filmed twice (to little critical acclaim), and has had many theatre, opera, and radio adaptations as well.[82] At the other end of the spectrum one can posit putative connections between *The Magic Mountain* and texts that are, say, also set in a sanatorium and display some features comparable to Mann's work, but do not explicitly allude to it.[83] In between these two poles there are numerous texts and artworks in different genres and media that explicitly engage with *The Magic Mountain*, to varying degrees. I have identified over a hundred such artworks: paintings, poems, songs, short stories, essays, but mostly novels and films, spanning ten decades, ten languages, and fifteen countries on five continents. The most interesting among these texts create new imaginary worlds inhabited by Mann's memorable characters from *The Magic Mountain* or fill Mann's remarkable setting on the 'Magic Mountain' with new characters and new stories. Some of these texts and films were written and directed by canonical figures, including Vladimir Nabokov, Erich Maria Remarque, Vittorio De Sica, Thomas Bernhard,

---

[82]   See Peter Zander, *Thomas Mann im Kino* (Berlin: Bertz + Fischer, 2005). See also Philip Kitcher, *Deaths in Venice: The Cases of Gustav von Aschenbach* (New York: Columbia University Press, 2016) for a recent discussion of *Death in Venice* alongside its two famous adaptations, Luchino Visconti's film from 1971 and Benjamin Britten's opera from 1973.

[83]   On the central position of *The Magic Mountain* in the micro-genre of sanatorium novels, see Vera Pohland, *Das Sanatorium als literarischer Ort* (Frankfurt am Main: Peter Lang, 1984) and Jens Herlth, 'Słodko-gorzkie heterotopie. Bruno Schulz i "tekst sanatoryjny" w europejskiej literaturze okresu międzywojennego', *Wielogłos: Pismo Wydziału Polonistyki UJ*, 2 (2013), 25–37. See also Karolina Watroba, 'Blind Spots on the Magic Mountain: Zofia Nałkowska's *Choucas* (1926)', *The Slavonic and East European Review*, 99.4 (2021), 676–98.

and Alice Munro; others by contemporary best-selling authors and Hollywood directors ranging from the popular Japanese writer Haruki Murakami to Gore Verbinski, of *Pirates of the Caribbean* fame; and others by little-known or forgotten authors, such as A. E. Ellis—an Oxford graduate who wrote a version of *The Magic Mountain* populated by Oxbridge students. Yet this robust cultural phenomenon had gone practically unnoticed in the vast scholarship on *The Magic Mountain*. In *Thomas Mann: Epoche, Werk, Wirkung*, Kurzke claims that the novel has had no literary afterlife to speak of, and only cites one novel from my corpus (*Castorp* by Paweł Huelle) as 'eine kuriose Sondererscheinung', 'a peculiar exception to the rule'.[84] It is telling that a quick survey of Wikipedia entries on *The Magic Mountain* in various European languages yields a list of more texts inspired by Mann's novel than a leading academic monograph does. This academic misrepresentation of the cultural field indicates that our understanding of what *The Magic Mountain* is, what it does to its readers, and how it manages to affect all segments of our cultural system, has been limited by the blind spots and biases of traditional scholarship.

History of Academic Reception

Of course, academic interpretations of *The Magic Mountain* offer myriads of insights into various possible responses to the novel too. However, by placing this type of evidence of readerly encounters with *The Magic Mountain* in the context of all other types of evidence, we can fully appreciate how limited our perspective will remain if we only pay attention to other academic readers of Mann's novel. As fascinating and stimulating as many academic interpretations undoubtedly are, overall, the scholarship on *The Magic Mountain* is extremely unbalanced in that it tends to completely elide the experience of non-academic readers. One consequence of this is that, in stark contrast to the history of its non-academic reception, the history of its academic reception has been very well documented and studied. In English, the most extensive treatment can be found in Hugh Ridley's *The Problematic Bourgeois: Twentieth-Century Criticism on Thomas Mann's 'Buddenbrooks' and 'The Magic Mountain'*; in German, extensive bibliographies of secondary criticism on the novel are available and detailed literature surveys are regularly published.[85] They focus almost exclusively on academic scholarship in the German- and English-speaking world, with some

[84] Kurzke, *Thomas Mann: Epoche, Werk, Wirkung*, p. 322. See also Horton, *Thomas Mann in English*, p. 222.
[85] See Ridley, *The Problematic Bourgeois*; Herbert Lehnert, *Thomas-Mann-Forschung: Ein Bericht* (Stuttgart: Metzler, 1969); Hermann Kurzke, *Thomas-Mann-Forschung, 1969–1976: Ein kritischer Bericht* (Frankfurt am Main: Fischer, 1977); Hermann Kurzke, ed., *Stationen der Thomas-Mann-Forschung: Aufsätze seit 1970* (Würzburg: Königshausen & Neumann, 1985), pp. 7–14; Heinrich

attention paid to other major Western European languages, but almost none to countries further afield—even though Thomas Mann has been widely studied for decades in regions ranging from Eastern Europe to Latin America to East Asia, often with a particular emphasis on *The Magic Mountain*.[86]

In addition to a purely historical approach, the academic reception of Mann's novel can be studied as a sociocultural phenomenon. One could analyse trends in the study of Thomas Mann relative to other writers, considering the fluctuating numbers and shifting topics of doctoral theses, academic publications, and conferences on Mann compared to those on other writers.[87] One could also study the activities of the two major Thomas Mann societies—the Deutsche Thomas Mann-Gesellschaft (Lübeck) and Thomas Mann Gesellschaft Zürich—and the research activities undertaken by the Thomas Mann Archive at the ETH Zurich.[88] Another angle would be to gather data on when and where it has been taught as a set text, whether at school or university, as part of which degrees, in which classes or modules, alongside which other texts, and so on.

* * *

Most scholars of *The Magic Mountain* draw solely on other academic interpretations of the novel; in some cases, they mention in passing one or two of the other types of evidence I outlined above. In this study I make use of as many of them as I can, based on the availability of material and its interest in relation to my argument about academic and non-academic reading, and consider the potential for drawing intriguing connections between these different kinds of sources. This is what I take to be the greatest advantage of studying literature and culture from the perspective of their reception: that we can see how readers very different from ourselves respond to the texts we cherish, and can find a language for talking about these texts that makes sense to us as well as these other readers.

Detering and Stephan Stachorski, eds., *Thomas Mann: Neue Wege der Forschung* (Darmstadt: WBG, 2008) , pp. 7–12; and Helmut Koopmann, ed., *Thomas-Mann-Handbuch* (Stuttgart: A. Kröner, 2001), pp. 941–1007.

[86] See Changshan Shu, *Die Rezeption Thomas Manns in China* (Frankfurt am Main: Peter Lang, 1995); Tsunekazu Murata, 'Thomas Mann in Japan', in *Thomas Mann 1875–1975: Vorträge in München—Zürich—Lübeck*, ed. Beatrix Bludau, Eckhard Heftrich, and Helmut Koopmann (Frankfurt am Main: Fischer, 1977), pp. 434–46; Yasumasa Oguro, 'Die Brechungen der modernen japanischen Literatur: Thomas Mann bei Yukio Mishima, Kunio Tsuji und Haruki Murakami', *Neue Beiträge zur Germanistik*, 2.4 (2003), 107–21; Young-Ok Kim, 'Übernahme, Anverwandlung, Umgestaltung. Thomas Mann in der koreanischen Literatur', *Zeitschrift für Germanistik*, 7 (1997), 9–24; Katarzyna Bałżewska, '*Czarodziejska góra*' w literaturze polskiej: ślady/interpretacje/nawiązania (Katowice: Śląsk, 2018); Carlos Fuentes, 'How Zurich Invented the Modern World', *Salon*, 30 September 1997 <https://www.salon.com/1997/09/30/zurich> [accessed 10 May 2019].

[87] David Damrosch briefly discusses some data of this kind in *What Is World Literature?*, p. 188. Klaus Jonas and Holger R. Stunz, eds., *Die Internationalität der Brüder Mann: 100 Jahre Rezeption auf fünf Kontinenten (1907–2008)* (Frankfurt am Main: Klostermann, 2011), would be a useful resource for this kind of project.

[88] See Thomas Sprecher, ed., *Im Geiste der Genauigkeit. Das Thomas-Mann-Archiv der ETH Zürich 1956–2006* (Frankfurt am Main: Klostermann, 2006).

This common language will always be provisional and based on a narrow selection of all possible approaches to a given text. It is a recognition that is increasingly seen as central to any kind of meaningful comparative study. In the introduction to a recent issue of *Comparative Critical Studies*, the guest editors—who founded the Oxford Comparative Criticism and Translation research centre, of which I am a member—argue that 'to write comparative criticism is [...] to be aware of yourself as participating in the construction of one among many possible literary and cultural worlds'.[89] Accordingly, my goal in this study is not to provide a systematic overview of how *The Magic Mountain* has been read inside and outside academia. This is an impossible task: the data I have managed to access are extremely incomplete, often almost haphazard. On a more fundamental level, we will never identify *all* readers who have ever read *The Magic Mountain*, or chosen *not* to read it, and even if we could, we would still be faced with the problem that the experience of reading 'takes place inside a reader's mind and body, and must be represented in some form before we can access it'.[90] Rather than putting together a semblance of a taxonomy for my corpus of non-academic responses to *The Magic Mountain*, I set out to convey its excitement and whimsy. In short, I wanted to capture the appeal of culture, not destroy it.

Throughout this study I discuss novels and films that respond to *The Magic Mountain* and offer the most robust, complex, and imaginative perspectives on Mann's novel and what it means to its readers in my entire corpus. When interpreting these texts I often use traditional tools of comparative literature—the study of influences, similarities, and differences—to develop a more fine-tuned exploration of the uses to which Mann's novel has been put by its readers around the world over the past century. An integral part of my approach is that I relate these texts to various other types of accounts of reading experience, by both famous and ordinary readers of *The Magic Mountain*, including interpretations produced by academic readers. For example, I discuss the material history of the book and its use in tourist advertising alongside several novels and films that rework central motifs from *The Magic Mountain*; I relate psychological theories of why and how people read to models of reading in *The Magic Mountain* and its afterlives; I consider letters Mann received from his fans and recent blog posts about the book; I analyse a non-academic online book club and advertising campaigns and marketing strategies deployed by Mann's German and American publishers; and so on. By grouping disparate pieces of evidence together around a common thread, I uncover patterns in readerly engagement with *The Magic Mountain*.

---

[89] Matthew Reynolds, Mohamed-Salah Omri, and Ben Morgan, guest eds., 'Introduction', *Comparative Critical Studies*, 12 (2015), 147–59, p. 148.
[90] Ika Willis, *Reception* (Abingdon: Routledge, 2018), p. 39.

The concepts of world literature and closer reading go hand in hand in enabling us to do this. A 'closer reading' of Mann's novel as 'world literature', in the senses I have been outlining in this section, moves us beyond two unhelpfully narrow paradigms: that of academic reading and that of the national canon. In other words, enlarging the scope of the material that is potentially relevant to us as literary scholars enables us to cut new, more imaginative paths through it, rather than relying on a few well-established ways of categorizing culture. This is not to say that those established categories (national literature, literary period, and so on) should be abandoned altogether. Rather, the goal is to try and chart some new paths through the messy reality of reading to see Mann's novel afresh through the eyes of its many diverse readers.

In contemporary scholarship, the study of reception does not seem to have the same kind of cachet that world literature theory does, but its methods in fact undergird most of the best world literature studies. For example, all of the chapters in Damrosch's *What Is World Literature?* chart the reception of various books, starting with Eckermann's *Gespräche mit Goethe* (*Conversations with Goethe*, 1836) in the Introduction. In fact, Goethe himself used the term 'Weltliteratur' when telling Eckermann about his experience of reading Chinese and Serbian texts in translation, and soon Marx and Engels used the same term in *Das Kommunistische Manifest* (*The Communist Manifesto*, 1848) to describe the selling and buying of books around the world. World literature and reception go hand in hand, and my hope is that the term 'closer reading' recaptures some of the excitement that the best reception studies can generate.

3. Roadmap for the Journey Ahead

At the centre of this book are nine comparative readings of five novels, three films, and one short story that have been conceived as responses to *The Magic Mountain*. They provide access to distinct readings of Mann's text on three levels: they function as records of their authors' reading of Mann; they provide insights into broader, culturally and historically specific interpretations of the novel; and they—in most cases—feature portrayals of fictional readers of *The Magic Mountain*. These nine case studies are contextualized, complemented, enhanced, and expanded through references to dozens of other diverse sources that testify to a lively engagement with *The Magic Mountain* outside of academic scholarship. They include journalistic reviews, discussions on internet fora and blogs, personal essays and memoirs, marketing brochures from Davos (where the novel is set), advertisements used to sell the novel, Mann's fan mail and his replies to it, and other books and films that respond to *The Magic Mountain*. Most of the diverse sources discussed in this study have not been considered in the scholarship on Thomas Mann before.

This is also true of the main nine texts, which have been subject to little—in most cases no—critical commentary in the context of their relationship to Mann's novel, even though they comprise works by critically acclaimed and widely read contemporary authors (Alice Munro, Paweł Huelle, Haruki Murakami), historically important writers (Erich Kästner, Konstantin Fedin, A. E. Ellis), and prize-winning contemporary directors (Paolo Sorrentino, Hayao Miyazaki, Gore Verbinski). Encompassing, among other countries, Germany, Britain, the United States, Canada, Russia, Poland, and Japan, as well as spanning the full century since *The Magic Mountain*'s publication (with sources dating from the 1920s to the 2010s), this study aims to be both highly specific, thanks to its focus on the afterlife of one text, and wide-ranging, this focus providing a framework for discussing a century of diverse global cultural production across various media.

Where it appeared particularly helpful, I contextualized my discussion of *The Magic Mountain* with reference to Mann's other texts: *Buddenbrooks* (1901), *Der Tod in Venedig* (*Death in Venice*, 1912), *Doktor Faustus* (1947), his essays, diaries, and letters. But this is done sparingly, and intentionally so. An important part of my strategy in this book is to reinvigorate the study of *The Magic Mountain* by placing it in a radically different set of texts and contexts than is usually the case. Here Mann's novel does not appear primarily as a crucial node in his long writing career, nor is it read alongside Proust, Joyce, Musil, Kafka, Woolf, and other classics of German, French, and English modernism. Instead, attention is directed to texts that respond to *The Magic Mountain*, whether literary works by critically acclaimed authors, contemporary films, memoirs of Mann's readers, or online reviews of the novel. Reading Mann's novel alongside those texts allows us to read it afresh.

Each of the book's three chapters focuses on one aspect of *The Magic Mountain* that is almost entirely absent from academic discussions about the novel but is central to many non-academic responses to it: economy, emotions, and erudition. Chapter 1 is about readers who respond strongly to the economic structure underlying Mann's novel. Chapter 2 is about readers whose responses to the novel are highly emotional and inflected by personal experience. Chapter 3 is about readers who are particularly sensitive to the novel's intimations of erudition and intellectualism that can act as barriers to comprehension and pleasure. In this way, each chapter responds to an aspect of the reading experience that mainstream literary scholarship often ignores: what it takes to afford to read books—in terms of money, time, education, social and cultural capital; how books make people feel; and how academic reading advocated by literary scholars compares to what non-academic readers do with books.

Chapter 1: Economy

I start by outlining Thomas Mann's concerns about the readability of *The Magic Mountain* and the readership that the novel would reach. I then move on to a close reading of the novel's first pages, which—in a classic opening move—describe Hans Castorp's literal transportation from his lowland hometown Hamburg to Davos in the Swiss Alps. The reader's gradual immersion in the story-world as she moves through those first pages is analogous to the protagonist's immersion in his new environment, but various aspects of Hans's experience can at the same time act as a barrier to readerly immersion. I discuss a selection of records left by readers who experienced this tension specifically in the context of class identity. These records range from short comments to a fully fledged novel from the late 1930s—*Sanatorium Arktur* by Konstantin Fedin, one of the founding fathers of socialist realism in Soviet Russia. Just like Mann's novel, it is set in Davos, at a sanatorium whose patients grapple with the ideology behind *The Magic Mountain*, a novel that they find uniquely immersive, but—to use Settembrini's characterization of the power of music—politically suspect.

I relate Fedin's novel to *Der Zauberlehrling* (*The Sorcerer's Apprentice*), a text written at about the same time by Erich Kästner, who received a commission from the tourist board of Davos for an upbeat novel set in the town to counter the morbid association with tuberculosis supposedly propagated by *The Magic Mountain*. I place Fedin's propagandistic text and Kästner's commission along-side other traces of engagement with the novel, ranging from records of a Davos summer school in the 1920s, where a famous discussion between Martin Heidegger and Ernst Cassirer was seen by many to symbolically encapsulate the divergence of continental and analytical philosophical traditions in Europe, to the inception of World Economic Forum meetings. Taken together, all these pieces of evidence show how exceptionally effective Mann was at world-making: in his novel, he created a story-world so robust that it overshadowed the reality of Davos, and determined its public image and tourism marketing for years to come.

Mann was fully aware of the dynamic he had tapped into. Commenting on the novel's early sales, he wrote to a friend: 'ich habe, unter uns gesagt, an Eintrittsgeldern in mein mystisch-humoristisches Aquarium schon einige siebzig-tausend Mark verdient' ('between you and me, I have already made some 70,000 Marks on entry fees into my mystical-humorous aquarium').[91] His book was bringing in handsome profits—in 1925, 70,000 Marks was roughly five hundred times the monthly salary of a worker[92]—and its price was the entry fee into a

[91] Mann, *Selbstkommentare*, p. 56.
[92] See Gerd Hardach, '1929: Wirtschaft im Umbruch', in *Die Welt spielt Roulette. Zur Kultur der Moderne in der Krise 1927 bis 1932*, ed. Werner Möller (Frankfurt am Main: Campus, 2002), pp. 20–31, p. 22.

story-world in which a reader could be immersed as in an aquarium. Gore
Verbinski's recent Hollywood horror film *A Cure for Wellness*, which I discuss
at the end of this chapter, offers an arresting parallel to Mann's aquarium
metaphor. In a key scene the protagonist—a young banker, called Hans Castorp
in the original screenplay—enters a float tank as part of his water cure in a
luxurious Swiss spa, as the technician in charge of his treatment flips open a
copy of *The Magic Mountain*.

In Chapter 1, I analyse themes ranging from money, class, and ideology to
tourism and marketing, and explore what is at stake in the decision to enter the
immersive world of Mann's novel.

Chapter 2: Emotions

In this chapter, I trace the consequences of the decision to enter the world of *The
Magic Mountain*, whether with enthusiasm, diffidence, or reluctance. I discuss one
particular subset of readers who have found the novel uniquely engaging: readers
who have suffered from tuberculosis or another long-term illness themselves.
I move from fan mail which Thomas Mann received at various points in his life
from tubercular readers of *The Magic Mountain* to much more recent online
accounts of reading the novel by people convalescing from complicated surgeries
or suffering from terminal diseases. I extend my analysis of these individual cases
to more public-facing instances of the novel being perceived in this way, from the
more inconsequential, for example, the 2011 review in *The Guardian* that recommended *The Magic Mountain* as 'an essential purchase for every sickbed this
winter',[93] to the more profound, for example, the new art installation in the
Cancer Centre at Guy's Hospital in London, which was inspired by Mann's
novel. These real-life examples of engagement with *The Magic Mountain* set the
stage for a discussion of three literary texts that respond to Mann's novel in a
similar way—using it as a tool to navigate and negotiate culturally acceptable ways
of expressing, managing, and coming to terms with physical and psychological
suffering.

I first look at how Hans Castorp deals with his feelings in *The Magic Mountain*
at three different points in the novel: when he observes Clawdia Chauchat's
departure from the sanatorium, when he interacts with Ferdinand Wehsal after
her return, and when he listens to classical music after Joachim's death. These
examples showcase the productive ambiguities surrounding the culturally

---

[93] W. B. Gooderham, 'Winter Reads: *The Magic Mountain* by Thomas Mann', *The Guardian*, 14
December 2011 <http://www.theguardian.com/books/2011/dec/14/winter-reads-thomas-mann-magic-
mountain> [accessed 10 May 2019].

contested issue of emotional expression in Mann's novel. I then move on to show how three very different responses to *The Magic Mountain* use Mann's novel, alongside various other cultural texts, to navigate crises of their own. The three texts are A. E. Ellis's *The Rack* (1958), a half-forgotten English novel which was once included in the Penguin Modern Classics series; Haruki Murakami's *Norwegian Wood* (1987), a global bestseller from Japan, which sold more than ten million copies worldwide; and Alice Munro's short story 'Amundsen' (2012), published just a few months before the Canadian author was awarded the Nobel Prize in Literature.

In a gesture not dissimilar to the Davos tourist board's commissioning of Kästner to write an upbeat version of *The Magic Mountain*, Ellis unsuccessfully attempts to reject Mann's portrayal of a Swiss sanatorium and overwrite it with his own story. In contrast to Ellis, Murakami shows a young man who deeply engages with Mann's novel. The protagonist of *Norwegian Wood* reads *The Magic Mountain* while his love interest leaves for an isolated sanatorium in the Japanese mountains during the 1968 student movement. Similarly, Munro writes about a young woman who takes up a job at a tuberculosis sanatorium in rural Canada during the Second World War and attempts to make her new environment more manageable by likening it to the setting of *The Magic Mountain*. While this proves impossible, she ends up navigating her strained relationship with the head doctor through competing readings of *The Magic Mountain*, and thus—like young Munro herself, as we find out from 'Dear Life', an autobiographical essay published in the same collection as 'Amundsen'—carving out some intellectual independence for herself.

In Chapter 2, I consider themes of illness, suffering, heartbreak, marginalization, and entrapment to look at how some of the most engaged readers of *The Magic Mountain* have imaginatively written themselves into Mann's novel.

Chapter 3: Erudition

Having analysed the complexities of entering the story-world and motivations behind it in Chapter 1, and a range of deeply emotional encounters with *The Magic Mountain* in Chapter 2, in Chapter 3 I discuss the widespread scholarly assumption that the opposite of an emotionally engaged reading, which snaps the reader out of it, is critical reflection. This notion has a long history. At the time of *The Magic Mountain*'s publication, for example, Bertolt Brecht was insisting that modern theatre should prevent the spectator from emotionally engaging with a play's events (being 'in eine Bühnenaktion verwickelt' or 'hineinversetzt') and instead turn her into a critical observer, and early film theory was painting a chilling picture of an impressionable, defenceless spectator who surrenders herself to the spectacle ('sich [dem] Schauspiel hingibt').[94] Drawing on *The Magic Mountain* and the history of its reception, I destabilize the opposition between emotions and critical reflection.

I start by challenging a widely held view that *The Magic Mountain* privileges critical reflection over immersive reading and thus appeals only to highly erudite readers, drawing on Mann's own conception of his work, the metaphorical connotations of the novel's title and their impact on readers, advertising campaigns and marketing strategies deployed by Mann's German and American publishers, and various records of reading encounters with the novel. A key resource that I draw on here is Goodreads, a website where readers form online book clubs and together read a book, discussing it in real time over the course of a few months. I analyse the forum devoted to debates between Settembrini and Naphta and argue that *The Magic Mountain* was designed to make its reader feel like an intellectual imposter, but in the process the reader gets an exciting chance to dissect the cultural politics of erudition. I develop this argument by considering three recent afterlives of *The Magic Mountain* that are sensitive to this issue: Paweł Huelle's Polish novel *Castorp* (2004), Hayao Miyazaki's Japanese animated film *The Wind Rises* (2013), and Paolo Sorrentino's British/Italian film *Youth* (2015).

Castorp and *The Wind Rises*—a prequel and a sequel to *The Magic Mountain*, respectively—both feature Hans Castorp as a figure who is at once uniquely immersed in and reflective about his cultural environment. In Huelle's novel, Castorp—a young student in Danzig—rereads Theodor Fontane's *Effi Briest* (1895) and finds the novel singularly engaging, but this emotional experience of reading teaches him about the reality of German imperial expansion in Eastern Europe. In Miyazaki's film, Castorp—a dissident who has escaped from Nazi Germany to Japan—sings a German song about the attraction of immersion, but at the same time is the only character in the film fully aware of the fraught political situation in the run-up to the Second World War. Sorrentino's film, while a much more distant relative of Mann's novel, stages cultural anxiety about the relative merits of intellectualism and levity in art in a similar way, which suggests that this is one of the most powerful cultural tropes activated by *The Magic Mountain*. All three texts enter into a playful dialogue with Mann's novel, probing the boundary between emotions and critical reflection, and ultimately demonstrating that it is more porous than critics usually assume.

---

[94] Bertolt Brecht, 'Anmerkungen zur Oper *Aufstieg und Fall der Stadt Mahagonny*', in *Werke: Große Kommentierte Berliner und Frankfurter Ausgabe*, ed. Werner Hecht and others (Frankfurt am Main: Suhrkamp, 1988–98), xxiv: *Schriften 4: Texte zu Stücken*, ed. Peter Kraft (Frankfurt am Main: Suhrkamp, 1991), pp. 74–86, pp. 78 and 85; Hugo von Hofmannsthal, 'Der Ersatz für die Träume', in *Gesammelte Werke*, ed. Bernd Schoeller (Frankfurt am Main: Fischer, 1979–80), ix: *Reden und Aufsätze II: 1914–1924* (Frankfurt am Main: Fischer, 1979), pp. 141–45, p. 144.

In Chapter 3, I discuss themes of erudition, intellectualism, levity, reflection, and critique. I show how scholars, writers and readers have tried to delineate the boundaries of immersion, and argue that this issue is at the very heart of *The Magic Mountain* itself.

* * *

One of the main aims of my study is to show that all these records of reception— both real-life readers' records and cultural representations of *The Magic Mountain*'s readership—do not take us outside of the novel, but rather deeper inside it. *The Magic Mountain* registers with seismographic sensitivity cultural anxieties around the notions of erudition, sophistication, and taste—in short, it is about the anxiety of not being a good enough reader. This unresolved, pressing cultural anxiety embodied so eloquently and provocatively in and by *The Magic Mountain* comes to life again when I compare various encounters with Mann's novel, ranging from academic debates to online reading groups and from literary afterlives to Hollywood blockbusters. My analysis of them can help us better understand the book, which describes and produces an uncommonly immersive reading and learning experience. My recontextualization of Mann's novel shows that this text is much more receptive towards various unorthodox models of culture and learning than academic discussions of it would have us believe. Considering non-academic responses to *The Magic Mountain* alongside its reception in literary criticism affords a fresh perspective on what it means to interact with culture—which, as I argue, is what Mann's book is all about.

1
Economy

1. Introduction: Ordinary Young Man
with a Crocodile-skin Handbag

The train that Hans Castorp boards in Hamburg whisks him away from his
hometown and by the time he gets off at Davos, his final destination, he has
been transported into an entirely new realm. The opening chapters of *The Magic
Mountain* chronicle the mountain's magic as it inexorably pulls Hans into its
orbit. The crisp thin air makes him dizzy; the opulent meals slow down his
digestion; the camel's hair blanket he wraps himself in on the sanatorium balcony
is snug and cosy; he becomes obsessed with the striking cheekbones of an
unnerving Russian woman; gradual acquisition of the local lingo turns him into
an insider; time begins to flow differently. 'Hans Castorp is drawn into the world
of the sick, just as the reader is drawn into the world of the novel', one critic
observed with admiration.[1] It is 'a story of enchantment that induces enchantment', to borrow a term Rita Felski coined for another text.[2] But what magic does
it take for a reader who picks up *The Magic Mountain* to immerse herself in it,
mirroring Hans's immersion in the world of the sanatorium?

In this chapter, I approach this question from several different angles, and, as
befits a world literature approach, consider the circulation of Mann's novel in
1920s Germany and beyond: from inter- and postwar Switzerland to Soviet Russia
to twenty-first-century Hollywood. I start by reconstructing Mann's own doubts
as to whether the reading public would engage with *The Magic Mountain* and the
strategies he put in place to ensure the novel's success. Through a close reading of
the novel's opening pages, I then show that Mann's real-life efforts to give his
novel both a whiff of exclusivity and a broad appeal are reflected in his design of
the story-world and characterization as well. Hans Castorp is introduced as 'ein
einfacher junger Mensch' ('an ordinary young man'), a modern-age 'Everyman'
figure representative of his generation, but at the same time he is clearly marked as
a wealthy and well-connected man of privilege. It is not just that Hans's own social
status is made clear, but the boundaries of his identity are also carefully delineated
to distinguish him from groups to which he does not belong: women, workers, and

---

[1] Michael Minden, *The German Bildungsroman: Incest and Inheritance* (Cambridge: Cambridge
University Press, 1997), p. 206.
[2] Rita Felski, *Uses of Literature* (Oxford: Blackwell, 2008), p. 65.

Mann's Magic Mountain: World Literature and Closer Reading Karolina Watroba, Oxford University Press.
© Karolina Watroba 2022. DOI: 10.1093/oso/9780192871794.003.0002

colonial subjects. From its first pages *The Magic Mountain* postulates a universal possibility of a deeply engaging experience of culture, learning, and self-reflection, while at the same time restricting it to a well-to-do, upper-class, young, white German man. This contradiction is a source of productive tensions in the novel, which calls into question models of stable identity and cultural superiority: Hans Castorp's bourgeois stability will be marred by queer sexual desires; he will get involved in an interracial romance with a woman for whose attention he will compete with a Dutch colonialist from Java; and he will learn from a Jew-turned-Jesuit and communist. The question whether Hans's experience is universal or exclusive creates the space for reworkings and interventions by generations of diverse readers.

A particularly interesting cluster of such readerly responses engages with the interrelated questions of money, class, and economy in *The Magic Mountain*. Unlike in the case of *Buddenbrooks*, these aspects have so far been seen as secondary (at most) in the scholarship on the novel. In his famous 1933 monograph, Hermann J. Weigand marvelled at what he perceived to be the 'almost complete omission of the economic realm from the range of [the novel's] discussion'—an assessment which has not been challenged much in later scholarship.[3] Michael Minden qualified it more than six decades later by observing that 'the economic theme is driven out of the explicit world of the novel because it is all-conditioning upon the implicit level', but his treatment of it remained largely implicit itself.[4] This chapter aims to make it explicit: it will demonstrate that the portrayal of the economic realm in *The Magic Mountain* has been central to the novel's overall design and impact.

A recurring trope in the responses of various Marxist and socially critical readers to Mann's novel, ranging from Bertolt Brecht to Thomas Bernhard, is a tension between passionate ideological opposition to Mann's public persona and writing style and an involuntary attraction towards *The Magic Mountain*. This tension can be explored most fully by juxtaposing two novelistic responses to *The Magic Mountain* written some fifteen years after its publication. They are *Der Zauberlehrling*, a little-known short novel (or 'Romanfragment'—I will return to this classification later) written by Erich Kästner in 1938,[5] and *Sanatorii Arktur*

---

[3]   Hermann J. Weigand, '*The Magic Mountain': A Study of Thomas Mann's Novel 'Der Zauberberg'* (Chapel Hill, NC: University of North Carolina Press, 1964), p. 13. For later discussions of this topic, see Eckhard Heftrich, 'Der *Homo oeconomicus* im Werk von Thomas Mann', in *Der literarische Homo oeconomicus*, ed. Werner Wunderlich (Bern: Haupt, 1989), pp. 153–69; Thomas Sprecher, 'Kur-, Kultur- und Kapitalismuskritik im *Zauberberg*', *Thomas-Mann-Studien*, 16 (1997), 187–249; Anna Kinder, *Geldströme: Ökonomie im Romanwerk Thomas Manns* (Berlin: De Gruyter, 2013), pp. 93–112; and Björn Weyand, *Poetik der Marke: Konsumkultur und literarische Verfahren 1900–2000* (Berlin: De Gruyter, 2013), pp. 97–167.

[4]   Minden, *The German Bildungsroman*, p. 243.

[5]   Erich Kästner, *Der Zauberlehrling*, in *Kästner für Erwachsene: Ausgewählte Schriften*, ed. Luiselotte Enderle (Stuttgart: Deutscher Bücherbund, 1984), iii: *Fabian—Der Zauberlehrling—Die Schule der Diktatoren*, pp. 203–97. Quotations given in my text are taken from this edition. Its text used to be

(*Sanatorium Arktur*), another little-known short novel, written between 1937 and 1940 by one of the founding fathers of socialist realism, Konstantin Fedin.[6] Kästner was commissioned by the 'Verkehrsverein' (tourist board) of Davos to write a cheerful counterpart to Mann's *The Magic Mountain*, which, the writer was told, 'den Ort in gesundheitlicher Hinsicht in Verruf gebracht hatte' ('had brought the town into bad repute with regard to health').[7] *Der Zauberlehrling* has received almost no critical attention and has never been discussed in the context of its inception as a paid commission and a version of *The Magic Mountain*,[8] but it is a fascinating case study of the interplay between artistic creativity, literary tradition, and economic incentives. Konstantin Fedin, who suffered from tuberculosis, spent a year in a sanatorium in Davos in the early 1930s with the assistance of Maxim Gorky. *Sanatorium Arktur* was inspired by his own stay in Davos, but *The Magic Mountain*, a subject of heated discussions among the patients and doctors at the Arktur, clearly served as a blueprint for Fedin's novel.[9]

Kästner's text was supposed to become 'ein heitere[r] Gegenroman' ('a cheerful counterpart') to *The Magic Mountain*,[10] or a hyper-commercialized replacement for it. Fedin's book stages itself as a staunch anti-capitalist counterpart to Mann's novel. Read alongside each other, *Der Zauberlehrling* and *Sanatorium Arktur* represent the range of possible responses to the underlying economic system in *The Magic Mountain*, but their relationships to Mann's novel are much more complex than they might seem at first glance. Both texts grow out of an illicit attraction to the world of *The Magic Mountain*: putting into practice the approach I termed 'closer reading' in the Introduction, I interpret them as fascinating records of involuntary attraction to Mann's novel, held in check by the

dated to 1936, but Sylvia List found strong evidence that it was in fact written in 1938; see Erich Kästner, *Kästner im Schnee*, ed. Sylvia List (Zurich: Atrium, 2011), pp. 197 and 140–42. The text remained unpublished for many years. The first four chapters appeared in 1959, and the latter six were first added in a 1966 edition; see Renate Benson, *Erich Kästner: Studien zu seinem Werk* (Bonn: Bouvier, 1973), pp. 50–57. The novel has not been translated into English; all translations of quotations from it are mine.

[6] Konstantin Fedin, *Sanatorium Arktur*, trans. Olga Shartse (Moscow: Foreign Languages Publishing House, 1957). Quotations in the text are given from this edition. I also consulted the Russian original: Konstantin Fedin, *Sanatorium Arktur*, in *Sobranie sochinenii* (Moscow: Khudozh. lit-ra, 1969–73), v: *Sanatorii Arktur—Pervye radosti* (1971), pp. 7–134.

[7] Sven Hanuschek, *Keiner blickt dir hinter das Gesicht* (Munich: Hanser, 1999), pp. 236–37.

[8] The only more sustained discussion of *Der Zauberlehrling*, in Dieter Mank, *Erich Kästner im nationalsozialistischen Deutschland: 1933–1945, Zeit ohne Werk?* (Frankfurt am Main: Peter Lang, 1981), pp. 169–81, is not very persuasive, mainly because it entirely ignores the fact that it is a humorous text. Rex William Last, *Erich Kästner* (London: Wolff, 1974), pp. 38–68, and Benson briefly discuss it alongside Kästner's other works from the period.

[9] The relationship between *Sanatorium Arktur* and Mann's novel has been noted in the scholarship on *The Magic Mountain* on a few occasions. T. J. Reed has a footnote on it in T. J. Reed, *Thomas Mann: The Uses of Tradition* (Oxford: Clarendon Press, 1996), p. 273. See also Esther N. Elstun, 'Two Views of the Mountain: Thomas Mann's *Zauberberg* and Konstantin Fedin's *Sanatorium Arktur*', *Germano-Slavica*, 3 (1974), 55–71.

[10] Barbara Piatti, 'Erich Kästners Davos' <http://www.literatur-karten.ch/de/schauplatz/erich-kaestners-davos> [accessed 10 May 2019].

contradictory impulse to reject its appeal. In other words, the readerly encounter with *The Magic Mountain* that can be reconstructed based on Fedin's and Kästner's texts is one that lingers on the threshold of the text.

Whether fairly or not, some readers—such as Brecht and Fedin—sneered at Mann's complicity with capitalist modes of cultural production and circulation. Other readers—such as members of the Davos 'Verkehrsverein'—perceived Mann's novel as a threat to their own profits. Still other readers (including, in time, the 'Verkehrsverein') tried to capitalize on Mann's literary and commercial success with *The Magic Mountain*, and I will discuss three such examples, evenly spread across the century that has passed since the novel's publication. In the late 1920s, plans were made to found a prestigious international university in Davos, in the hope that young tuberculosis patients would be more likely to stay in the sanatorium town—which was by then suffering from serious financial troubles—if they could continue their education there. In the end, a series of annual week-long 'Hochschulkurse' took place, consisting of lectures given by high-profile German, French, and Swiss academics to a group of international students. A contemporary account of the 1929 'Hochschulkurse' in Davos demonstrates the extent to which this venture was perceived by its participants as an immersive re-enactment of Mann's novel.

In a striking parallel, German economist and engineer Klaus Schwab, who decided in 1971 to host in Davos the first meeting of what later became the World Economic Forum, claims to have been inspired by the atmosphere of *The Magic Mountain*. He was eager to recreate for his guests 'a place of recreation and relaxation, where people took in clean mountain air to restore their health and recharge their minds'.[11] Set in what the *Australian Financial Review* described as 'a retirement home for veterans of the Davos Economic Forum',[12] Gore Verbinski's 2016 Hollywood horror film *A Cure for Wellness* is my most recent example of a commercially motivated desire for a re-enactment of *The Magic Mountain*. The film reimagines Mann's sanatorium treatment as a water cure in a luxurious Swiss spa. These three projects—'Davoser Hochschulkurse', World Economic Forum, and *A Cure for Wellness*—suggest three very different readings of Mann's novel, each showcasing a different route to entering the world of *The Magic Mountain*, and—as I will demonstrate—all of them ultimately lingering on the threshold of the text, much like Fedin or Brecht, albeit for the opposite reason: not out of contempt for bourgeois capitalism, but in an attempt to benefit from it.

*   *   *

[11] [Anon.], 'The Beginning' <https://widgets.weforum.org/history/1971.html> [accessed 10 May 2019].

[12] John McDonald, 'Movie Review: *A Cure for Wellness* (2016) Offers a Nightmarish View of Wall St', *Australian Financial Review*, 24 March 2017 <https://www.afr.com/lifestyle/arts-and-entertainment/film-and-tv/movie-review-a-cure-for-wellness-2016-20170322-gv3fhj> [accessed 10 May 2019].

Thomas Mann was much preoccupied with readers' ability to enter his story-world in the long years that it took him to write *The Magic Mountain*. He wanted it to be readable, gripping, even; he was very pleased when one early reader took a break from the novel to let its author know that he was finding it 'fesselnd' ('gripping'). The author wrote back with a disarming lack of false modesty, 'Daß *Der Zauberberg* Sie fesselt, freut mich. Es geht ja offenbar mehr Menschen so, und ich muß sagen, wenn ich hineinsehe, so fesselt er mich selber' ('I am happy to hear that *The Magic Mountain* has gripped you. Apparently other people are also experiencing it; I have to say, when I look into it, it grips me too').[13] In 1917, while taking a break from the draft of *The Magic Mountain* to work on his mammoth political treatise *Betrachtungen eines Unpolitischen* (*Reflections of a Nonpolitical Man*), Mann explained in a letter to a friend that he had to write the latter 'weil infolge des Krieges der Roman sonst intellektuell überlastet worden wäre' ('because the novel would have otherwise become intellectually overloaded as a result of the war').[14] At work on *The Magic Mountain* again, in 1922, he wrote to another friend: 'das tolle Buch und die Frage seiner Lesbarkeit machen mir oft schwere Sorgen' ('the wild book and the question of its readability worry me a lot').[15] A year later he described the novel to the same friend as 'das verschleppte Roman-Untier, das in großen Partien sicher langweilig ist' ('this beast of a novel, much delayed, certainly with many boring stretches').[16] Another year went by—the publication of *The Magic Mountain* was now only a few months away—and Mann wrote to his editor about his worries that 'das Werk große Schwächen und Längen hat' ('the work has serious weaknesses and at times drags').[17] Finally, the book was published and began to sell remarkably well. But Mann still had his doubts: 'ob dieser Anfangserfolg sich hält, ist zweifelhaft, denn die Leute seufzen nicht wenig über die langen, langen Diskurse' ('I doubt that this initial success will last because people have been complaining quite a bit about the long, long philosophical discussions').[18] The book did continue to sell very well, which Mann still found surprising years later; in 1940, he marvelled at the fact that so many people had been ready for 'eine so wunderliche Unterhaltung, die mit gewohnter Romanlektüre fast nichts mehr zu tun hatte' ('an odd kind of entertainment which had hardly anything to do with the usual reading of novels').[19]

But it was more than the question of readability that bothered Mann. He was worried that the book might end up too long or boring, but also aware of barriers to entry into his magical story-world that were in place long before a reader would ever open up his novel. In November 1924, mere days after *The Magic Mountain* hit the shelves, Mann wrote in a letter to a friend: 'das Buch ist heraus, ich hörte

---

[13] Thomas Mann, *Selbstkommentare: 'Der Zauberberg'*, ed. Hans Wysling and Marianne Eich-Fischer (Frankfurt am Main: Fischer, 1993), p. 72.
[14] Ibid., p. 15.   [15] Ibid., p. 28.   [16] Ibid., p. 36.
[17] Ibid., p. 43.   [18] Ibid., p. 49.   [19] Ibid., p. 135.

schon manches Wohltuende, aber der Preis macht mir Sorgen' ('the book is out, I have already heard some nice things, but I am worried about the price').[20] Those who bought the book were enjoying reading it, but Mann wanted more readers, and that meant more buyers. When expressing his anxiety over the novel's initial success due to 'die langen, langen Diskurse', Mann went on to add: 'auch ist der Preis doch ein Hemmnis. Fischer denkt von Weitem auf eine einbändige Ausgabe auf Dünndruckpapier' ('the price is a constraint after all. Fischer is beginning to consider a thin-paper edition in one volume').[21] When he recalled the book's success in 1940, he listed two different types of investment that readers had to make in it: 'Zeit und Geld'[22]—the time it took to read nearly 1000 pages of the novel, and the 20 Marks that the first edition cost.[23]

In the novel itself, Naphta memorably attacks Settembrini's ideals of demo-cratic humanism by pointing out that only a select few can in fact afford the kind of education that Settembrini postulates: 'Bildung und Besitz—da haben Sie den Bourgeois!' ('education and property—behold the bourgeoisie!') (p. 773/p. 608). However, there is little to suggest that Mann was worried about *The Magic Mountain*'s price because he was committed to making his work accessible to the worse-off; rather, he was a savvy marketer, hyper-conscious of his own brand, and hard at work to produce a bestseller. He meticulously traced the sales of *The Magic Mountain*. Before the novel came out, his publishing house had received 5000 preorders, 'sodaß Fischer gleich 20 Tausend druckt' ('so that Fischer is printing 20,000 copies straight away'), Mann noted excitedly.[24] That first print run sold out within three months, earning Mann 70,000 Marks, with which he promptly bought a six-seater Fiat.[25] He kept tabs on the sales even over Christmas that year: 'das 26. Tausend ist im Handel' ('26,000 copies are out now'), he noted down on 26 December, undoubtedly pleased about the numerical coincidence.[26] In Germany alone, the book went through one hundred reprints and had sold 100,000 copies by 1928, 125,000 copies by 1930, and 135,000 copies by 1936, when Mann was expatriated. Between 1933 and 1936, Mann was already in exile, but 'could not bring himself to denounce the Nazi regime publicly, despite consider-able moral pressure from various quarters for him to do so, because this would have been to relinquish all access to his readers in Germany'.[27]

[20] Ibid., p. 48.   [21] Ibid., p. 49.   [22] Ibid., p. 135.

[23] Peter de Mendelssohn, *Nachbemerkungen zu Thomas Mann* (Frankfurt am Main: Fischer, 1982), vol. i, p. 93.

[24] Mann, *Selbstkommentare*, p. 46.

[25] Wilhelm Haefs, 'Geist, Geld und Buch. Thomas Manns Aufstieg zum Erfolgsautor im S. Fischer Verlag in der Weimarer Republik', in *Die Erfindung des Schriftstellers Thomas Mann*, ed. Michael Ansel, Hans-Edwin Friedrich, and Gerhard Lauer (Berlin: De Gruyter, 2009), pp. 123–59, pp. 138–39. See also de Mendelssohn, *Nachbemerkungen*, pp. 93–95, on the novel's commercial success.

[26] Mann, *Selbstkommentare*, p. 49.

[27] Michael Minden, ed., *Thomas Mann* (London: Longman, 1995), p. 8.

The Magic Mountain was also almost immediately available in catalogues of lending libraries,[28] and its various editions ranged from the 1926 'einbändige Ausgabe auf Dünndruckpapier', which Mann had been eager to have from the very beginning, to a linen-bound limited edition included in Mann's 1925 collected works for almost 100 Marks. The novel was one of the top five bestselling novels published in the Weimar Republic between 1925 and 1930. All other top titles were historical novels or novels about the First World War that are now largely forgotten, with the exception of Remarque's *Im Westen nichts Neues* (*All Quiet on the Western Front*), which sold an astonishing million copies within a year of its publication in 1929 and dwarfed in sales all other German novels published at the time.[29] (Incidentally, Remarque greatly admired *The Magic Mountain*. Traces of his fascination with Mann's novel can be found in many of his own books and stories from the 1930s, 1940s, and 1950s.)[30]

Even the sales of *Buddenbrooks*—by far Mann's biggest bestseller and, at 1,350,000 copies, the biggest German bestseller in the first half of the twentieth century—only skyrocketed after Mann managed to persuade Fischer to publish an extraordinarily cheap 'Volksausgabe' ('popular edition') in 1929, less than a week before he was awarded the Nobel Prize. Before that, it had taken a full twenty years to sell the first 100,000 copies—something which *The Magic Mountain* had achieved in just three. As Tobias Boes explains, Mann had been 'chastened by his experience with his debut novel *Buddenbrooks*', whose sales had only picked up after its 1903 reissue in a cheaper edition in only one volume.[31] After that, Mann 'paid extraordinarily close attention to the physical aspects of the publishing trade', trying to target different sectors of the book-reading public. On the one hand, he 'push[ed] for status-enhancing luxury editions'—for example, the first American editions of his books were printed on 'richly textured paper' with 'carefully designed covers';[32] on the other hand, Mann 'convince[d] S. Fischer to

[28] See Haefs, pp. 152–53.
[29] See Kornelia Vogt-Praclik, *Bestseller in der Weimarer Republik 1925–1930* (Herzberg: Bautz, 1987), pp. 134–35. See also Donald Ray Richards, *The German Bestseller in the 20th Century: A Complete Bibliography and Analysis 1915–1940* (Bern: H. Lang, 1968), which lists more data for a longer time period. On the pitfalls of these types of bestseller compilations, see Christian Adam, '"Nach zwei Jahren spricht von diesem Buch kein Mensch mehr". Kurzer Ruhm und langes Leben zwischen Bestsellerliste und Longsellerdasein', in *Text und Kritik: Sonderband Gelesene Literatur: Populäre Lektüre im Zeichen des Medienwandels*, ed. Steffen Martus and Carlos Spoerhase (Munich: Edition Text + Kritik, 2018), pp. 21–30.
[30] See Wilhelm von Sternburg, *Als wäre alles das letzte Mal: Erich Remarque* (Cologne: Kiepenheuer & Witsch, 2010), p. 299.
[31] Tobias Boes, 'Thomas Mann, World Author: Representation and Autonomy in the World Republic of Letters', *Seminar: A Journal of Germanic Studies*, 51 (2015), 132–47, p. 136.
[32] David Horton, *Thomas Mann in English: A Study in Literary Translation* (New York: Bloomsbury, 2016), p. 31. See also Catherine Turner, *Marketing Modernism Between the Two World Wars* (Amherst, MA: University of Massachusetts Press, 2003).

allow Reclam to print a mass-market edition of his novella *Tristan* in the Universalbibliothek'.[33]

In a similar vein, in 1927, Mann edited, together with George Scheffauer— whom he had initially envisaged as the English translator of *The Magic Mountain*—a book series published by Knaur Verlag, called 'Romane der Welt' ('Novels of the World').[34] This was a highly controversial venture: at 2.85 Marks apiece, these books were five to ten times cheaper than comparable titles published by other publishing houses—including Mann's own novels at S. Fischer Verlag. In the preface to the first volume in the series, Hugh Walpole's 1925 Gothic novel *Portrait of a Man with Red Hair* (in its German title of *Bildnis eines Rothaarigen*), Mann asked rhetorically, 'könnte das Massenhafte, das Massengerechte, nicht einmal gut sein?' ('could things that are popular with the masses not be good for once?'), and postulated: 'rümpfen wir nicht esoterisch die Nase! Flüchten wir nicht auf ein Elfenbeintürmchen!' ('let's not turn up our noses at this! Let's not flee up our little ivory towers!')[35] Even though Thomas Mann is usually seen as an elitist writer and *The Magic Mountain* as something of an ivory tower, in fact he relentlessly pursued a mass readership. As Michael Minden put it, 'Goethe exploited the popular novel to make it serious[;] Mann exploited the serious novel to make it popular.'[36] In Mann's lifetime, many other German-language modernists, including Robert Musil, Alfred Döblin, and Hermann Broch, were very critical of his popular success.[37]

Mann's market-conscious approach to the writing process intensified in the 1920s due to the unstable economic situation. He was 'forced to scavenge for additional sources of revenue' and did this by 'implementing a multimedial strategy designed to create an international reputation'.[38] It included 'extended lecture tours to foreign countries, a job as the German correspondent for the American little magazine *The Dial*, and negotiations with Hollywood studios about film adaptations of his stories'.[39] He was even close to releasing his own brand of cigars. In an intriguing study, *Poetik der Marke: Konsumkultur und literarische Verfahren 1900-2000*, Björn Weyand reconstructed Mann's collabor- ation with the German tobacco industry to release a limited edition of Thomas Mann–Maria Mancini cigars, which would recreate Hans Castorp's favourite brand in the novel.[40] Indeed, years before it was even published, *The Magic*

---

[33] Boes, 'Thomas Mann, World Author', p. 136.

[34] See Stefan Rehm, '"Könnte das Massenhafte, das Massengerechte nicht einmal gut sein?" Thomas Mann und die Massenkultur des Literaturmarktes der Weimarer Republik', *Düsseldorfer Beiträge zur Thomas Mann-Forschung*, 2 (2013), 199–209.

[35] Thomas Mann, 'Romane der Welt: Ein Geleitwort', in *Weimarer Republik: Manifeste und Dokumente zur deutschen Literatur 1918-1933*, ed. Anton Kaes (Stuttgart: Metzler, 1983), pp. 287–89, p. 287.

[36] Minden, *The German Bildungsroman*, p. 244.   [37] See Minden, ed., *Thomas Mann*, p. 22.

[38] Boes, 'Thomas Mann, World Author', pp. 141–42.   [39] Ibid.

[40] See Weyand, *Poetik der Marke*, pp. 102–04 and 166–67. See also Mann, *Selbstkommentare*, pp. 81–82.

Mountain had been a part of this wide-ranging marketing strategy. Mann read from his draft on his book tours as early as 1920 and had extracts from it published in the press. In the words of Peter de Mendelssohn, 'nun wußte die ganze literarische Welt, daß mit dem *Zauberberg* etwas für die deutsche Literatur Hochbedeutsames im Kommen war' ('now the whole literary world knew that something highly significant for German literature was about to occur with the publication of *The Magic Mountain*').[41] In the words of marketing strategists of today, Mann was building up the hype for the launch of his product.

It was to be a luxurious product—from its sophisticated, elegant prose and astonishing range of coverage to its sheer length and the time it took to write and read. But Mann was also eager for his product to be mass-marketed, with affordable editions available, and a comprehensive advertising campaign targeting all sorts of potential readers. Advertisements for the forthcoming book had been in circulation as early as 1913, at a time when Mann conceived of it as a novella, a humorous counterpart to *Death in Venice*.[42] In 1920, he explained to the organizers of his Swiss book tour that he tended to adjust the contents of his public readings 'je nach dem Publikum, das ich vor mir habe' ('according to the public that I have in front of me'); 'wohl mit Recht nehme ich an, daß es fehlerhaft wäre, etwa in Aarau oder Solothurn dasselbe zu bieten, wie in Bern und Basel' ('surely I am justified in assuming that it would be a mistake to offer in, say, Aarau or Solothurn the same reading that I do in Bern and Basel').[43] Two provincial, largely industrial towns of 10,000 inhabitants versus two cultural metropoles at least ten times their size: Mann was very much aware of the diversity of his audiences and eager to cater to their differing expectations. He would acquire a similar reputation in the United States; in 1947, Charles Neider claimed that 'Mann has the distinction of simultaneously appealing to the person of esoteric learnings as well as the general reader.'[44]

None of this is, strictly speaking, new to academic criticism on Thomas Mann. 'It can easily be documented that Mann was actually as concerned to reach a wide public as he was to lend intellectual refinement to his work', wrote Michael Minden in the Introduction to his popular English-language handbook on Mann from the 1990s.[45] And yet, especially in the most influential German studies of Mann, this crucial aspect of his writing—its orientation towards the broadest possible readership—has been glossed over, underplayed, or downright repressed over and over again. It is bewildering that even those scholars who explicitly analyse Mann's success as a mass-marketed modernist—such as Minden, who

[41] De Mendelssohn, *Nachbemerkungen zu Thomas Mann*, p. 72.
[42] Michael Neumann, *Thomas Mann, 'Der Zauberberg': Kommentar*, GKFA (Frankfurt am Main: Fischer, 2002), pp. 19 and 58–59, and Mann, *Selbstkommentare*, pp. 8–9.
[43] Mann, *Selbstkommentare*, p. 23.
[44] Charles Neider, ed., *The Stature of Thomas Mann* (New York: New Directions, 1947), p. 11.
[45] Minden, ed., *Thomas Mann*, p. 3.

says that Mann 'should be valued as an outstanding popular writer, not revered as a literary classic'[46]—do not discuss any tangible evidence of how and why his mass readership has related to his writing, and instead rely on their own conjectures, as well as Mann's self-interpretations.[47] It is an understandable temptation in the case of a writer who produced copious amounts of writing on his own writing throughout his life. But ultimately Mann is just one reader of his own work—an important reader whose views are well documented, but nevertheless only one reader among many.

This is, again, by no means a novel recognition. In fact, it is the conclusion reached in the first major examination of Mann's 'doppelte Optik' ('double optics' or 'dual perspective')—an approach to making art that is attractive to highbrow critics as well as the wider public, which Mann arrived at by studying Wagner and Nietzsche. Eberhard Lämmert listed various biases in the critical tradition, largely resulting from the Romantic cult of a genius artist, which had led to an unhelpful fixation on authorial intention, so that:

> andere Bereiche der Interpretation, etwa die der Wirkungsgeschichte bedeuten-
> der Werke und damit die Geschichte ihrer Neuinterpretation durch das lesende
> Publikum, Fakten also, die letzten Endes das 'Leben' der Dichtung und ihre
> soziale Bedeutung ausmachen, ungebührlich vernachlässigt [wurden].

> other areas of interpretation have been unreasonably neglected, for example, the
> reception history of significant works, and thereby the history of their changing
> interpretations by the reading public; facts, that is, that ultimately determine the
> 'life' of literature and its social significance.[48]

Despite this recognition, Lämmert himself, as well as later scholars of Mann's 'doppelte Optik', focused exclusively on the origin of this idea and Mann's own understanding of it, and never wrote about Mann's writings from the perspective of his diverse readers, who, as Lämmert points out so aptly, 'ultimately determine the "life" of literature and its social significance'.

---

[46] Ibid., p. 22.

[47] See Eberhard Lämmert, 'Doppelte Optik. Über die Erzählkunst des frühen Thomas Mann', in *Literatur, Sprache, Gesellschaft*, ed. Karl Rüdinger (Munich: Bayerischer Schulbuch-Verlag, 1970), pp. 50–72; Michael Minden, 'Popularity and the Magic Circle of Culture', *Publications of the English Goethe Society*, 76.2 (2007), 93–101; Achim Hölter, *'Doppelte Optik und lange Ohren*—Notes on Aesthetic Compromise', in *Quote, Double Quote: Aesthetics between High and Popular Culture*, ed. Paul Ferstl and Keyvan Sarkhosh (Amsterdam: Rodopi, 2014), pp. 43–63; Paolo Panizzo, 'Ambiguität und Doppelte Optik', in *Thomas Mann Handbuch: Leben, Werk, Wirkung*, ed. Andreas Blödorn and Friedhelm Marx (Stuttgart: Metzler, 2015), pp. 281–83.

[48] Lämmert, 'Doppelte Optik', pp. 66–67. Shortly before Lämmert, Helmut Koopmann discussed the term 'doppelte Optik' in the context of Mann's writing in Helmut Koopmann, *Die Entwicklung des 'intellektuellen Romans' bei Thomas Mann* (Bonn: Bouvier, 1980), but he defined it as having to do with the ambivalence or ambiguity of Mann's writing.

As Haefs's analysis of Mann's position within the book market of the Weimar Republic amply demonstrates, Mann 'gehörte [...] zu den wenigen Autoren, bei denen die Akkumulation ökonomischen Kapitals zeitgleich mit dem des symbolischen Kapitals erfolgte' ('was among the few authors who simultaneously accrued economic and symbolic capital').[49] Mann wanted to create a product that would be luxurious and yet also mass-marketed, to write a book at once highbrow and popular, to tell a story that was both exclusive and inclusive. He considered this tension carefully and from many angles: he thought about its implications for the physical properties of different editions of his book, for its price, for the philosophical discussions in his novel, for its length, and for the kind of reading experience it would offer. His readers responded to this tension at the heart of *The Magic Mountain* with an intensity and insightfulness that have as yet gone unnoticed and unrecorded in the academic scholarship on Thomas Mann. But this tension, and its explosive potential, are hiding in plain sight—starting on the very first page.

*   *   *

'Ein einfacher junger Mensch reiste im Hochsommer von Hamburg, seiner Vaterstadt, nach Davos-Platz im Graubündischen. Er fuhr auf Besuch für drei Wochen' ('An ordinary young man was on his way from his hometown of Hamburg to Davos-Platz in the canton of Graubünden. It was the height of summer, and he planned to stay for three weeks') (p. 11/p. 3). These are the opening words of the first chapter of *The Magic Mountain*. There can hardly be a more generic, a more unassuming, a more understated characterization of a protagonist. Mann prepared the reader for the entrance of this character in the 'Vorsatz' ('Foreword'): 'der Leser wird einen einfachen, wenn auch ansprechenden jungen Menschen in ihm kennenlernen' ('the reader will come to know him as a perfectly ordinary, if engaging young man'), and his tale will be told 'nicht um seinetwillen [...], sondern um der Geschichte willen' ('not for his sake [...], but for the sake of the story itself') (p. 9/p. xxxv). Before I discuss the role of the Foreword more fully, let me dwell on the fact that Hans Castorp is first introduced as an emphatically ordinary person, a sort of modern-day 'Everyman' who is subsidiary to his own story. The adjective 'einfach' can mean several things. It can mean 'simple' in a pejorative sense (not very bright); or, more positively, it can denote somebody who is unassuming and generally content with life.[50] What both these meanings have in common is that they indicate a lack of distinction, a certain generalizable quality.

Thomas Mann is at great pains to characterize Hans Castorp as a common man, perhaps the epitome of the common man. This is crucial to the book's overall purport: 'der einfache junge Mensch' will prove highly susceptible to

[49] Haefs, 'Geist, Geld, und Buch', p. 154.
[50] See Horton, *Thomas Mann in English: A Study in Literary Translation*, p. 99, on different possible English translations of the adjective 'einfach' in *The Magic Mountain*.

intellectual adventures and uncommonly interested in every possible area of study ranging from biology, chemistry, medicine, and meteorology to classical music, medieval Church history, and the complexities of French vocabulary and Russian pronunciation. The reader will gradually discover Hans's morbid fascination with death and his capacity for deep self-reflection. Hans Castorp's example apparently shows that learning, culture, and knowledge are for everyone, literally, for 'Everyman'; that knowledge is attractive and alluring, far from dry, dispassionate, and matter of fact; that culture is a tool for exploration of the self and the world, and learning is an adventure, a temptation, a pleasure, and an indulgence available to the common man.

But is Hans really an 'Everyman'? The details of his background and appearance which the reader glimpses in the novel's first few paragraphs situate him firmly in a very specific social context. Hans's 'krokodilslederne Handtasche' ('alligator valise') (p. 11/p. 3) would be enough to establish him as a man of wealth; if we had any doubts, we soon learn that the crocodile-skin handbag is a gift from his uncle, a 'Konsul'; and a few lines further down we find out from a relative clause—Mann's characteristic way of subtly conveying a telling detail by making it sound like an unimportant aside—that Hans Castorp is clad in a 'modisch weiten, auf Seide gearbeiteten Sommerüberzieher' ('silk-lined [...] fashionably loose summer overcoat') (pp. 11–12/p. 3). Quite a dandy, this 'ordinary young man', clearly a wealthy man, and a bit spoilt at that; he is a 'Familiensöhnchen und Zärtling' ('coddled scion of the family'), we are told as he pulls up the collar of his valuable overcoat (p. 12/p. 3). But for all the fragility and effeminacy that this passage attributes to Hans, he is also depicted in the position of symbolic mastery over the entire globe. Hans comes from Hamburg, a wealthy Hanseatic city. His props—a crocodile-skin handbag and a silk-lined overcoat—connote Africa and Asia, the two continents most palpably associated with nineteenth-century colonial exploitation.[51] Hans's travel reading of choice is an English textbook about ocean steamships—a means of transport that connects European port cities like Hamburg with the entire world, so that no place is out of bounds. The fact that the textbook is in English subtly introduces the theme of the naval race between Britain and Germany at the beginning of the twentieth century, placing Hans—freshly out of marine engineering school—at the forefront of this rivalry.[52]

[51] On the topic of Germany's imperial projects and colonial expansion as reflected and problematized in Mann's novel, see Kenneth Weisinger, 'Distant Oil Rigs and Other Erections', in *A Companion to Thomas Mann's Magic Mountain*, ed. Stephen Dowden (Columbia, SC: Camden House, 1999), pp. 177–220, Todd Kontje, *Thomas Mann's World: Empire, Race, and the Jewish Question* (Ann Arbor, MI: University of Michigan Press, 2011), pp. 85–117, and Debra N. Prager, *Orienting the Self: The German Literary Encounter with the Eastern Other* (Rochester, NY: Camden House, 2014), pp. 220–82.
[52] See Weisinger, 'Distant Oil Rigs', pp. 186–88.

Hans's mastery over the world is also encoded in the novel's opening paragraphs through a careful separation of his identity from its 'Others'. But these exclusions are so perfectly executed that they paradoxically leave indelible traces on the surface of the text. The language of the first pages of *The Magic Mountain* is defensively sexist in that it highlights Hans's paternal lineage and the patriarchal political order of his world: Hamburg is his 'Vaterstadt' ('hometown', literally 'father city'), he travels to Davos through 'mehrerer Herren Länder' ('many a landscape', literally 'lands of many masters'), and the only family member we hear about at this point is his 'Onkel und Pflegevater' ('uncle and foster father') (p. 11/ p. 3). In Andrew Webber's words, 'in spite of the focal female figure of Clawdia Chauchat or the female anatomy given to the allegory of life, *The Magic Mountain* is essentially a narrative between men'.[53] This gender imbalance of Hans's world is emphatically present in the opening lines.

The contrast between the world of hard physical labour and the material profits that the bourgeoisie draw from it is similarly hidden on the surface of the text. The description of Hans's overcoat—'[sein] auf Seide gearbeiteter Sommerüberzieher'—contains a linguistic trace of the labour ('Arbeit') that went into making it. Hans's *Ocean Steamships* book lies on the side and 'der hereinstreichende Atem der schwer keuchenden Lokomotive [verunreinigte] seinen Umschlag mit Kohlenpartikeln' ('the cover [was] dirtied by soot drifting in with the steam of the heavily puffing locomotive') (p. 12/p. 4). The personification 'der Atem der schwer keuchenden Lokomotive' (literally 'the breath of the heavily puffing locomotive') evokes the hard physical labour of the stokers who keep the coal-fired steam engine running so that Hans can make his train journey. It also conjures up the physical toil of the stokers who work on the steamships that engineers like Hans design, and perhaps even the strain of those who had to work harder still before the steam engine replaced the power of their muscles. The carbon particles that are dirtying the cover of Hans's book penetrate into the lungs of the working masses every day, contributing to the kind of respiratory illnesses that will be suffered by the working-class protagonist of *Una breve vacanza* (*A Brief Vacation*, 1973), Vittorio De Sica's cinematic response to *The Magic Mountain*.[54]

Mann gestures to the universality of his story and his protagonist, while with the other hand withholding the possibility of this experience from countless faceless 'Others'. But those excluded from Hans's story still lurk in the blind corners of the text: the women elided from Hans's family tree and the political organization of Germany with its 'Vaterstädte' and 'mehrerer Herren Länder'; the

---

[53] Andrew J. Webber, 'Mann's Man's World' in *The Cambridge Companion to Thomas Mann*, ed. Ritchie Robertson (Cambridge: Cambridge University Press, 2001), pp. 64–83, p. 78.

[54] See Karolina Watroba, 'Reluctant Readers on Mann's *Magic Mountain* (Ida Herz Lecture 2020)', *Publications of the English Goethe Society*, 90.2 (2021), 146–62, where I discuss de Sica's film.

colonial 'Others' who left their invisible touch on Hans's crocodile-skin handbag before a steamship brought it from Africa to the Hanseatic port of Hamburg; the coal miners and stokers who keep Hans's train going, who load the coal into the steam engines of the ships that Hans learned to build, and who might end up suffering from a far less glorious form of respiratory illness than Hans's rarefied, arguably self-proclaimed tuberculosis. Hans benefits from patriarchy, capitalism, and colonialism, and there is something simultaneously triumphant and self-deprecating about the way he is introduced: on the one hand, with the bold claim that he is 'ein einfacher junger Mensch', an 'Everyman'; on the other hand, by making the forces that shape his privileged situation visible on the surface of the text.

The narrative is in fact very sensitive to the issue of social mobility. In the novel's opening pages the narrator announces:

> Der Raum [löst] die Person des Menschen aus ihren Beziehungen und [versetzt] ihn in einen freien und ursprünglichen Zustand,—ja, selbst aus dem Pedanten und Pfahlbürger mach[t] er im Handumdrehen etwas wie einen Vagabunden.
>
> (p. 12)
>
> Space [removes] an individual from all relationships and [places] him in a free and pristine state—indeed, in but a moment it can turn a pedant and philistine into something like a vagabond.   (p. 4)

The wide semantic range of the term 'Vagabund' into which Mann taps here moves from 'a homeless person' to a metaphor for 'somebody who likes travel-ling', and especially the Romantic 'Wanderer', a popular type in German literature in the early nineteenth century.[55] It is precisely because Hans is very rich and well connected that he can now become a 'Vagabund' at a whim (he can be called a 'Pfahlbürger', a petty bourgeois, only in the sense of being a somewhat narrow-minded 'Spießbürger', or philistine, who conforms to social norms and rejects unfamiliar concepts, and not in the sense of belonging to the lower strata of the bourgeoisie). The text seemingly does not reflect the crucial difference between being forced into homelessness and choosing a vagabond lifestyle to experience freedom. There is a strong sense, however, that these are Hans's own thoughts, and that he is not critical enough to realize that it is not just temporal and geographic distance that enable people to make those lifestyle changes. The broader narrative perspective, meanwhile, keeps open the possibility of a more socially critical assessment of Hans's self-understanding.

---

[55] On the motif of the German Romantic 'Wanderer', see Andrew Cusack, *The Wanderer in Nineteenth-Century German Literature: Intellectual History and Cultural Criticism* (Rochester, NY: Camden House, 2008).

At the beginning of the Foreword the reader learned that Hans's story would be told 'not for his sake [...], but for the sake of the story itself'. This statement is followed by an important qualification: 'wobei zu Hans Castorps Gunsten denn doch erinnert werden sollte, dass es *seine* Geschichte ist, und dass nicht jedem jede Geschichte passiert' ('although in Hans Castorp's favor it should be noted that it is *his* story, and that not every story happens to everybody') (p. 9/p. xxxv). Academic readers of the novel usually interpret this passage as Mann's nod to the tradition of the German 'Bildungsroman', a genre that asks about the relationship between an individual and his environment, the social and cultural forces that are brought to bear on his development.[56] It is understandable that literary scholars find the intricacies of Mann's relationship to an older literary genre particularly intriguing. But in my reading of the opening pages of *The Magic Mountain*, I have been arguing that it is also possible to confront the crucial question that the novel poses from the start—namely, what makes this story happen to Hans?—by thinking about Hans's gender, class, and racial identity.

What makes my case stronger is that many of *The Magic Mountain*'s readers have followed precisely this line of thought, especially in terms of class—an issue, as I will demonstrate, far more resonant with non-academic readers than Mann's attitude towards the 'Bildungsroman'. Already in 1926, a reviewer for the left-wing Berlin magazine *Die neue Bücherschau* sneered at Mann's protagonist—'einen jungen großbürgerlichen Gent [... unter dem] Glassturz eines Luxussanatoriums' ('a young, upper-class dandy under the glass cover of a luxurious sanatorium')— whose story is described at great length because 'der Roman, um dir was einzubringen, mindestens zwei Bände stark sein muß' ('to earn you anything, the novel must be made up of at least two volumes').[57] It is worth adding that this review, barely ever discussed in the scholarship on Mann, was rather prescient: its last sentence reads: 'und womöglich kriegst du dann den nobelsten Preis?'—'and possibly you'll end up getting the noblest prize?' At the same time a reviewer for another left-wing Berlin magazine—*Die Weltbühne*—described Hans Castorp as 'ein junger Durchschnittsmensch', 'an average young man', or even 'Everyman'.[58] Which is it, then? Who is Castorp, the protagonist with whom the reader is invited

---

[56] See, for example, Martin Swales, *Mann: 'Der Zauberberg'* (London: Grant & Cutler, 2000), pp. 59–61. See also Jürgen Scharfschwerdt, *Thomas Mann und der deutsche Bildungsroman: Eine Untersuchung zu den Problemen einer literarischen Tradition* (Stuttgart: Kohlhammer, 1967), W. H. Bruford, *The German Tradition of Self-Cultivation: 'Bildung' from Humboldt to Thomas Mann* (Cambridge: Cambridge University Press, 1975), Martin Swales, *The German Bildungsroman from Wieland to Hesse* (Princeton, NJ: Princeton University Press, 1978), Michael Beddow, *The Fiction of Humanity* (Cambridge: Cambridge University Press, 1982), Minden, *The German Bildungsroman*, and Russell A. Berman, 'Modernism and the Bildungsroman: Thomas Mann's *Magic Mountain*', in *The Cambridge Companion to the Modern German Novel*, ed. Graham Bartram (Cambridge: Cambridge University Press, 2004), pp. 77–92.

[57] Salomo Friedländer [Mynona], 'Zauberpredigt eines ungläubigen Thomas an Mannbare: Rezept zum Kitsch allerersten Ranges', *Die neue Bücherschau*, 4 (1926), 186–87.

[58] Hans Reisiger, '*Der Zauberberg*', *Die Weltbühne*, 21 (1925), 810–15, p. 810.

to identify? Who is the immersive 'Magic Mountain' experience for—in the double sense of Hans's experiences in the sanatorium, and the experience of reading about his experiences? Who can afford to embark on this magical journey—to go for a long sanatorium stay, to buy an expensive book, to embark on a series of intellectual adventures? Erich Kästner and Konstantin Fedin offer two extreme answers to these questions, and it is to their texts that I now turn, situating *Der Zauberlehrling* and *Sanatorium Arktur* in the context of other similar responses to *The Magic Mountain*.

2. No Communism Without *The Magic Mountain*

Konstantin Fedin (1892–1977) was a seminal writer of the socialist-realist movement in Soviet literature and the longest-serving chairman of the Union of Soviet Writers. He believed that bourgeois art could and should be 'co-opted and reworked for the purposes of the working masses',[59] travelled extensively around Europe, especially Germany and Switzerland (he was fluent in German), and wrote several novels and short stories juxtaposing Soviet Russia with Western Europe. Fedin's typical plot revolves around a Russian intellectual learning to live up to the ideal of 'the new Soviet man'. His most famous novel, *Goroda i gody* (*Cities and Years*), was published in 1924—the same year as *The Magic Mountain*. In a letter to a friend from November 1929, Fedin noted that the Nobel Prize in Literature had just been awarded to Thomas Mann; 'kakaia svin'ia!', he wrote, an invective literally meaning 'what a pig!', and went on to fantasize about winning the prize himself.[60] A few months later Fedin started looking into tuberculosis cures in Switzerland, and—with financial assistance from Maxim Gorky—in 1931 arrived in Davos, where he started writing *Sanatorium Arktur*, a novel fashioned as a communist response to *The Magic Mountain*. One might be tempted to laugh it off as a squarely ideological exercise with no intrinsic appeal for a modern-day reader. T. J. Reed dismissed Fedin's take on the historical and philosophical basis of the sanatorium lifestyle as a simplistic, 'out of proportion [less] valuable' counterpart to Mann's novel.[61] While Reed is right about the limitations of Fedin's ideological stance, I consider *Sanatorium Arktur* to be one among many traces left by reluctant readers of *The Magic Mountain* and believe that we can learn a lot about Mann's novel by listening carefully to them.[62]

[59] Ruth Wallach, 'Konstantin Aleksandrovich Fedin (12 February 1892–15 July 1977)', in *Russian Prose Writers Between the World Wars*, ed. Christine Rydel (Detroit, IL: Thomson Gale, 2003), pp. 88–100, p. 91.

[60] N. V. Kornienko and I. E. Kabanova, eds., *Konstantin Fedin i ego sovremenniki: iz literaturnogo naslediia XX veka* (Moscow: Institut mirovoi literatury im. A. M. Gor'kogo RAN, 2016), p. 453.

[61] Reed, *Thomas Mann*, p. 273.

[62] Parts of this section, as well as the Conclusion, were first published in Watroba, 'Reluctant Readers', where I discuss Fedin alongside Vittorio De Sica and Thomas Bernhard, among others.

The protagonist of *Sanatorium Arktur*, a tubercular Russian patient called Levshin, is an engineer—but, unlike Hans Castorp, he is determined to overcome his illness, return to his homeland, and further progress by serving society. It is as though Settembrini's admonitions to Hans to leave the sanatorium and take up his engineering job have finally reached a sympathetic ear. But, in an ironic twist, it is a Russian—a representative of the nation branded by Settembrini as idle, anti-rationalist, and obscurantist—who sets off to literally carry the light of progress into his native country: the big task awaiting Levshin upon his return to Soviet Russia is the electrification of remote Siberian villages (pp. 114–15). Early on in *The Magic Mountain*, Settembrini performs a symbolic act that marks him out as a champion of the Enlightenment: he switches on the electric light in the dim bedroom where Hans is brooding about desire, decay, and death. This act is repeated towards the end of the novel by Hans himself, who switches on the light to interrupt a mystical séance. But what good are such empty gestures, Fedin seems to suggest, when *his* enlightened engineer can build actual power plants and install transmission lines? Levshin therefore outdoes Mann's Settembrini, Fedin must have thought, and has nothing at all to do with Naphta, the caricature of a communist in *The Magic Mountain*. Instead, Levshin enacts Lenin's famous slogan from 1920: 'communism is Soviet government plus the electrification of the whole country.'[63] With what I imagine must have been a wry smile, Fedin set out to counter Settembrini's racist and nationalist binary rhetoric on the active and industrious Westerners and the passive and idle Easterners with his portrayal of a Stakhanovite, an uncommonly diligent and enthusiastic Soviet worker.

Present-day readers of *Sanatorium Arktur* might be sceptical about the communist glorification of strenuous labour for the benefit of the regime, and rightly so, especially given that the USSR's economy in the 1930s relied heavily on the labour of more than two million prisoners in the inhumane conditions of the Gulag camps. Levshin's work to electrify Siberia would effectively consist in commanding an army of such prisoners—a reality that Fedin's novel conveniently glosses over. And yet *Sanatorium Arktur*, one-sided as it is itself in many ways, puts pressure on the ambiguities inherent in Settembrini's position, which, following Mann's interpretation of his own novel, is still widely read as an allegory of progressive humanist values that Mann came to embrace after the First World War. In 1919, Mann wrote in his diary that Settembrini's views would be 'das sittlich einzig Positive' ('the only morally positive aspect') in the novel;[64] to this day, most critics would largely agree with Martin Swales that 'there are immense reserves of goodness, courtesy and likeability in Settembrini. He is a profoundly decent person' and that 'Settembrini means well. His views may not always be

---

[63] Quoted in David Lane, *Leninism: A Sociological Interpretation* (Cambridge: Cambridge University Press, 1981), p. 72.
[64] Quoted in Neumann, *Thomas Mann*, p. 33.

convincing, but the human behaviour that flows from them deserves respect, even perhaps love.'[65] Fedin's novel is a reminder that it is hard to love Settembrini if one happens to be Asian—which in Settembrini's expansive definition starts in Eastern Europe. (Konrad Adenauer was similarly said to 'close the curtains in his train compartment whenever he passed eastwards across the Elbe, muttering: "schon wieder Asien"'—'Asia yet again.'[66])

To add to this complicated picture of Fedin's ideological allegiances, if we take a step back and examine Levshin's role in the novel as an exemplary Soviet citizen—the equivalent of Mann's 'Everyman' Castorp—it becomes apparent that in fact, just like Hans, Levshin must be an unusually privileged citizen of his country.[67] Even though he is presented as a humble engineer, any Soviet reader would know that it was only the Party elites and their influential supporters who could hope to go for a cure in the Alps; not only was travelling abroad unaffordable for most citizens, but getting a passport for foreign travel was also nearly impossible for those with no connections.[68] In other words, Fedin—a famous author compliant with the regime's propaganda and financially supported by Maxim Gorky—is able to stay in Davos, but it is rather unrealistic that his protagonist Levshin—an ordinary Soviet engineer—gets to go there too. In the context of Soviet ideology, no matter how critical Levshin's view of the sanatorium is, his mere presence in Davos marks him out as a duplicitous figure. A real Stakhanovite should not be in the position to resist the attractions of Western culture because he should not set foot in Davos at all. This ideological inconsistency was not lost on Soviet readers of *Sanatorium Arktur*: 'Levshin constitutes the only Soviet element in this most European of all Fedin's novels, and the portrayal has confused and annoyed Soviet critics, as in fact has the novel', noted an early American critic in an essay entitled 'A Soviet Magic Mountain'.[69] To Soviet critics, it would have made much more sense if Fedin had shown Levshin in action, electrifying those Siberian villages, not just thinking about his lofty mission spread on a deck chair in a Swiss sanatorium.[70] A Swiss sanatorium is 'kein sibirisches Bergwerk' ('not a Siberian salt mine') (p. 273/p. 212), after all, as the Berghof's head doctor Behrens

[65] Swales, *Mann: 'Der Zauberberg'*, pp. 23–26. For a standard account of Settembrini's character, see Thomas Sprecher, '"Ich glaube an den Fortschritt, gewiß". Quellenkritische Untersuchungen zu Thomas Manns Settembrini-Figur', *Thomas-Mann-Studien*, 11 (1995), 79–116. But see Hermann Kurzke, ed., *Stationen der Thomas-Mann-Forschung: Aufsätze seit 1970* (Würzburg: Königshausen & Neumann, 1985), p. 65, on the sceptical reception of Settembrini at the time of the novel's publication.
[66] James Hawes, *The Shortest History of Germany* (London: Old Street Publishing, 2017), p. 150.
[67] I am indebted to Maciej Jaworski for this observation.
[68] See Iurii Oklianskii, *Fedin* (Moscow: Molodaia gvardiia, 1986), pp. 182–86 on Fedin's money troubles and Gorky's assistance. I am indebted to Marina Soroka, who pointed me towards the relevant passages in Oklianskii's book and helped me translate them.
[69] Ernest J. Simmons, *Russian Fiction and Soviet Ideology: Introduction to Fedin, Leonov, and Sholokhov* (New York: Columbia University Press, 1958), p. 55.
[70] See Monika Zielińska, *Twórczość Konstantego Fiedina w okresie międzywojennym* (Wrocław: Zakład Narodowy im. Ossolińskich, 1983), p. 133.

says in Mann's novel, albeit with the very different intention of scolding a patient eager to quit the cure.

How to make sense of *Sanatorium Arktur*—a novel whose very premise seems more dubious the more closely one considers it? Fedin's novel stages the drama of an impossible attraction. As his essay in celebration of Mann's eightieth birthday demonstrates, Fedin was critical of Mann's bourgeois ideology and yet was an admirer of his writing.[71] A comparison between Levshin and Mann's Castorp, Settembrini, and Naphta shows that Fedin was critical of Mann's cavalier portrayal of characters who succumb to the corrupt world of capitalist excess and self-indulgence, fall into a stupor, and forfeit all agency when it comes to their health. At the same time, however, *The Magic Mountain* is a topic of heated discussions in the Arktur and praised there not only as a powerful indictment of the medical profession's greed and dishonesty but also as a uniquely engrossing novel. Its first mention comes in a conversation between two patients, a young German woman called Inga and an older man from Montenegro known as Herr Major, who shows her a list of the books he read in the trenches of the First World War. Some titles are marked with an asterisk—these are the ones 'which I read in one go but did not understand', explains Herr Major (pp. 101–02). Inga notices that one title even has two asterisks next to it, presumably to single it out as the most memorable of these books. It is *The Magic Mountain*. This must be one of the most curious fictional accounts of reading Mann's novel: 1000 pages of intricate prose devoured in one sitting, unintelligible yet magnetic, and—even more strikingly—the reading takes place several years before Mann had written the novel! This account of reading *The Magic Mountain* is fictional in a double sense—it takes place in a work of fiction, but it is also entirely unrealistic. Herr Major's encounter with the novel, however engrossing he finds it, is a temporal impossibility.

One way to make sense of this scene of an impossible reading is to see Herr Major's *Magic Mountain* as a version of Mann's *Magic Mountain*—much like Fedin's *Sanatorium Arktur* is also a version of it. *The Magic Mountain* multiplies in the hands of its readers: every reader produces her own version. This interpretation is strengthened by the fact that in *Sanatorium Arktur* Thomas Mann is never explicitly identified as the author of *The Magic Mountain*. In fact, at one point, a character claims that *The Magic Mountain* does not exist at all. That is Doctor Klebe, the head doctor of the sanatorium, who soon joins Inga and Herr Major's conversation about *The Magic Mountain*. Herr Major points out that he and Doctor Klebe have talked about *The Magic Mountain* many times before, but now Klebe tries to discourage Inga from reading it: first by pretending that he has not read it himself, then claiming that he has never heard of it, and finally asserting that the book does not exist at all: 'there is no such novel' (pp. 108–09).

[71] See Konstantin Fedin, 'Thomas Mann: Zu seinem achtzigsten Geburtstag', in *Dichter, Kunst, Zeit*, trans. Georg Schwarz (Berlin: Aufbau, 1959), pp. 212–21.

Klebe's frustration with the very existence of *The Magic Mountain* is symptomatic of a wider trend among early readers of Mann's novel. The medical community was outraged upon its publication and many doctors protested against it vehemently. Here was a group of readers decidedly unimpressed with *The Magic Mountain* and so vocal about their exasperation that Mann found himself publishing an open letter in the press to address criticisms from medical circles.[72] Meanwhile, he was chuffed to hear an anecdote that showed just how impactful his fictional sanatorium had become: 'in Davos trifft ein Engländer ein, dessen erste Frage am Bahnhof lautet' ('an Englishman arrives in Davos and his first question at the train station is') '"where ist the German Sanatorium of Dr. Mann?"'[73]

What was it that so enraged many doctors who read *The Magic Mountain*? Mann's novel laid bare the fact that tuberculosis had become a lucrative business opportunity towards the end of the nineteenth century.[74] This highly contagious disease had begun to spread more rapidly in the nineteenth century, especially in large, overcrowded European cities with poor sanitation. The sick had to be isolated from the healthy to stop the spread of the illness, but public sanatoria established for this purpose were miserably decrepit. When doctors started to associate the clean mountain air with salutary effects on respiratory health, private sanatoria for the rich began to sprout, especially in the Alps. These institutions were a cross between a hospital and a hotel, and offered good amenities, personal medical care, hearty meals, various forms of entertainment, and life among an international upper-class clientele. Many patients stayed in the sanatoria for years and did not fancy leaving them even when given the doctor's permission. Due to a lack of reliable diagnostic methods, the decision as to whether somebody was sick or healthy was to a great extent arbitrary, so there was a lot of leeway for doctors and patients to prolong the sanatorium stay.

In a letter about his own short stay in Davos—it was where he accompanied his ailing wife Katia in 1912, stayed for a few weeks, and first came up with the idea for what would become *The Magic Mountain*—Thomas Mann described how a local

---

[72] See Malte Herwig, 'The "Magic Mountain Malady": *The Magic Mountain* and the Medical Community, 1924–2006', in *Thomas Mann's 'The Magic Mountain': A Casebook*, ed. Hans Rudolf Vaget (Oxford: Oxford University Press, 2008), pp. 245–64.

[73] Mann, *Selbstkommentare*, p. 95.

[74] On the cultural history of tuberculosis sanatoria, see Vera Pohland, *Das Sanatorium als literarischer Ort* (Frankfurt am Main: Peter Lang, 1984); Clark Lawlor, *Consumption and Literature: The Making of the Romantic Disease* (Basingstoke: Palgrave Macmillan, 2006); Katherine Byrne, *Tuberculosis and the Victorian Literary Imagination* (Cambridge: Cambridge University Press, 2011); Helen Bynum, *Spitting Blood: The History of Tuberculosis* (Oxford: Oxford University Press, 2012); Daniel M. Thomas, *Captain of Death: The Story of Tuberculosis* (Rochester, NY: University of Rochester Press, 1997); and Alison F. Frank, 'The Air Cure Town: Commodifying Mountain Air in Alpine Central Europe', *Central European History*, 45 (2012), 185–207. All these authors see *The Magic Mountain* as the most interesting and the most influential cultural portrayal of a tuberculosis sanatorium.

doctor '[ihn] profitlich lächelnd für etwas tuberkulös und einer längeren Kur bedürftig erklärte' ('smiled greedily and pronounced him somewhat tubercular and in need of a longer cure').[75] Every long-term rich patient meant a steady flow of income for doctors, many of whom could not hope for employment outside of the sanatoria towns because they suffered from tuberculosis themselves. The Berghof sanatorium's head doctor, Hofrat Behrens—with his bloodshot, watery eyes and bluish cheeks—also seems sickly; indeed, he is suspected to be 'einer der Ärzte, die Leidensgenossen derjenigen sind, deren Aufenthalt sie überwachen' ('one of those physicians who not only supervises people's stay here, but also shares their sufferings') (p. 202/p. 156). Mann's novel captured the mercantile aspect of sanatorium life with ruthless precision. Doctors felt attacked; in the 1920s their income was stalling even without the added negative publicity. As Vera Pohland explains in her study of literary sanatoria, the serious reputation of Davos as a high-altitude health resort was changing around 1920 because of the simultaneous development of the town into a winter sports centre.[76] No wonder doctors wished Mann's novel away and sought to discredit its author.

Fedin wrote in his letters from Davos that *The Magic Mountain* was not available in any bookshops in the town; doctors forbade their patients to read it, he explained, and therefore every patient had read it.[77] In the 1930s, when Fedin's novel is set, the heyday of sanatoria in Davos is over; but Fedin—and his characters in *Sanatorium Arktur*—recognize the manipulative and mercantile attitude of doctors from *The Magic Mountain*, written a decade earlier, based on experiences of two decades earlier, and set three decades earlier. This is how Herr Major describes the novel to Inga:

'Ever read it? Here, on the magic mountain, it's taboo. It's about people like you and me. But here they pretend it doesn't exist.'

'Is it hard to get?'

'Try.'

'Is it harmful?'

'For doctors. But they say it's harmful for patients. [...] Medicine feels it has been wronged by *The Magic Mountain*, because the writer wrote his book without obtaining the blessing of the Davos Medical Association first. But, I must admit, I did not understand the book. Destiny ruled by chance is a philosophy which deprives the patient of his will.'

'And the doctors of their income,' Inga supplemented with scorn.   (p. 102)

---

[75] Mann, *Selbstkommentare*, p. 7.   [76] Pohland, *Das Sanatorium*, p. 38.
[77] See Oklianskii, *Fedin*, p. 191.

The 'they' mentioned by Herr Major are the doctors—especially Doctor Klebe, who will pretend that *The Magic Mountain* does not exist a few pages later. Inga discovers that the book is indeed impossible to buy in Davos. Herr Major finally brings it back from Locarno towards the end of the novel, after Inga's death. 'How fortunate that she did not taste this sea of pessimism', comments Klebe bitterly (p. 207).

Klebe is a doctor, but he suffers from tuberculosis himself, and his surname playfully indicates that he clings on to his patients and does everything he can to keep them at his declining institution, which is threatened by a looming bankruptcy. In the opening passage of *Sanatorium Arktur*, artfully designed in the English edition, Klebe pores over a stack of financial documents that paint a gloomy picture of his prospects:

> Doctor Klebe was fast becoming insolvent. His creditors had appointed administrators and once a week their accountant presented himself at the sanatorium to check the receipts from patients and to deduct as much as possible towards the settlement of Klebe's debts.   (p. 9)

He goes on to mull over what he perceives to be the gradually increasing stinginess of his patients: 'they were saving even on medicine, to say nothing of their feigned indifference to such things as a glass of Italian vermouth or a ride on a horsedrawn sleigh with bells jingling in the harness' (p. 10), he grudgingly says to himself. This scene is a reversal of an episode in *The Magic Mountain* towards the end of the fourth chapter—a fortnight into Hans Castorp's stay in the sanatorium—in which his weekly payments are described:

> die bescheidene Wochenrechnung von rund 160 Franken, bescheiden und billig nach seinem Urteil, selbst wenn man die Unbezahlbarkeiten des hiesigen Aufenthalts, eben ihrer Unbezahlbarkeit wegen, überhaupt nicht in Anschlag brachte, auch nicht gewisse Darbietungen, die wohl berechenbar gewesen wären, wenn man gewollt hätte, wie zum Exempel die vierzehntägige Kurmusik und die Vorträge Dr. Krokowskis, sondern allein und ausschließlich die eigentliche Bewirtung und gasthausmäßige Leistung, das bequeme Logis, die fünf übergewaltigen Mahlzeiten.   (pp. 245–46)
>
> the modest weekly sum of 160 francs. And it was modest and fair to his mind, even if you disregarded the priceless benefits of his stay—which were not on the bill because they were priceless; but then neither were certain other entertainments, which could very well have been calculated, the band concerts every two weeks, for example, or Dr. Krokowski's lectures. The bill was solely for room and board, for the basic services of the hotel—comfortable lodging and five prodigious meals.   (p. 190)

When Hans lists all the amenities available at the Berghof, all the sanatorium routines and activities—five hearty meals a day, Krokowski's fortnightly lectures on psychoanalysis, regular X-ray scans, and check-ups with the doctors—appear not as Wagnerian leitmotifs, but as cyclical expenses that must be budgeted for.[78] In Anthony Heilbut's words, Mann made psychoanalysis 'a part of commercial history, a tourist's entertainment along with mountain hikes and afternoon tea'.[79] In stark contrast to Doctor Klebe's patients, Hans finds his 'Wochenrechnung' very reasonable. He then goes on to estimate how much it would cost to live in the sanatorium for a month—and for a full year. Hans presents his calculations as though coming up with them on the spot to get a better understanding of his cousin Joachim's expenses, but it turns out that he has done the maths beforehand and checked it against his own income:

> [er hatte] festgestellt, daß sein Vetter, oder vielmehr, daß man überhaupt hier alles in allem 12 000 Franken pro Jahr benötige und sich zum Spaße innerlich klargemacht, daß er für seine Person dem Leben hier oben wirtschaftlich mehr als gewachsen sei, da er sich als einen Mann von 18–19 000 Franken jährlich betrachten durfte. (p. 247)

> he had determined that his cousin, or rather, anyone just in general would need, all things considered, twelve thousand francs a year here. Just for the fun of it, he had pointed out to himself that his own funds were more than adequate for a life up here, seeing as he was a man with an annual income of eighteen to nineteen thousand francs. (p. 191)

Fedin turns this scene on its head, and it is Doctor Klebe who must count his assets—but, unlike Hans Castorp, he cannot be satisfied with his calculations. By the end of the novel Klebe will have gone bankrupt and died by suicide. As the design of the first page of the novel's English edition illustrates, he is destined to linger awkwardly on the threshold of the luxurious lifestyle of sanatorium novels—longingly looking at the characteristic spires of Davos from his small, claustrophobic balcony, but ultimately fended off by the spiky balustrade.

Nods to the economic basis of the sanatorium lifestyle were a staple element in the micro-genre of the interwar sanatorium novel. Knut Hamsun, the author of *Siste Kapitel* (*Chapter the Last*, 1923), the best-known sanatorium novel before *The Magic Mountain*, brought it into sharp focus by beginning his book with a chapter about local farmers and landowners negotiating with a doctor and a

---

[78] Scholars usually describe recurring thematic and structural elements in the novel as Wagnerian leitmotifs; some have argued, however, that it is a device Mann learned from Dickens. See U. Janssens-Knorsch and L.R. Leavis, '"Buddenbrook & Son": Thomas Mann and Literary Influence', *English Studies*, 82.6 (2001), 521–38.

[79] Anthony Heilbut, *Thomas Mann: Eros & Literature* (London: Macmillan, 1996), p. 426.

lawyer who want to buy a plot for a sanatorium. The whole enterprise is purely mercantile in nature; the lawyer is at great pains to woo the right kind of patients—preferably well-known aristocrats whose names will in turn attract wealthy bourgeoisie.[80] The opening paragraph of Mann's 1903 novella *Tristan* captures a similar impression—it reads like a promotional brochure: 'Hier ist "Einfried", das Sanatorium! Weiß und geradlinig liegt es mit seinem langgestreckten Hauptgebäude und seinem Seitenflügel inmitten des weiten Gartens' ('Here we are at "Einfried", the well-known sanatorium! It is white and rectilinear, a long low-lying main building with a side wing, standing in a spacious garden').[81] Fedin read *Chapter the Last* and thought very highly of it;[82] Mann had a lot of respect for Hamsun too.[83] Hamsun, Mann, and Fedin make it clear in their different ways that the sanatorium as a business model and a lifestyle choice was only possible due to the surplus wealth that upper-class patients had access to. Their families' income, inheritance, and substantial interest rates provided for them. In the lecture on *The Magic Mountain* that he gave at Princeton in 1939, Mann explained:

> es [...] handelte sich bei diesen Instituten um eine typische Erscheinung der Vorkriegszeit, nur denkbar bei einer noch intakten kapitalistischen Wirtschaftsform. Nur unter jenen Verhältnissen war es möglich, daß die Patienten auf Kosten ihrer Familien Jahre lang oder auch ad infinitum dies Leben führen konnten.

> such institutions [...] were a typical pre-war phenomenon. They were only possible in a capitalistic economy that was still functioning well and normally. Only under such a system was it possible for patients to remain there year after year at the family's expense.[84]

One might wonder, as Eckhard Heftrich did, whether Thomas Mann or his characters had any moral scruples about this state of affairs;[85] but from the perspective of reception studies, it is more fruitful to ask how the text registers these issues so that readers can engage with them.

---

[80] See Knut Hamsun, *Chapter the Last*, trans. Arthur G. Chater (London: A. A. Knopf, 1930), pp. 46–47.

[81] Thomas Mann, 'Tristan', in *Frühe Erzählungen: 1983–1912*, ed. T. J. Reed, GKFA (Frankfurt am Main, 2004), p. 319. Thomas Mann, 'Tristan', in *Death in Venice and Other Stories*, trans. David Luke (London: Vintage, 1998), p. 93.

[82] See Oklianskii, *Fedin*, p. 192.

[83] For a discussion of contemporary reviews that drew comparisons between Hamsun and Mann, see Neumann, *Thomas Mann, 'Der Zauberberg'*, p. 109.

[84] Thomas Mann, 'Einführung in Den Zauberberg für Studenten der Universität Princeton', in *Der Zauberberg* (Frankfurt am Main, 1962), pp. ii–xiv, p. v; Thomas Mann, 'The Making of *The Magic Mountain*', in *The Magic Mountain*, trans. H. T. Lowe-Porter (London: Vintage, 1999), pp. 719–29, p. 721.

[85] See Heftrich, 'Der *Homo oeconomicus* im Werk von Thomas Mann', p. 161.

Mann's sanatorium is a world of surplus wealth and excessive consumption. Time and again, its underlying economic forces are brought to light. In her recent monograph, *Geldströme: Ökonomie im Romanwerk Thomas Manns*, Anna Kinder discussed 'Hans Castorps Flucht aus der kapitalistischen Stromsphäre hinauf auf den Zauberberg' ('Hans Castorp's flight from the sphere of capitalistic currents onto the Magic Mountain').[86] This is certainly how Hans Castorp perceives his own situation; he gradually comes to define his identity in terms of a radical break with the world of work, money, and capital. But is it a fair assessment of his circumstances? Hans and other wealthy patients might wish to forget the links that tie them very closely to their social context, but the novel does not elide this aspect of their existence. Hans's transition from visitor to patient is usually discussed with reference to his adoption of certain habits of speech ('wir hier oben'—'we up here'—becomes his personal pronoun of choice) and of other habits: he measures and records his temperature twice a day religiously, follows the regime of the 'Liegekur' ('rest cure'), and attends regular check-ups with the doctors. But the scene in which Hans counts his assets to make sure that he can afford to become a patient at the sanatorium forms an integral part of this transition too. The result is satisfactory: Hans will be able to live comfortably off the interest on the capital accumulated over several generations by his merchant family.[87]

Several cultural critics writing about tuberculosis have noted that its other name in English, 'consumption', is polysemous: it is also used, among other things, to describe the process of buying and using goods. Katherine Byrne writes that in Victorian novels tuberculosis/consumption is closely associated with capitalism:

> consumption works as both a disrupter of the capitalist, commercial world, and a metaphor for it [...] consumption's ability to infect all social spheres rendered it a perfect symbol for the capitalist system as a whole, rather than just a means of expressing its effect upon one section of the population [...] the process of consumption [...] is as dangerous as the process of production: capitalism [...] is pathological at any stage of the system.[88]

In *The Magic Mountain*, however, tuberculosis is not quite the great leveller: its experience is heavily conditioned by the patient's class. Not long after counting his assets Hans buys a thermometer. Given a choice between one for three francs and fifty cents and another for five francs, Hans—who 'wußte, was er sich und seinem Ansehen schuldig war' ('knew what he owed himself and his social station')

---

[86] Kinder, *Geldströme*, p. 93.

[87] For more details on Hans's background and wealth, see Sprecher, 'Kur-, Kultur- und Kapitalismuskritik im *Zauberberg*'.

[88] Byrne, *Tuberculosis and the Victorian Literary Imagination*, pp. 5–6.

(p. 256/p. 198)—does not even look at the cheaper thermometer and decides to purchase the more expensive item right away. The purchase will be on his bill, Hans is told—the weekly bill that he had been considering. The thermometer is a material symbol of Hans's transformation into a patient, and the economic dimension of this process is again highlighted. Hans's new thermometer is a luxurious and valuable commodity, compared to a piece of jewellery: 'schmuck wie ein Geschmeide lag das gläserne Gerät in die genau nach seiner Figur ausgesparte Vertiefung der roten Samtpolsterung gebettet' ('the glass instrument lay bedded like a precious gem in its red velvet cushion, the indentation exactly matched to its form') (p. 256/p. 198). While asserting his newly acquired identity as a patient rather than guest in the sanatorium, Hans also asserts his identity as a wealthy bourgeois man. Yet again the experience of life in the sanatorium is linked to a particular social class and economic status.

The luxurious world of the Berghof sanatorium and the refined novel that describes it are alienating and alluring at the same time: they tempt the reader with a promise of a uniquely attractive experience, and thereby pose a threat to those critical of the bourgeois lifestyle and mindset. Fedin was not the only reader faced with this dilemma. 'Der arme, unglückliche Georg Lukács hat den größten Teil seines arbeitsamen Lebens der Frage gewidmet, auf welche Weise man gleichzeitig Thomas Mann und Lenin lieben könnte' ('Poor, hapless Georg Lukács dedicated most of his industrious life to the question of how one can simultaneously love Thomas Mann and Lenin'), wrote Leszek Kołakowski—himself a prominent historian of Marxism, and an avid reader of Mann—in a special section of the *FAZ* edited by Marcel Reich-Ranicki to commemorate the hundredth anniversary of Mann's birthday.[89] In the same issue of the *FAZ*, Peter Rühmkorf wrote of a 'language' or even 'class barrier' that separated him from Mann's writing, from Mann's 'Ausdrucksweise' ('manner of expression') which was '[ihm] beinahe physisch zuwider' ('almost physically repulsive to him').[90]

Ten years later, however, Rühmkorf changed his view and wrote another essay on Mann, entitled 'Die neugewonnene Wertschätzung des Prosaartisten' ('The Newly Found Appreciation of a Prose Master').[91] Scholars of Mann's work have often reacted with vitriol and hostility to such assessments. Eckhard Heftrich, for example, wrote of Rühmkorf's change of heart:

[man würde] Rühmkorfs Selbstbewußtsein falsch einschätzen, wollte man ihm unterstellen, es habe ihn allmählich die Furcht beschlichen, er könne am Ende in die Literaturhistorie nur als eine Fußnote der Rezeptionsgeschichte Thomas

[89] Marcel Reich-Ranicki, ed., *Was halten Sie von Thomas Mann?* (Frankfurt am Main: Fischer, 1988), p. 48. For a discussion of the relationship between Mann and Lukács, see Judith Marcus, *Georg Lukács and Thomas Mann: A Study in the Sociology of Literature* (Amherst, MA: University of Massachusetts Press, 1987).
[90] Reich-Ranicki, *Was halten Sie*, p. 69.   [91] Ibid., p. 121.

Manns eingehen, so daß er es vorzöge, ganz aus den Annalen zu verschwinden, anstatt allein durch ein gespreiztes Fehlurteil unsterblich zu werden.

[one would misjudge] Rühmkorf's self-awareness if one were to imply that he had been gradually overcome by fear of going down in literary history as a mere footnote to the reception history of Thomas Mann's works, so that he preferred to disappear entirely from the annals rather than becoming immortal through a gross misjudgement alone.[92]

Similarly, Kurzke wrote bitterly of Martin Walser's rejection of *The Magic Mountain*—'*Der Zauberberg* gefällt ihm nicht, weil Castorp soziologisch ein Parasit ist und weil nichts dabei herauskommt' ('*The Magic Mountain* does not take his fancy because Castorp is a social parasite and in the end not much comes out of it all')—and chided him for not appreciating Mann's critique of the pre-war world.[93]

But such a closer reading—listening carefully to the readers who struggle to engage with Mann's writing for ideological reasons—can yield interesting insights. Yet another essay in Reich-Ranicki's section on Mann in the *FAZ* was contributed by Wolfgang Harich—an East German philosopher and member of the Sozialistische Einheitspartei Deutschlands (SED), albeit with a troubled relation-ship to the party elites—who reminisced about a conversation he had had with Hanns Eisler on Brecht and Mann, in which Eisler expressed admiration for Mann and apparently asked rhetorically: 'glauben Sie, dass Brecht sich [die höchste Stufe des Kommunismus] ohne den *Zauberberg* vorstellt?' ('do you think that Brecht imagines the highest stage of communism without *The Magic Mountain*?').[94] In 1920, the young Brecht wrote an article about an event in Munich at which Thomas Mann read from his draft of *The Magic Mountain*.[95] Rather amusingly, scholars of Mann have tended to describe it as a positive, even admiring early review of the novel, while scholars of Brecht have mostly described it as sarcastic. Mann critics thought it was 'eine verständige Rezension des sehr beeindruckten [...] Bert Brecht' ('a judicious review by Bert Brecht, who was much impressed'),[96] that Brecht's 'Reserve [verhehlte] noch nicht den Respekt' ('his respect was not yet masked by his reserve');[97] that 'noch ohne [...] Häme [...] äußert sich Brecht durchaus bewundernd' ('Brecht still speaks [of Mann] without

[92] Eckhard Heftrich, 'Der gehaßte Kollege: Deutsche Schriftsteller über Thomas Mann', *Thomas-Mann-Studien*, 7 (1987), 351–69, p. 353.
[93] Kurzke, *Stationen der Thomas-Mann-Forschung*, pp. 233–34.
[94] Reich-Ranicki, *Was halten Sie?*, p. 35. For an overview of Mann's reception in the GDR, see Georg Wenzel, *Gab es das überhaupt? Thomas Mann in der Kultur der DDR* (Gransee: Schwarzdruck, 2011).
[95] Bertolt Brecht, 'Thomas Mann im Börsensaal', in *Werke*, ed. Werner Hecht and others, xxi: *Schriften 1: 1914–1933* (Frankfurt am Main: Suhrkamp, 1992), pp. 61–62.
[96] De Mendelssohn, *Nachbemerkungen zu Thomas Mann*, p. 72.
[97] Neumann, *Thomas Mann, 'Der Zauberberg'*, p. 103.

malice and with clear admiration').[98] Brecht critics thought that he 'äußert [...] sich hier noch zurückhaltend, jedoch eindeutig ironisch-ablehnend' ('speaks still with some restraint, but sarcastically and dismissively without any doubt');[99] that he wrote of Mann 'mit listiger Ironie' ('with sly irony'), and of the novel 'im großen ganzen noch wohlwollend' ('on the whole still in favourable terms'), but 'den Mannschen Stil behutsam parodierend' ('scrupulously parodying Mann's style');[100] that he suggested that *The Magic Mountain* was boring.[101]

Later animosity between the two writers, fuelled by ideological differences (emphasized by Brecht critics) and possibly jealousy (often suggested by Mann critics), has been chronicled in much detail.[102] It is impossible now to reconstruct with certainty what Brecht felt as he listened to Mann's reading in that Munich hall in 1920, or when he read the novel later on, or, indeed, whether he imagined Hans's sanatorium lifestyle when thinking about 'die freie Entwicklung eines Jeden' ('the free development of each')—the strangely imprecise phrase in the last sentence of the second chapter of the *Manifest der Kommunistischen Partei* (*The Communist Manifesto*) which conjures up Marx's vision of a classless communist society.[103] In the *Grundrisse der Kritik der Politischen Ökonomie* (*Fundamentals of a Critique of Political Economy*), an unfinished manuscript from 1857–58, Marx developed a vision of 'a post-scarcity age, when men can turn from alienating and dehumanizing labor to the free use of leisure in the pursuit of the sciences and arts'.[104] The main thrust of this vision is presented in the so-called 'Maschinenfragment', which now attracts a lot of interest in our age of automation, artificial intelligence, and unprecedented wealth. Marx revisited his terms from *The Communist Manifesto* there, writing about the goal of 'die Arbeitszeit für die ganze Gesellschaft auf ein fallendes Minimum zu reduzieren und so die Zeit aller frei für ihre eigne Entwicklung zu machen' ('reducing working time for the whole of society to a minimum and thus making everyone's

---

[98] Johannes Roskothen, '"Der Stehkragen sprach": Die unproduktive Spannung zwischen Thomas Mann und Bertolt Brecht—eine Rekonstruktion', *Düsseldorfer Beiträge zur Thomas Mann-Forschung*, 2 (2013), 61–78, p. 63.

[99] Jürgen Hillesheim, *Augsburger Brecht-Lexikon* (Würzburg: Königshausen & Neumann, 2000), p. 115.

[100] Klaus Völker, *Bertolt Brecht. Eine Biographie* (Munich: Hanser, 1976), p. 109.

[101] Jost Hermand, *Die Toten schweigen nicht: Brecht-Aufsätze* (Frankfurt am Main: Peter Lang, 2010), p. 149.

[102] See Roskothen, '"Der Stehkragen sprach"', as well as Hans Mayer and Jack Zipes, 'Thomas Mann and Bertolt Brecht: Anatomy of an Antagonism', *New German Critique*, 6 (1975), 101–15.

[103] Karl Marx and Friedrich Engels, 'Manifest der Kommunistischen Partei', in *Ausgewählte Werke in sechs Bänden* (Berlin: Dietz, 1972), vol. i, pp. 383–451, p. 438; Karl Marx and Friedrich Engels, *The Communist Manifesto*, trans. David McLellan (Oxford: Oxford University Press, 2008), p. 26.

[104] D. C. Lee, 'On the Marxian View of the Relationship between Man and Nature', in *Karl Marx's Social and Political Thought*, ed. Bob Jessop and Russell Wheatley (London: Routledge, 1999), viii: *Nature, Culture, Moral, Ethics*, pp. 1–15, p. 9. On Marx's utopian ideas, see Gregory Claeys, *Marx and Marxism* (London: Penguin, 2018), pp. 231–40.

time free for their own development'),[105] and the vision of 'die künstlerische, wissenschaftliche etc. Ausbildung der Individuen durch die für sie alle freigewordne Zeit und geschaffnen Mittel' ('all members of society [being able to] develop their education in the arts, sciences, etc., thanks to the free time and means available to all').[106]

While contemporary theorists of post-scarcity economy debate whether this really is how most people would choose to spend their leisure time, it is a recurring fantasy of many Marxist critics. In an essay published in *The New York Times*, Elif Batuman wrote of Fredric Jameson's interpretation of Proust:[107]

> I still remember how moved I was by Jameson's description, in a passage on Proust, of the Guermantes salon—a world utterly devoted to 'interpersonal relationships, to conversation, art, [...] fashion, love'—as a 'distorted' reflection of the Marxist Utopia: 'a world in which alienated labor will have ceased to exist, in which man's struggle with the external world and with his own mystified and external pictures of society will have given way to man's confrontation with himself' [...] I love this passage, because it finds such a simultaneously meaningful and absurd justification for Proust's worship of the aristocracy: that leisure class was, for better or worse, Proust's only available 'source of concrete images' of the classless Utopia.[108]

It is in this sense that one might question the common view of Mann as a writer who, in Michael Minden's words, 'remain[ed] interested in the individual rather than the larger social formation, and was never able to convince himself that economic interventions were equal to modifying the human condition'.[109] The reading of *The Magic Mountain* that I have outlined in this section suggests that Mann and his readers had a palpable sense that Hans's intellectual and emotional adventures on the 'Magic Mountain' were only possible because of his social status. Russell A. Berman has been one of the few critics to comment on this anxiety inherent in Mann's novel. According to him, 'can social equality and quality of education be combined?' is among the fundamental questions that the novel asks.[110] Hans lives out 'die freie Entwicklung' envisioned by Marx, but the question of whether this free development can belong to 'each' is much more vexed.

[105] Karl Marx, *Grundrisse der Kritik der politischen Ökonomie* (Berlin: Dietz, 1974), p. 596; Karl Marx, *The Grundrisse*, trans. and ed. David McLellan (New York: Harper Torchbooks, 1971), p. 144.
[106] Marx, *Grundrisse*, p. 593. Marx, *The Grundrisse*, p. 142.
[107] Jameson is also an avid reader of *The Magic Mountain*. See Fredric Jameson, *Modernist Papers* (London: Verso, 2007), pp. 55–95.
[108] Elif Batuman, 'From the Critical Impulse, the Growth of Literature', *The New York Times*, 31 December 2010 <https://www.nytimes.com/2011/01/02/books/review/Batuman-t-web.html> [accessed 10 May 2019].
[109] Minden, ed., *Thomas Mann*, p. 4.
[110] Russell A. Berman, 'Modernism and the Bildungsroman: Thomas Mann's *Magic Mountain*', in *The Cambridge Companion to the Modern German Novel*, ed. Graham Bartram (Cambridge: Cambridge University Press, 2004), pp. 77–92, pp. 90–91.

Just as Marxist readers might feel simultaneously drawn to and critical of bourgeois narratives in this way, an episode at the end of *Sanatorium Arktur* encapsulates Levshin's ambiguous relationship towards Western European society and culture. He takes his last walk around Davos with Fräulein Hoffman, an assistant physician at the sanatorium with whom he has had an affair; they walk along an avenue lined with trees and 'heavy, tall masts supporting high voltage transmission lines'. Levshin stops 'to take a closer look at the porcelain insulators on which the wires were suspended', bravely disregarding a sign 'with a frightening zigzagging arrow and the word "Danger" on it' (p. 237). Just as Fedin attempts to appropriate the 'Magic Mountain' archetype for his own ends—to juxtapose Soviet Russia and Western Europe, demonstrating the advantages of the former, and to create the new socialist realist literature informed by prestigious modernist forms—so Levshin is contemplating Western technology with an eye to transplanting it onto Soviet ground. But a hint of ambiguity remains: if socialist realism is dependent on bourgeois literature and a Soviet engineer looks up to Western technology, who emerges victorious from this confrontation?

Fedin's novel registers an uneasiness about bourgeois culture, but also about the social role of culture more generally. Towards the beginning, Doctor Klebe talks to Herr Major (soon revealed as an avid reader of *The Magic Mountain*) about a 'shocking' and 'licentious' French novel he has recently read—about 'a respectable, wealthy gentleman [...] living in sin with his servant'; the servant 'gets pregnant and the gentleman throws her out into the street' (p. 15). Doctor Klebe concludes that from now on he will only ever read Edgar Wallace novels—popular English pulp fiction ranging from countless detective stories to a series of adventure novels set in Africa—and offers to lend one to Herr Major. But to Klebe's distress, Herr Major shyly asks if he could borrow the French novel 'about the respectable and wealthy gentleman' first. From the first pages of *Sanatorium Arktur*, Fedin confronts us with the question of why people read novels, and what kind of novels they are attracted to—which is all the more striking given that these questions are posed in a novel fashioned as a response to another novel.

The problem that Fedin faces is the tension between prescriptive and descriptive visions of the role of culture. It is the tension between what people think or are told they *should* read and what they *actually* read; what they *should* enjoy and what they *actually* enjoy. According to an amusing anecdote—or 'legend', as John Willett calls it[111]—on one occasion Kurt Weill saw 'a book lying on the bedside table in [Brecht's] flat and picked it up. The dust jacket said "Karl Marx: *Das Kapital*". Inside was an Edgar Wallace thriller.'[112] What should one read in one's free time indeed? What role should culture play in our lives? Responding to Rita

---

[111] John Willett, *Brecht in Context: Comparative Approaches* (London: Methuen, 1984), p. 28.

[112] Ronald Taylor, *Kurt Weill: Composer in a Divided World* (London: Simon & Schuster, 1991), p. 102. I am grateful to Kevin Hilliard for sharing this anecdote with me.

Felski's *Limits of Critique*, Bruce Robbins insisted that the job of culture is to provide a 'critical distance from the present society'[113] and the job of literary scholars is to be 'edgy' and 'distanc[e] ourselves from the values of the society around us', something which 'distinguishes us as academics from fans as well as from most reviewers, belletrists, and other adjuncts to the publishing industry'.[114] In her response, Rita Felski retorted that 'conceiving of culture and society, or art and society, as two mutually opposed blocks is [...] part of the problem, not the solution'.[115] Their disagreement illuminates the same problem that I have been describing in this section: what is the job of culture? What is the danger of pleasure? Who should decide?

For Fedin and Soviet critics, attraction to the bourgeois world of *The Magic Mountain* is a problem because it weakens the socially critical impulse that culture should foster. For present-day readers critical of the Soviet regime and their cultural policies, however, it is the fact that books such as *Sanatorium Arktur* responded to official regulations issued by the Politburo that is likely to appear the far greater problem. And somewhere in the middle of all this is *The Magic Mountain* itself—blissfully indifferent to all these debates about which books readers should and should not read. In fact, no long-term patients of the Berghof read books at all—'sie erklärten es für das Ungeschick von Stümpern, sich [...] an ein Buch zu klammern' ('[they] declared openly that only clumsy bunglers in the art needed a book to hang on to') (p. 413/p. 324). Novels are taken out of the local library and make rounds around the sanatorium, but the long-term patients satisfy themselves with simply having a copy lying around nearby, 'auf dem Schoß oder dem Beitischchen' ('on their lap or within reach on a table')—'das genüge vollauf, sich versorgt zu fühlen' ('that sufficed for them to feel their reading needs were taken care of'); there is no need to open a book and read it. Looking at the chain of responses to *The Magic Mountain*, one could quip that Mann's characters do not have to worry about their attitude towards immersive novels because they already live in one. Other readers who have been discussed in this chapter linger awkwardly on the threshold—tempted by the world on the 'Magic Mountain' and yet critical of it or excluded from it. Fedin's Levshin chooses to resist the temptation and leaves his sanatorium—but Fedin himself, after his own departure from the sanatorium, goes on to write a version of *The Magic Mountain*. He dives into Mann's enchanted world one more time, in a bid to enter the centre stage of world literature beside the 'pig' with his Nobel Prize.

[113] Bruce Robbins, 'Not So Well Attached', *PMLA*, 132.2 (2017), 371–76, p. 371.
[114] Ibid., p. 372.   [115] Rita Felski, 'Response', *PMLA*, 132.2 (2017), 384–91, p. 387.

3. Intellectual Tourists

Section 2 grouped together readers who linger on the threshold of Mann's text because, while they can feel the pull of the novel, they also feel a sense of ideological opposition to it. In this section, I consider readers who also linger on the threshold of the text, but for a very different reason. These are readers who are not at all critical of the ideology of bourgeois consumerism which forms the backbone of *The Magic Mountain*. On the contrary, these readers want to recreate Mann's enchanting story-world so they can profit from it themselves. To put it figuratively, they dip their toes in Mann's immersive aquarium, but their true goal is to go swimming in a very different pool altogether.

My first example here, *Der Zauberlehrling* by Erich Kästner, is an intriguing counterpart to *Sanatorium Arktur*. Kästner wrote it in the late 1930s, at the same time as Fedin, his almost exact contemporary, was at work on his novel. Both texts are set in Davos in the 1930s, and both are responses to *The Magic Mountain* based on their authors' visits to the Swiss town. It might seem that the similarities between them end here: *Sanatorium Arktur* is a sanatorium novel, but Kästner's characters never set foot in a sanatorium; in Fedin's book, *The Magic Mountain* is discussed several times, but there is no explicit mention of it in *Der Zauberlehrling*; Fedin's novel condemns capitalism, whereas Kästner's novel wholeheartedly embraces it. By the end of this section, however, I hope to have demonstrated that these two texts have much more in common than might at first appear to be the case.

Erich Kästner (1899–1974) was one of the best-known writers in the Weimar Republic. He published novels, satirical poetry, newspaper feuilletons, and bestselling children's detective stories which helped transform the conventions of children's literature. Kästner identified as a left-wing pacifist and anti-fascist, but he refused to go into exile after 1933 and stayed in Berlin, where he was subjected to political repression. Even though most of his books were officially banned in Nazi Germany, he continued to write and, under his own name, published some less overtly political texts with a Swiss publisher. More problematically, under various pseudonyms he also wrote numerous simple theatre plays and film screenplays which fuelled the Nazi entertainment industry and enabled Kästner to make a living.[116] His economic situation was precarious: it comes as no surprise, then, that in 1936 he accepted the invitation of the 'Verkehrsverein' of Davos to come visit the town, give a public lecture, and write a cheerful counterpart to *The Magic*

---

[116] This problematic issue remained almost completely unknown for decades, mainly because Kästner never owned up to these texts after the war. See Stefan Neuhaus, *Das verschwiegene Werk: Erich Kästners Mitarbeit an Theaterstücken unter Pseudonym* (Würzburg: Königshausen & Neumann, 2000), and Hermann Kurzke's review of it: Hermann Kurzke, 'Der mit den Wölfen heulte', *FAZ*, 3 January 2001 <http://www.faz.net/aktuell/feuilleton/buecher/rezension-sachbuch-der-mit-den-woelfen-heulte-11267861.html> [accessed 30 May 2017].

Mountain—the novel which, according to the tourist board, had painted an unsympathetic and off-putting picture of Davos.

Kästner went to Davos in 1938 and wrote a manuscript entitled *Der Zauberlehrling*. Doctors in the 1920s had been bothered by Mann's novel because they wanted to attract more patients and worried that Mann had discredited their sanatoria; members of the tourist board in the 1930s were bothered by the novel because they wanted to attract more tourists and worried that Mann had discredited the town with his descriptions of its sanatoria. Their desire to counteract the cultural influence of Mann's novel was not as unusual as it might seem to a reader of today. In the 1920s and 1930s leading magazines for hoteliers ran review columns about books set in hotels with the intention of helping hoteliers decide which books to stock in their hotel libraries. A novel described as a 'fröhlicher Hotel-Roman' ('cheerful novel set in a hotel') would qualify, whereas a book critical of hotel life would be discouraged.[117] Meinrad Inglin's 1928 novel *Hotel Excelsior* did not appeal to one reviewer in such a magazine: 'wer nie in einem Schweizer Hotel gewesen ist, konnte einen üblen Eindruck von einem solchen Werk erhalten' ('such a novel could make a negative impression on a reader who has never stayed in a Swiss hotel').[118] Similarly, Hugo Marti complained in 1935 after the publication of his novel *Davoser Stundenbuch* (*The Davos Book of Hours*): 'Davos versteckt das Buch so diskret wie möglich und macht mir den Vorwurf, propagandistisch schlecht gewirkt zu haben' ('Davos hides my book as discreetly as possible and accuses me of having spread negative propaganda').[119]

With the benefit of historical hindsight, the tourist board's concern about the impact of *The Magic Mountain* and other novels on the town's reputation seems rather misplaced. Davos made the headlines when, in February 1936, David Frankfurter, a student at the University of Bern, killed Wilhelm Gustloff, the Nazi 'Gauleiter' of Switzerland, in the town. At the time, Davos was home to the Swiss Nazi Party headquarters and a beloved tourist spot for Hitler's fascists, which would become a much more significant threat to Davos's reputation in the long run. A recent documentary by Danielle Jaeggi, entitled *A l'ombre de la montagne* (*In the Shadow of the Mountain*, 2009), explores this problematic past.

But there seem to be no Nazis in *Der Zauberlehrling*. The protagonist of the story, Alfons Mintzlaff, is a thirty-year-old German art historian. Just like Erich Kästner in real life, Mintzlaff gets an invitation to give a public lecture in Davos; he accepts, then at the last minute postpones it by two weeks, but in the end travels to the town a week before the new date of the lecture; the confusion about the date of his arrival proves crucial later in the story. On his way to Davos, Mintzlaff meets a

---

[117] Quoted in Seán M. Williams, 'Home Truths and Uncomfortable Spaces: Swiss Hotels and Literature of the 1920s', *Forum for Modern Language Studies*, 55.4 (2019), 444–65, p. 452.

[118] Ibid., p. 461.

[119] Quoted in Thomas Sprecher, *Davos im 'Zauberberg': Thomas Manns Roman und sein Schauplatz* (Munich: Fink, 1996), p. 32.

mysterious man who introduces himself as Baron Lamotte. It quickly turns out that Lamotte has supernatural powers—he can read people's minds and control people's bodies—but it long remains uncertain who he really is, until the revelation that he is none other than...the Greek god Zeus in disguise. Lamotte/Zeus wants to help Mintzlaff, who has renounced emotions and relationships with other people, become happier. In Davos, they discover that somebody has taken advantage of the confusion about the date of Mintzlaff's lecture, has been impersonating him, and is to give the lecture under Mintzlaff's name, entitled 'Der Humor als Weltanschauung' ('Humour as Worldview'). Mintzlaff and Lamotte decide to expose the false professor during the lecture. In the meantime they enjoy themselves in Davos; the book showcases all kinds of entertainment awaiting tourists in the town—skiing, hiking, ice skating, and fancy-dress balls. Finally, all the main characters attend the lecture and the false professor is denounced.

This is how the text ends or—perhaps I should say—how it breaks off. Kästner published the text subtitling it as 'ein Fragment', but the book feels complete: it has got exactly ten chapters and is framed by Mintzlaff's public lecture engagement, so that the entire plot is contained between Mintzlaff's journey to Davos to give the lecture and the lecture itself, given by the false professor. Even if Kästner had planned to write a longer book, he found quite an ingenious way to deal with the premature ending. Towards the end of the story, the false professor is exposed and introduces himself as 'Prinz Friedrich von Ofterdingen', a descendant of an old aristocratic family. The name is a blend of Heinrich von Ofterdingen—the protagonist of Novalis's famous book under the same title—and Friedrich von Hardenberg, Novalis's real name. Novalis's *Heinrich von Ofterdingen* (1802) is the most famous Romantic 'Romanfragment', published posthumously by Friedrich Schlegel. The term 'Romanfragment' describes an unfinished piece of work, but it also evokes early Romantic aphoristic 'Fragmente', a highly prestigious literary genre, famously theorized by Schlegel as possessing unity without creating a false impression of totality, 'von der umgebenden Welt ganz abgesondert und in sich selbst vollendet wie ein Igel' ('entirely isolated from the surrounding world and [...] complete in itself like a porcupine').[120] So, rather amusingly, Kästner chooses to break off his witty, playful, and light-hearted text, his supposed 'Fragment' (which, however, does not seem incomplete), with a reference to the solemn, almost mystical conception of the Romantic 'Fragment'.[121]

---

[120] Friedrich Schlegel, *Kritische Ausgabe seiner Werke*, ed. Ernst Behler and others (Padeborn: F. Schöningh, 1958-), ii: *Charakteristiken und Kritiken I: 1796–1801*, ed. Hans Eichner (1967), p. 197; Friedrich Schlegel, 'From "Athanaeum Fragments" (1798)', trans. P. Firchow, in *Classic and Romantic German Aesthetics*, ed. J. M. Bernsetin (Cambridge: Cambridge University Press), pp. 246–60, p. 251.
[121] Another nod to German Romanticism in the text is Baron Lamotte's name which evokes the Romanic writer Friedrich de la Motte Fouqué, most famous for his 1811 novella 'Undine'.

Der Zauberlehrling is full of clever intertextual allusions of this kind—to Thomas Mann and *The Magic Mountain*, as we will see, but also to Goethe, Nietzsche, Greek mythology, and more. Greek mythology plays a particularly big role—unsurprisingly so, given that one of the main characters is Zeus. We briefly get a glimpse of other gods discussing Zeus's manifold love affairs. Mintzlaff is also able to list the names of fifteen mythological women seduced by Zeus under various guises. In response, Zeus comments bitterly: 'ich finde es nicht sehr fein, daß man in Ihren Schulen derartige Dinge ausplaudert. Was sollen denn die Gymnasiasten von mir denken!' ('I find it rather distasteful that you should gossip about such things in your schools. What must your pupils think of me!') (p. 278). This remark draws attention to the fact that the cultural allusions that Kästner makes in *Der Zauberlehrling* are very transparent—especially to the German middle class: the 'Bildungsbürger' who attended 'Gymnasien', the people long perceived to form the core of Thomas Mann's readership (and who can afford a trip to Davos). The portrayal of culture as an easily accessible, familiar, and undemanding territory recurs throughout the book: at one point, Mintzlaff ponders the question of why we all like to 'lesen und reisen' ('read and travel') in regions that we know well (p. 215). Kästner's model of engagement with culture in *Der Zauberlehrling*, then, is that of modern-day tourism. If Fedin's text, while registering *The Magic Mountain*'s allure, constantly pushes against the temptation to re-enact Mann's novel, Kästner's book gives in to the temptation and not only indulges in transforming many tropes from *The Magic Mountain* into marketable tourist attractions but, as I will argue, also moves towards becoming its 'Doppelgänger'.

Many tropes from Mann's novel are easily recognizable in Kästner's book. There are upper-class guests from all over Europe and beyond (including Germany, England, Scandinavia, the Netherlands, the USA, India, and Argentina); there is the multilingualism of Davos, which occasionally permeates the text itself, so that Kästner's German includes various foreign words; there are winter sports, the same kinds of comments about the weather, 'Fasching' fancy-dress parties; and there is the Schatzalp sanatorium located high in the mountains above the town—the only one mentioned in *The Magic Mountain* by its real name, and often featured in films and novels set in Davos. In Mann's novel the Schatzalp is memorably described as a sanatorium located so high up in the mountains that the corpses of the patients who die there during the winter must be transported to the town in bobsleds. The Schatzalp is not the sanatorium where Mann's wife, Katia, stayed between 1912 and 1914, and where Thomas visited her for a few weeks. The Berghof sanatorium in the novel is fictional. But the Schatzalp is still associated with *The Magic Mountain*; indeed, this is how the hotel is described on Davos's official tourist website: 'the Schatzalp, where readers of Thomas Mann's best-selling novel will find the magic mountain'.[122]

[122] [Anon.], 'Thomas Mann & The Magic Mountain' <https://www.davos.ch/en/davos-klosters/portrait-image/storytelling/thomas-mann-the-magic-mountain/> [accessed 20 May 2016].

Many such details can be attributed to a shared experience of Davos. But in *Der Zauberlehrling* there are many closer parallels to *The Magic Mountain* as well. Mintzlaff's attitude towards life resembles Hans Castorp's isolated existence in the mountains. Neither wishes to get involved in the business of the world, and both avoid emotional engagement with people around them. One American critic, despite knowing only the first four chapters of *Der Zauberlehrling* and being unaware that it had been written as a reply to *The Magic Mountain*, still called the setting 'a kind of magic mountain'.[123] Just as in *The Magic Mountain*, Mintzlaff's spiritual sickness is accompanied by an organic malfunction, and just as in Mann's novel, it is a symbolic one: not tuberculosis, with its implications of decadence and moral decay, but a 'Herzensschwäche' ('a heart defect'), which corresponds to Mintzlaff's emotional inhibitions in his relationships with other people.[124]

There are other less obvious but even more illuminating connections between *The Magic Mountain* and *Der Zauberlehrling*. The title of Kästner's book alludes to a famous ballad by Goethe, in which an apprentice tries his master's magic tricks,[125] but this title has further significance. As mentioned earlier, when Thomas Mann started writing *The Magic Mountain*, he envisioned it as a comical and light-hearted counterpart to *Death in Venice*: 'eine Art von humoristischem, auch groteskem Gegenstück zum *Tod in Venedig*' ('a kind of humorous, grotesque counterpart to *Death in Venice*').[126] Due to a misunderstanding, *Die neue Rundschau*, S. Fischer Verlag's prestigious literary magazine which was supposed to publish Mann's new text, announced it in 1913 as a forthcoming novella, the title of which was mistakenly given as, of all things, 'Der Zauberlehrling'. It was advertised as 'eine Novelle von Thomas Mann, die eine Art groteskes Gegenstück zum *Tod in Venedig* bildet' ('a novella by Thomas Mann which provides a grotesque counterpart to *Death in Venice*').[127] Other newspapers and magazines quickly spread the news before Mann could intervene. Ultimately, however, his conception of *The Magic Mountain* was transformed during the First World War, a novella grew to become a long novel, and it was not published until ten years later. It is tempting to imagine Kästner, fourteen years old at the time, reading about Mann's plan for a novella entitled 'Der Zauberlehrling' in 1913,

---

[123] See Last, *Erich Kästner*, p. 42.

[124] This is also similar to Kästner's *Fabian* and the protagonist of *Die Doppelgänger*, another work that he wrote around the same time as *Der Zauberlehrling*; see Benson, *Erich Kästner*, p. 54.

[125] Little seems to allude to Goethe's ballad beyond the basic character constellation: we have the powerful Baron Lamotte who has supernatural powers—but he is a Greek god, not a sorcerer—and we have Mintzlaff, a sort of apprentice who gets to observe Lamotte's magic tricks. *Der Zauberlehrling* oftentimes seems to resemble Goethe's *Faust* more than his famous ballad. There are traces of Faust and Mephistopheles in the pair Mintzlaff-Lamotte: Lamotte offers Mintzlaff supernatural help because Mintzlaff is dissatisfied with his life and feels that he does not know the hidden laws of life and the world.

[126] Mann, *Selbstkommentare*, p. 7.

[127] Neumann, *Thomas Mann*, pp. 19 and 58–59, and Mann, *Selbstkommentare*, pp. 8–9.

and twenty-five years later setting out to write 'das groteske Gegenstück zum *Tod in Venedig*' that Mann never ended up writing. If this really is the genesis of Kästner's title, it was not the last time that he parodied Mann in this way. In 1946, he wrote a harsh polemic against Mann's choice to go into exile in the 1930s; its title—'Betrachtungen eines Unpolitischen'—was a (not particularly subtle) reminder of Mann's controversial ideological declarations during the First World War.[128]

In what ways might *Der Zauberlehrling* allude to *Death in Venice*? Both texts start in Munich with a protagonist suddenly experiencing a surge of 'Reiselust' ('desire to travel') and setting out on a journey, and even though Mann's Gustav von Aschenbach is a famous writer and Kästner's Mintzlaff an art historian, Mintzlaff is also described as an 'Ästhetiker' ('aesthete'). In *Der Zauberlehrling*'s opening scene, Mintzlaff analyses his 'Reiselust' in very curious terms. He pulls out a big poster with a scheme he has designed:

ein System, in dem die Skala der menschlichen Gemütslagen und das Spektrum gewisser künstlerischer Kategorien—wie beispielsweise des Tragischen, des Komischen, des Satirischen, des Humoristischen—einander rechtwinklig und übersichtlich zugeordnet wurden.   (p. 206)

a system which, squarely and transparently, maps the scale of human emotions onto the spectrum of certain artistic categories, for example, tragedy, comedy, satire, and humour.

Mintzlaff goes on to match his mood to a suitable aesthetic category in which to express it, and decides on 'die apollinische Haltung' ('the Apollonian attitude'). The whole scene seems to subtly mock Mann's plan to take the experience of sex and death drives and express it first as a tragedy in *Death in Venice* and then as a comedy in *The Magic Mountain*, as well as Mann's well-known predilection for aesthetic dichotomies, such as that of the Apollonian and Dionysian drives.

This dichotomy sends us back to Nietzsche and his famous treatise in which he developed it: *Die Geburt der Tragödie aus dem Geiste der Musik* (*The Birth of Tragedy from the Spirit of Music*, 1872). Kästner seems to enjoy allusions to Mann via Nietzsche: he does it again in a scene where Mintzlaff has a strange dream about Mount Olympus.[129] The German word 'Zauberberg', which Mann chose as the title of his novel, had previously been recorded only a handful of times—and the most famous of those early instances is its use by Nietzsche, when, again in *The Birth of Tragedy*, he calls Mount Olympus a 'Zauberberg'. In Mintzlaff's dream, Greek gods gossip about Zeus's love affairs, which makes him so angry that—as is

---

[128] Guy Stern, 'Exile Honoris Causa: The Image of Erich Kästner among Writers in Exile', in *Flight of Fantasy: New Perspectives on Inner Emigration in German Literature 1933–1945*, ed. Neil H. Donahue and Doris Kirchner (New York: Berghahn, 2003), pp. 223–34, pp. 227–29.

[129] Lamotte also assures Mintzlaff that he is not an 'Übermensch' (p. 222).

his custom—he strikes thunderbolts, causing a huge storm on Mount Olympus, and creating a mocking version of Hans Castorp's dreamy vision of ancient Greece in the famous snowstorm chapter of *The Magic Mountain*.

Zeus is also used in the book to introduce the 'Doppelgänger' motif: he is often associated with it because of the mythical story of how he impregnated Alcmene with Hercules, under the guise of her husband Amphitryon—a story familiar from Heinrich von Kleist's *Amphitryon* (1807). But Zeus is not the only 'Doppelgänger' in *Der Zauberlehrling*: there is also the false professor who is Mintzlaff's 'Doppelgänger', Mintzlaff himself resembles Hans Castorp in many ways, as I discussed earlier, and the entire book is a 'Doppelgänger' of sorts, given its relationship to *The Magic Mountain*. An amusing episode highlights this even more: when Mintzlaff must come up with a false identity to be able to spy on the false professor, he introduces himself as a publisher working on a book about Robert Louis Stevenson, author of *Treasure Island* (1883) and *The Strange Case of Dr Jekyll and Mr Hyde* (1886). His book is supposed to be about the writing that Stevenson completed while staying in Davos in the 1880s. Kästner has his protagonist pretend that he came to Davos to do research on a famous author writing a book in Davos, which is very fitting for an author who is himself writing a book which lives off *The Magic Mountain*—another famous book inspired by its author's stay in Davos. It is hard to imagine a more immersive approach to the task the Davos 'Verkehrsverein' set Kästner.

But what role is played by Kästner's clever allusions to Mann, Goethe, Nietzsche, and Greek mythology? Readers may be unsure what to make of this strange mixture of famous cultural intertexts with a tourist brochure—for *Der Zauberlehrling* does read like a tourist brochure at times. The book opens with Mintzlaff's inner monologue about the advantages of travelling. When he and Lamotte reach Davos, a very favourable description of the town is given, culminating in an exclamatory narratorial remark about all its metropolitan conveniences: 'es unterlag keinem Zweifel: Sie befanden sich, obwohl sechszehnhundert Meter hoch, in einer Stadt!' ('there was no doubt: even though at an altitude of 1600 metres, they were in a city!') (p. 224). When Mintzlaff tells the hotel manager that he cannot go skiing due to a heart defect, it seems to be just a pretext to list numerous other enjoyable activities that tourists can engage in while in Davos, like going on walks or sunbathing (p. 233). When Mintzlaff does go for a walk, he passes by the brand-new ski lift anyway and a detailed description of the new technology is given, ending in another enthusiastic exclamation-cum-product placement—'die Bergwelt war wirklich mit jeglichem Komfort ausgestattet!' ('the alpine world was truly equipped with every imaginable comfort!') (p. 247). In such passages Kästner is clearly responding to his commissioners' interest in changing Davos's reputation. Former sanatoria were being transformed into hotels for healthy tourists; the association with tuberculosis, wasting away, and death had become problematic. And yet an early reviewer of *The Magic Mountain* described the novel's setting as 'ein mit allem Comfort ausgestattetes Lungensanatorium auf der Höhe von Davos' ('a sanatorium for lung patients high up in Davos, equipped with every imaginable comfort');[130] so perhaps even this aspect of Kästner's text has been prefigured by Mann's novel and its reception after all.

In the many years since Kästner received his commission and tuberculosis ceased to be an imminent threat, the tourist authorities in Davos clearly changed their approach—*The Magic Mountain* is nowadays a constant point of reference in the town's official promotional materials. *The Magic Mountain* is described as 'a literary memorial in honour of the mountain health resort Davos' in a recent tourist catalogue.[131] But in the 1930s it seemed that a new cultural advertisement for Davos was needed. While *Der Zauberlehrling* grows out of this commercial interest, it also registers Kästner's awareness of the relationship between culture and its social uses. At a ball in Davos, Mintzlaff and Lamotte sit at one table with the false professor, the director of the 'Verkehrsverein', and the head physician of a local sanatorium. At one point,

> man begann […] die bange Frage zu diskutieren, ob die wirklich große Kunst und das Urteil des jeweils zeitgenössischen Publikums einander wesentlich beeinflußt hätten und ob sich, im Laufe der überschaubaren Kunstgeschichte, das Verhältnis zwischen den beiden Faktoren grundsätzlich und inwieweit es sich graduell gewandelt habe.   (p. 244)

> they began to discuss the difficult question whether truly great art and the judgement of each subsequent generation of readers and spectators had significantly influenced each other and whether, in the course of recent art history, the relationship between these two had changed fundamentally or rather gradually.

We never get to hear how the discussion develops, and 'endgültige Schlüsse ließen sich naturgemäß nicht ziehen' ('naturally, definite conclusions could not be drawn'). But it is remarkable that this group of people—an art historian, a false art historian, the director of the Davos tourist board, and the head physician of a sanatorium (a character who really seems to have walked straight out of *The Magic Mountain*—he is also the chairman of the local art society and art collector— associations with Behrens are hard to resist!)—should sit together and discuss the extent to which 'highbrow' art ('die wirklich große Kunst') succumbs to the

---

[130] Reisiger, '*Der Zauberberg*', p. 812.
[131] See, [Anon.], '100 Jahre Faszination Zauberberg und Thomas Mann' <http://www.davos.ch/fileadmin/user_upload/medien/texte_und_themen/Medientext_100JahreZauberberg_d.pdf> [accessed 30 May 2017]; see also Herwig, 'The "Magic Mountain Malady"', p. 246. A similar change of heart can be traced in the way *Buddenbrooks* has been perceived in Lübeck; the initial accusations that Mann had fouled his own nest were followed by a reappraisal of his achievement, and the Buddenbrookhaus is now one of the main tourist attractions in the city.

commercial pressures of the book market, and how culture and its consumers affect each other to engender some standard of taste. Kästner knows that his *Zauberlehrling* is an extreme example of precisely this process.

But his book also implies that this is a much more universal description of the workings of culture. As Mintzlaff observes, people like to read books that seem familiar to them; culture and society, books and their readers, constantly influence each other. And so *Der Zauberlehrling* combines a witty and light-hearted tone with innumerable intertextual references to 'highbrow', canonical culture, but, as the text itself announces through the mouth of Zeus, these are the kinds of references that are drilled into pupils' heads in every German 'Gymnasium', which dismantles the pretence of intellectualism and erudition. *Der Zauberlehrling* poses as a 'Doppelgänger' of *The Magic Mountain*, as the unwritten satirical 'Gegenstück' to *Death in Venice*, but this revisiting of Mann's writing is firmly anchored in the emergent commercial world of mass tourism.

This closer reading of *The Magic Mountain* as reworked by Kästner casts new light on Hans Castorp—as the first tourist on Mann's 'Magic Mountain', travelling on the train from Hamburg to the enchanting fictional world which Mann is about to conjure up in his extraordinary novel like a true magician, or, dare we say, like a hotelier. In 1913, Robert Musil commented bitterly: 'ein vom Publikum favorisierter Schriftsteller hat heute durchschnittlich das Einkommen eines Hoteldirektors' ('nowadays a writer favoured by the public enjoys on average an income of a hotelier').[132] When academic critics discuss the term repeatedly used to describe Hans in the novel—'Bildungsreisender'—they focus on the first part of this compound noun, as it suggests a link to the tradition of the 'Bildungsroman'. For example, Debra N. Prager criticizes John E. Woods's choice to translate this term as a 'tourist thirsting for knowledge' because 'the wording is clearly meant as a reference to the "Bildungsroman" and its youthful hero's inner journey'.[133] But it seems that, at least for non-academic readers, the second part of this term— 'Reisender', a 'traveller' or a 'tourist'—is much more intriguing. Generations of readers will want to follow in Hans Castorp's footsteps, eager to recreate his experience in Davos. For a critic like Bruce Robbins, such non-academic uses of books are irrelevant to the business of literary scholarship because they fail to fulfil the role of culture, which is to provide a critical distance from social practices. For a critic like Rita Felski, the way that people use books *is* what constitutes culture. Social practices *are* culture. Demanding critical distance is a social practice and one example of a cultural use of literature. But there are others—and it is to one such other cultural use of literature, marginalized in mainstream literary scholarship, that I now turn.

---

[132] Quoted in Haefs, 'Geist, Geld und Buch', p. 127.   [133] Prager, *Orienting the Self*, p. 281.

4. Magic Mountain Pilgrims

The touristic enterprise that Kästner's novel chronicles—ostensibly to suppress associations with *The Magic Mountain* but, as I have shown, in fact playfully imitating Mann's novel—lives on. Every year a sizeable group of guests in Davos's Hotel Schatzalp (the former sanatorium mentioned in *The Magic Mountain*) consists of Thomas Mann fans or, as a recent article in *The New Yorker* puts it, 'Magic Mountain pilgrims'.[134] They include academics working on Thomas Mann's oeuvre: between 1994 and 2012 biannual academic conferences on Mann were held in Davos. They were organized with the support of the Davos tourist board and initiated by a Swiss doctor, an avid reader of *The Magic Mountain*, who wanted to organize an event that would bring together doctors and literary scholars interested in the novel. The participants would stay in Hotel Schatzalp, eat together in the hotel dining hall, and go for walks around Davos in Hans Castorp's footsteps. The first event in 1994 attracted 600 participants and many more guests had to be turned away.[135] Even leading scholars of *The Magic Mountain*, keen to present the book as a novel of ideas and the towering intellectual achievement of twentieth-century German literature, are up for an immersive re-enactment of Mann's enchanted story and eagerly participate in the commercial afterlife of the novel. This is a long way from doctors writing angry letters about *The Magic Mountain* and the tourist board of Davos commissioning a novel that would replace it as the chief cultural reference for the town. As a recent critic put it, 'Davos's transition from medical to intellectual tourism was in the long run successful.'[136]

But it was not at the 'Davoser Literaturtage' ('Davos Literature Days'), as these conferences were called, that academic scholarship was for the first time discussed in the shadow of Mann's 'Magic Mountain'. After the First World War, 'town planners [...] thought of founding an "international high-alpine University" in Davos, chiefly to convince the younger tuberculosis patients to remain for the full length of their cures' and thus 'replenish town revenues, which had been depleted due to falling tuberculosis rates across Europe'.[137] By 1927, it was clear that the project was too ambitious; instead, plans were laid out to found a series of annual week-long 'Hochschulkurse' consisting of lectures given by high-profile German, French, and Swiss academics to a group of international students. The

[134] Sally McGrane, 'To the Magic Mountain!', *The New Yorker*, 17 February 2014 <http://www.newyorker.com/books/page-turner/to-the-magic-mountain> [accessed 30 May 2017].
[135] Sprecher, *Davos im 'Zauberberg'*, p. 65.
[136] David Nirenberg, 'When Philosophy Mattered', *The New Republic*, 13 January 2011 <https://newrepublic.com/article/81380/heidegger-cassirer-davos-kant> [accessed 10 June 2019].
[137] Peter E. Gordon, *Continental Divide: Heidegger, Cassirer, Davos* (Cambridge, MA: Harvard University Press, 2010), p. 91.

'Hochschulkurse', which took place between 1928 and 1931, attracted the attention of European upper-class intelligentsia; one of the first lectures was given by
Albert Einstein on the topic of general relativity. Thomas Mann himself sent a
telegram to congratulate the founders.[138]

In 1929, two influential philosophers were among the lecturers: Martin
Heidegger and Ernst Cassirer. Their debate in Davos came to be seen as a symbolic
expression of the divide between continental and analytic philosophy. In his 2010
study of this event, Peter E. Gordon devoted a whole chapter to describing the
analogies between the debate between Heidegger and Cassirer and the debates
between Settembrini and Naphta in *The Magic Mountain*. These analogies, as he
writes, were 'not lost on those attending the debate';[139] quite to the contrary, 'it
was almost as if *The Magic Mountain* furnished a ready-made script for understanding the exchange'.[140] The length of the 'Hochschulkurse' was three weeks,
Hans Castorp's intended length of stay in Davos, and Martin Heidegger was
himself an admirer of Mann's novel.[141] One of the attending students
described how

> nearly all the students who found themselves here for the 'Hochschulkurse' spent
> the last weeks before their departure buried in Thomas Mann's *Magic Mountain*
> (if they hadn't done this already) so as to be sure not to enter this mysterious
> atmosphere unprepared. Indeed, one must rightly say that even in the first days
> we were all impressed by how much the *genius loci* of Davos is captured in this
> novel, and we all felt ourselves drawn in by its infamous atmosphere of time-
> lessness and eternal dialectic. For days and a great portion of the nights one saw
> students and professors in discussion, the high point of the daily events for us just
> as for Hans Castorp [...] If one wished to present these discussions in a truly
> charming fashion, one might easily write a sort of sequel to Thomas Mann
> entitled *The University on the Magic Mountain*.[142]

This first-hand account of *The Magic Mountain*'s impact anticipates the wave of
responses to the novel discussed in this book (although I am yet to encounter a
spin-off in the form of a campus novel) and sheds some light on the motivations
behind them. Just five years after its publication, the experience afforded by
Mann's novel came close to monopolizing the cultural perception of erudition
and intellectualism. Mann created an influential archetype which the local

[138] See Sprecher, *Davos im 'Zauberberg'*, p. 32.   [139] Gordon, *Continental Divide*, p. 89.
[140] Ibid., p. 90.   [141] Neumann, *Thomas Mann*, pp. 114–15.
[142] Quoted in Gordon, *Continental Divide*, p. 90. See also Ludwig Englert, 'Als Student bei den
Zweiten Davoser Hochschulkursen März 1929', in *Nachlese zu Heidegger* (Bern: [n. pub.], 1962), ed.
Guido Schneeberger, pp. 1–6; Toni Cassirer, 'Cassirer und Heidegger in Davos', in *Nachlese zu
Heidegger* (Bern: [n. pub.], 1962), ed. Guido Schneeberger, pp. 7–9; Otto Friedrich Bollnow,
'Gespräche in Davos', in *Erinnerung an Martin Heidegger*, ed. Günther Neske (Pfullingen: Neske,
1977), pp. 25–29.

authorities in Davos were only too happy to harness in their marketing activities. This 'Magic Mountain' archetype came to be expressed in similar terms repeatedly over the years—in press articles about Davos, promotional materials for the World Economic Forum, programmes of the 'Davoser Literaturtage', and in numerous novels and films.

The 'Davoser Hochschulkurse' were short-lived; the topic of the fourth and final meeting in 1931 was, rather fittingly, the crisis of 'Bildung'. But it was not the last time that weighty ideas were to be discussed in a series of structured seminars atop the 'Magic Mountain'. In 1971, Klaus Schwab, a German engineer and economist, invited 444 executives from Western European companies to the newly opened Davos Congress Centre for an event which he called the European Management Forum. The purpose of the meeting was explained in a book published to commemorate its fortieth anniversary, which opens with a pompous quote misattributed to Goethe: 'boldness has genius, power and magic in it'. The aim was to allow 'top managers of corporations to interact with all their stakeholders' and 'senior European managers to learn about the latest management techniques and concepts from the most engaging thought leaders in business, including prominent professors from the top US business schools'.[143]

That first meeting would turn into the famous (or perhaps infamous) annual event known as the World Economic Forum, where 'business, government and civil society leaders' meet to 'consider the major global issues of the day and to brainstorm on solutions to address these challenges'.[144] For its many critics, however, the WEF is itself a symptom of the problems it claims to want to solve, such as dramatic global inequalities in wealth and the environmental crisis due to irresponsible use of natural resources. In 2019, climate activist Greta Thunberg made the headlines when she criticized the ultra-rich participants of the WEF for their disingenuity in discussing the climate crisis while arriving in Davos in private jets.

Even from this brief description of the WEF, one might start to detect some superficial parallels with *The Magic Mountain*. Both the WEF participants and the sanatorium patients in Mann's novel are, broadly speaking, a group of highly privileged people who meet in the Swiss Alpine resort and discuss the most pressing political and social issues of the day, while themselves being securely lifted above these very concerns. (This is meant both figuratively and literally— Davos is more than 1500 metres above sea level.) But the link between the WEF and *The Magic Mountain* is in fact more robust. In an anniversary publication

[143] [Anon.], 'The World Economic Forum: A Partner in Shaping History. The First 40 Years, 1971–2010' <http://www3.weforum.org/docs/WEF_First40Years_Book_2010.pdf> [accessed 10 June 2019], p. 8.
[144] Ibid., p. 1.

released by the WEF, the choice of Davos as the location for the meetings is explained as follows:

> The venue had to be accessible and comfortable enough so as not to deter attendance yet sufficiently removed to foster among participants a feeling of seclusion and camaraderie. The resort of Davos, a picturesque town nestled along a valley surrounded by peaks, was the setting of Thomas Mann's *The Magic Mountain* (*Der Zauberberg*). It was—and remains—a place of seclusion, contemplation, recreation and relaxation, the crisp, clean mountain air vital to restoring health and clear thinking. And in 1971, it had recently opened a congress centre. Davos had all the elements for hosting a productive working retreat for top CEOs.[145]

Klaus Schwab wanted to capitalize on Davos's association with Mann's novel— with its intellectual credentials (elsewhere in the promotional materials the 'Davoser Hochschulkurse' are mentioned as another precursor to the WEF meetings), its mix of heady discussions and an air of relaxation, and its depiction of the town's therapeutic properties. Readers of *The Magic Mountain* might realize that few patients ever recover in Mann's sanatorium and most of them do not even seem particularly committed to the idea of recovery, a fact which might invite rather snide comparisons to the participants of the WEF.

But the aspect of Davos that is first highlighted in the extract quoted above draws attention to another feature of the town: it is 'accessible' and 'secluded' at the same time. It is a variation on the tension between inclusivity and exclusiveness that I outlined in Mann's own thinking about his novel, and in many readers' responses to it. While there is no question that Klaus Schwab's reading of *The Magic Mountain* was largely driven by commercial interests, his sense of the appeal of Mann's novel is surprisingly perspicacious. The WEF website describes the inception of the meetings in similar words:

> Davos, the setting of Thomas Mann's *Der Zauberberg* (*The Magic Mountain*), was a place of recreation and relaxation, where people took in clean mountain air to restore their health and recharge their minds. Schwab wanted participants in the European Management Symposium to feel relaxed enough to speak frankly, while maintaining camaraderie of purpose and mutual respect. This became known as the 'Davos Spirit', still the hallmark of all Forum gatherings.[146]

The invention of the 'Davos Spirit'—a phrase widely used in press reporting on the WEF, from *The New York Times* to *China Daily*—is traced back to Mann's

[145] Ibid., p. 8.   [146] [Anon.], 'The Beginning'.

novel. Similarly, in the press materials released for the 2017 meeting, a section entitled 'Why Davos?' reads:

> The average temperature in January is -5 degrees centigrade, it's over two hours by train from the nearest major airport, but the Swiss resort town has a long history as a meeting place for the exchange of ideas. In the 19th century, Davos became well known for its sanatoria, where TB sufferers—including writers—sought a cure in the cool, clear air. Thomas Mann's 1924 novel, *The Magic Mountain*, which explored the clash of ideas in a modernizing Europe, was set in Davos. In the same decade, Einstein lectured at a philosophical conference there. The isolated setting is supposed to help visitors to look beyond their everyday concerns.[147]

Throughout its promotional materials the WEF uses the rhetoric familiar from *The Magic Mountain*, and so do international media outlets, as well as many WEF participants. Davos is repeatedly called 'a magic mountain', as opposed to the 'flatlands' of the outside world in *The Economist* and the *Financial Times*, *Time* and the BBC, *Die Zeit* and *Die Neue Zürcher Zeitung*.

But, as one commentator asked in *The Guardian* in 2011, 'how many of the government ministers, the multinational executives, the NGO heads, the journalists gathered in Davos [...] have read *The Magic Mountain*?' The commentator answers his own question with 'Not many, would be a safe bet', and goes on to hypothesize what these unlikely readers could get out of Mann's novel, 'should any of the powerbrokers chance upon a stray copy'.[148] They could draw parallels between the historical moment in which *The Magic Mountain* was written (in the aftermath of the First World War) and their own times (the aftermath of the 2008 economic crisis), as well as between the range of 'competing viewpoints and backgrounds' represented by Mann's characters and the increasing diversity of the WEF participants. The use of *The Magic Mountain* in the WEF's promotional materials strikes many readers as a misreading of the novel. And yet this reading and the reactions to it tell us something interesting about the book itself: *The Magic Mountain* can easily be weaponized as a symbol of intellectual superiority. The organizers of the WEF use it to prop up their own intellectual credentials—and in response, the journalist from *The Guardian* uses it to attack these very credentials. One might argue that both parties end up staying on the surface of the text, sacrificing its depth in the interest of their own rhetorical power. But does

---

[147] Ceri Parker, 'Everything you need to know about Davos 2017', 10 January 2017 <https://www.weforum.org/agenda/2017/01/everything-you-need-to-know-about-davos-2017> [accessed 10 June 2019].

[148] [Anon.], 'In Praise of... The Magic Mountain', *The Guardian*, 27 January 2011 <https://www.theguardian.com/commentisfree/2011/jan/27/the-magic-mountain-thomas-mann> [accessed 10 June 2019].

this very dynamic not capture something of the essence of *The Magic Mountain* and its portrayal of intellectual debates? I return to this question in Chapter 3.

The new interpretation of Davos as 'a Magic Mountain' of bankers, CEOs, and the rich world elite has influenced two recent big film productions which reimagine Mann's story as set in twenty-first-century luxurious Swiss spa resorts: *Youth* (2015), directed by Paolo Sorrentino, to be discussed in Chapter 3, and *A Cure for Wellness* (2016), directed by Gore Verbinski (b. 1964).[149] Verbinski's film has not been a success by any stretch of the imagination. It flopped at the box office, grossing $26 million against a production budget of $40 million; it garnered almost uniformly negative reviews; only a handful of cinemas in the world showed it for longer than two weeks; it did not win any prizes; and there is little to suggest that its fortunes will ever be reversed. (Peter Bradshaw of *The Guardian*, however, did single it out as the most likely film of 2016 to develop a cult status in the future,[150] and Kim Newman's review in *Sight and Sound* commended its thick web of intertextual allusions.[151]) This must have come as a disappointment to Verbinski, whose previous films—most notably *The Ring* (2002, a remake of a Japanese horror film) and the first three instalments of *The Pirates of the Caribbean* series (2003, 2006, 2007)—comfortably fit the Hollywood blockbuster formula, at the same time receiving widespread critical acclaim. So why was Verbinski unable to repeat those successes with *A Cure for Wellness*?

Discussing the film's engagement with *The Magic Mountain* will reveal the answer to this question. Verbinski has acknowledged that Mann's novel was his main source of inspiration for the story he wanted to tell in *A Cure for Wellness* (he described himself and his screenwriter, Justin Haythe, as fans of *The Magic Mountain*) but it seems that in the process of the film's production, this source was gradually but imperfectly suppressed, resulting in a film that is at times incomprehensible, incoherent, and confusing. Not enough of *The Magic Mountain* is left in *A Cure for Wellness* to make it into an attractive modern retelling of Mann's story, appreciated by those familiar with the novel; conversely, too much of *The Magic Mountain* is left in the film to make it easily digestible for a mass audience unfamiliar with Mann's book. In other words, the film is an attempt to repeat Mann's gamble in his novel—to be both accessible and exclusive at the same time—but it fails miserably. In this way, it is also another record of the drama of impossible immersion in *The Magic Mountain*, and in this case, as I will show, the drama of immersion is represented quite literally in a key scene in the film which features an outsized float tank. *A Cure for Wellness* seems destined to be enjoyed solely by those who like weird, imperfect movies—and by *Zauberberg*-buffs

[149] *A Cure for Wellness*, dir. by Gore Verbinski (20th Century Fox, 2017).
[150] See Peter Bradshaw, 'And the 2018 Braddies Go To...Peter Bradshaw's Films of the Year', *The Guardian*, 10 December 2018 <https://www.theguardian.com/film/2018/dec/10/braddies-peter-bradshaw-films-of-the-year> [accessed 10 June 2019].
[151] Kim Newman, '*A Cure for Wellness*', *Sight and Sound*, 27.4 (2017), 76.

fascinated by the novel's afterlives in contemporary culture. If nothing else, however, Verbinski's film is interesting for being yet another intriguing record of an economically motivated reading of *The Magic Mountain*.

The protagonist of *A Cure for Wellness*, Lockhart (played by Dane DeHaan), is a young New York banker whose career is on the rise. His company sends him to a luxurious spa sanatorium perched atop a Swiss mountain, but he is not there to take the waters. His task is quite the opposite: to bring back to New York the company's CEO (Harry Groener), who had refused to return from his vacation. Lockhart initially plans to visit Switzerland only for a day or two, but as soon as he gets off the train, the sinister spa town and the mysterious sanatorium draw him in and he becomes a patient there himself. The sanatorium is populated by international upper-class patients who willingly submit themselves to a complicated schedule of therapies and exercises, shown in painstakingly orchestrated sequences reminiscent of Sorrentino's *Youth* (itself borrowing them from Federico Fellini's *Otto e mezzo*). It appears that no one ever leaves the sanatorium—except as a corpse, and then always under the cover of night—ostensibly because they do not want to. In the sanatorium, time comes to a halt: indeed, soon after Lockhart is admitted as a patient, his expensive Rolex stops. But it is later revealed that the head doctor (Jason Isaacs) has an active interest in retaining his patients: 'it's bad for business when people start getting better', he says towards the end of the film.

This short summary of the film's plot makes it clear how it plays with *The Magic Mountain* in its basic premise. In Justin Haythe's original screenplay, developed together with Verbinski, the protagonist's name was Castorp. At one point in the film the indistinct voices of the nurses behind Lockhart's door are heard discussing—in German—a patient named Castorp. This might be an aural trace from the early stages of work on the film, or a subtle nod to Mann's story: in any case, the name's inclusion turns the film into a palimpsest, where *The Magic Mountain* seems to form its deepest layer. The main plot of the film, however, radically departs from the *Magic Mountain* template: what starts out as a modern-day tale of the decadence and self-indulgence of the rich and powerful soon turns into a Gothic horror about a 200-year-old German baron obsessed with the purity of his family line, undertaking horrendous medical experiments on unsuspecting local peasants and attempting to rape his own daughter. Before all of this is revealed in the film, Lockhart has to face the classic horror dilemma: is he imagining things, or are they actually true? This theme has been handled with much more elegance in many other films, including Stanley Kubrick's *The Shining* (1980), similarly set in a remote hotel.[152] But, as I will

---

[152] Incidentally, one scholar has argued that in *The Shining*, Kubrick made numerous covert references to *The Magic Mountain* to make a point about the Holocaust. See Geoffrey Cocks, 'Death by Typewriter: Stanley Kubrick, the Holocaust, and *The Shining*', in *Depth of Field: Stanley Kubrick, Film, and the Uses of History*, ed. Geoffrey Cocks, James Diedrick Cocks, and Glenn W. Perusek (Madison, WI: University of Wisconsin Press, 2006), pp. 185–217.

demonstrate, the convoluted and at times forced nature of Verbinski's plot derives, at least in part, from the fact that *A Cure for Wellness* is in conversation with *The Magic Mountain*.

In an interview given as the film was about to hit the screens, Verbinski reconstructed the process that led him and Justin Haythe to come up with the story for *A Cure for Wellness*. The director's description of the inception of his project is worth quoting in full, since it is a very detailed account of the creative transformation that the vision of culture in *The Magic Mountain* underwent in Verbinski's reading of the novel:

> Well, there's this book by Thomas Mann called *The Magic Mountain* that we're both fans of, and that book deals with people in a sanitarium in the Alps, clutching on to their sickness like a badge before the outbreak of World War I. *We wanted to explore this sense of denial and say, well, what if that was a genre? What if we splice that into a more decidedly goth — made it contemporary, made it gothic,* and explored this idea of sickness as a form of absolution? If you have a note from doctor, then you're not responsible. Because you're not well. And a place where we put all these CEOs and who by their very nature of succeeding have crushed skulls to get ahead, have made tough decisions—they're leaders of industry, and they end up at this place where the doctor says, we've all done terrible things but none of that matters because you're not responsible, because you're not well. You know, it's the great con, right? You know, you're not well, but there's a cure. So you're going to be caught in that loop. Saying, I'm here, but there's hope, right? So you're bleeding out with an internal sense of, I'm getting better, I'm getting better, just a few more weeks, just a few more weeks. It's lotus-eaters. Or it's an opiate drip. That denial, that sense of, there's a wonderful place, you know? It's a health spa. *Who doesn't like to put on a nice comfy robe and slip into a warm bath? But when you put a razor blade next to the bathtub, it changes the meaning completely.* I think to pervert and corrupt that sort of tranquility, or to at least say, look, the thing about denial is, that inevitability keeps marching forward. The truth keeps marching on. And I think as a society, we live in a time where we are perhaps in denial. We understand history, we understand how the world works, and yet we're sort of driving a car into a tree and we can't turn the wheel. *I think when the genre is elevated, it usually taps into some palpable feeling. Not as a social commentary, but just as a feeling.* You take it home. Three days later, you're still affected by that feeling in a subconscious way.[153]

[153] Angie Han, 'Interview with Gore Verbinski on Returning to Horror with *A Cure for Wellness*', 21 December 2016 <https://www.slashfilm.com/a-cure-for-wellness-gore-verbinski-interview/> [accessed 10 March 2018], my emphases.

Verbinski is clearly receptive to Mann's register, or story-telling mode, in *The Magic Mountain*: he articulates how Mann had found a way to monopolize a certain kind of cultural discourse to the extent that his Swiss sanatorium story contains the seeds of an entire new genre. For Verbinski, a genre originates in the cultural specificity and suggestive power of a narrative. The way he talks about an 'elevated'—or fully realized, ripened—genre 'tapping into some palpable feeling' rather than providing explicit 'social commentary' comes close to Raymond Williams's concept of 'structures of feeling'.[154]

Verbinski's own take on Mann's genre, as he envisages it in the interview, is to 'put a razor blade next to the bathtub'—to introduce a horror spin on Mann's sanatorium narrative, capitalizing on the sense of threat and suffocation that permeates *The Magic Mountain* in an implicit, subliminal way. Making a dys-topian horror film out of *The Magic Mountain* is an instinctively appealing idea, capturing as it would the sinister atmosphere permeating the sanatorium in the novel, but it is hard to resist the impression that *A Cure for Wellness* missed the mark. I will argue that this is because Verbinski chose the easy path of exploiting stereotypical and simplistic fears about the threat posed by German culture, in the process submitting the film completely to the logic of capitalism that he is trying to critique on the ideological plane.

To begin with, the use of the German language in the film is striking. Throughout the film, German is often spoken but never subtitled. Lockhart, who does not speak German, overhears spa workers' ominous whispers. They also shout at him aggressively whenever he is discovered exploring forbidden corridors in the sanatorium. German functions as the language of threat and barred entry. In the sanatorium Lockhart repeatedly encounters plaques saying 'ZUTRITT VERBOTEN' ('KEEP OUT'). When he asks one of the spa workers about an old crypt he has discovered, the only reply he receives is a firm 'Sie können hier nicht rein gehen' ('you can't go in there'). All the evil characters in the film speak with a German accent: this could be explained by the spa's location in Switzerland, except that one local character, Hannah (Mia Goth), who has lived her entire life in the sanatorium under the care of the German head doctor (later revealed to be her father), speaks with an impeccable British accent, and is the only innocent victim among the sanatorium's inhabitants. Moreover, the staff at the sanatorium and the locals in the town all speak with a high German rather than a Swiss accent—and the film, although ostensibly set in Switzerland, was filmed entirely in Germany, partly in Studio Babelsberg near Berlin, partly on location, including Burg Hohenzollern near Stuttgart. (A large proportion of the film's funding came from Germany—nearly €10 million from the German Federal Film Fund and the Medienboard Berlin-Brandenburg.)

---

[154] See Ian Buchanan, *Oxford Dictionary of Critical Theory* (Oxford: Oxford University Press, 2018), pp. 454–55.

The allusions to specifically German rather than Swiss culture are not restricted to the characters' accents. The police officer in the town in which the film is set has a large collection of 'Pickelhauben' (Prussian military helmets), prominently displayed in his office. Even more troubling is the fact that the German baron *cum* head doctor at the sanatorium is obsessed with blood purity and conducts medical experiments, first, on the peasants who belong to his lands, and then, two hundred years later, on his patients. The way that Verbinski mobilizes the cultural fear of Nazi ideology and the Holocaust is emphasized through visual evocation of this subtext: before Lockhart's tooth is violently pulled out, he catches a glimpse of a huge jar filled with human teeth, which clearly alludes to Nazi practices in concentration camps. The destructive fire at the end of the film as a direct consequence of the German baron's/doctor's obsession with blood purity also seems dangerously close to a distasteful metaphor for the Second World War—it is logical that the film's ending mirrors that of *The Magic Mountain*, the outbreak of the First World War, given that its beginning mirrors Hans's arrival in Davos at the beginning of Mann's novel. Other cultural myths of German violence are exploited in the film as well: during the baron's uncanny wedding celebration at the end of the film, all patients and sanatorium staff are wearing white capes which make them look like members of the Teutonic Order, minus the black crosses, which, taken together with the Hohenzollern castle in which the sanatorium is located and the Prussian helmets at the police station, creates a vague, and neither historically nor geographically accurate, echo of Prussian militarism through the ages.

As ahistorical as Verbinski's vision of German history's 'Gothic menace' is, it does have important historical precursors. Mary Shelley was inspired to write *Frankenstein* (1818) upon hearing local legends during a journey through Germany. In his preface to the *Tales of the Grotesque and Arabesque* (1840), Edgar Allan Poe commented on what critics had been calling his 'Germanism and gloom', 'that species of pseudo-horror which we are taught to call Germanic, for no better reason than that some of the secondary names of German literature have become identified with its folly'. Even though Poe went on to assert that 'if in many of my productions terror has been the thesis, I maintain that terror is not of Germany, but of the soul',[155] his preface testifies to the prevalent narrative of German culture's Gothic gloom. This narrative persists, and has only intensified after the horrors of the twentieth century. Writing in the first decade of the twenty-first century, Paul Cooke argued that 'the issue of Germany's problematic past was the "unique selling point" of German cinema as an internationally recognizable brand'.[156] This interpretation of German film, which Thomas

[155] Edgar Allan Poe, *Poetry and Tales* (New York: Literary Classics of the US, 1984), p. 129.
[156] Paul Cooke, 'Abnormal Consensus? The New Internationalism of German Cinema', in *German Culture, Politics, and Literature into the Twenty-first Century: Beyond Normalization*, ed. Stuart Taberner and Paul Cooke (Rocheste, NY: Camden House, 2006), pp. 223–36, p. 225.

Elsaesser described as a form of the 'historical imaginary', goes back to Siegfried Kracauer's influential book published just after the Second World War (when Kracauer was living in the USA), pointedly titled *From Caligari to Hitler: A Psychological History of the German Film* (1947).[157] The commodification of German history's 'Gothic menace' is a well-established phenomenon in the global, and especially US, culture of the past two centuries.

How is the accumulation of cultural clichés about German perversities in *A Cure for Wellness* relevant to my argument about the role that *The Magic Mountain* plays in the film? It shows how culture, in Verbinski's film, is reduced to facile and easily digestible bites, ready for the viewers' consumption. This vision of culture, reminiscent of Kästner's *Zauberlehrling*, is at its most intense in the film's only scene that features an explicit reference to *The Magic Mountain*, which directly follows Lockhart's admission to the spa as a patient. He undergoes his first water treatment—submersion in a float tank. The German technician who is supposed to monitor his heart rate—much like in the scientific experiments designed to test the power of literary immersion—picks up a copy of *The Magic Mountain*, then puts it down after a nurse enters and takes off her uniform; he begins to masturbate. *The Magic Mountain* is picked up just to be put down a few moments later when the character reading it starts to pleasure himself: the book is used as just another fetishistic prop in the film. The edition of the novel featured in the film is a recent limited bibliophile reprint with a woodcut of a sanatorium resembling the Schatzalp featured on the cover, stylized to look old-fashioned.

While the technician's immersion in *The Magic Mountain* proves to be very shallow, Lockhart's therapeutic immersion turns into dangerous, uncontrollable submersion when the technician stops paying attention to his heart rate. The demonic head doctor of the spa resort describes the float tank to Lockhart as follows:

Sensory deprivation chamber simulates a return to the embryonic state, a cleansing of the mind and body. Some patients experience increased heart rate, visions, even primal memories; but rest assured, it's just the toxins leaving the system. Give yourself over completely to the process and you will see the results.

The tank could be dubbed a narrative immersion machine: you dive into the water; it isolates you from your immediate surroundings; your heart rate goes up; you experience visions; forgotten memories rush back to you; you have a chance to experience catharsis. This is exactly what happens to Lockhart—except that something goes terribly wrong. Seemingly out of nowhere, a swarm of eels appears in the tank just as the nurse enters the room and the technician puts down *The*

---

[157] See Thomas Elsaesser, *Weimar Cinema and After: Germany's Historical Imaginary* (New York: Routledge, 2000).

Magic Mountain. Lockhart's immersion is disrupted when the technician operating the tank stops reading. Once Lockhart flatlines and nearly drowns, and the technician and the nurse finally rescue him, the technician apologizes profusely and says that 'something must have gone wrong with the machine'. But, as viewers, we have seen that Lockhart was close to drowning in the float tank because the technician was not sufficiently immersed in the novel he was reading, too prone to distractions, and not in control of his sexual urges.

Immersion that is too deep pitted against immersion that is too shallow: what a fitting metaphor for Verbinski's engagement with *The Magic Mountain* in *A Cure for Wellness*. The film was supposed to retell Mann's story in a different time and a different genre, but at some point in the production process *The Magic Mountain* was discarded and put away, much like the technician's copy, and replaced with a clichéd portrayal of German culture's 'Gothic menace'. Verbinski set out to make a modern-day recreation of Mann's novel, but he ended up only dipping his toes in it. A scenic take towards the beginning of the film features a split mirror-image of a train, as though capturing the way in which *A Cure for Wellness* mirrors *The Magic Mountain*, but ultimately departs from this model.

The Magic Mountain is no more than another fetishistic prop in a film whose visual surface is a carefully constructed, nostalgic recreation of an interwar sanatorium or spa hotel: almost all reviewers of the film noted the carefully orchestrated and painstakingly assembled scenography, some finding it to be the film's most attractive aspect, and others considering it pretentious. Richard Brody writing for *The New Yorker* thought it was 'cribbed' from Wes Anderson's *The Grand Budapest Hotel*.[158] This is an interesting comment: it draws attention to the fact that *A Cure for Wellness* belongs in a series of recent films and novels featuring strikingly similar sanatorium or spa hotel settings. In these modern versions of the sanatorium, tuberculosis—the white plague which marred the nineteenth and early twentieth centuries—is replaced by burnout and depression, which seem to have taken its place in the twenty-first century. There seems to be a significant cultural appetite for these types of narratives.

Seen in this light—the film itself being a consumable product responding to a certain cultural demand—Verbinski's critique of consumer culture in his film populated by rich CEOs and bankers who have lost the will to live is not particularly convincing. This paradox is encapsulated in the final scene of *A Cure for Wellness*. Lockhart and Hannah finally escape from the sanatorium on a bicycle, but on their way they quite literally collide with the world of capitalism, embodied by the CEOs from Lockhart's company driving up the mountain in a

---

[158] Richard Brody, 'The Tasteless Intricacies of *A Cure for Wellness*', *The New Yorker*, 16 February 2017 <https://www.newyorker.com/culture/richard-brody/the-tasteless-intricacies-of-a-cure-for-wellness> [accessed 10 March 2019].

limousine. Lockhart refuses to join them in the car and thus return to the position he had previously occupied on the capitalist market.

Is this the film trying to reject its own conditions of production? Lockhart's mad, sinister smile as he is pedalling away in the very last shot of the film is ambiguous—although it might be down to his new dentures, another fetishistic film prop. In any case, the financial fate of the film parallels its ending: Lockhart, the modern-day incarnation of Hans Castorp, rejects his profitable job as a banker, and the film ends up flopping at the box office.

On the one hand, then, the film is intent on critiquing the capitalist ideology that turns people into ruthless bankers and idle, rich pensioners wasting away in a luxurious spa. This model is underwritten by the economic exploitation that we see up close at the sanatorium. For the local town dwellers the sanatorium is a decisive contributor to the local economy, yet there is also inherent animosity between the town and the sanatorium. This is because, as the baron explains, his medical experimentation was initially conducted 'using the bodies of peasants that belonged to his lands'—which is how he 'managed to distil the water to its life-giving essence'. The upper class literally sucked life out of the poor. The film acknowledges this dynamic, but its own handling of cultural material—sampling it to extract a sellable product—is predicated on the same logic that the film seems to critique. Verbinski's desire for immersion in Mann's enchanted story-world, acted out through the theme of taking the waters and the float tank functioning as a narrative immersion machine, cannot ultimately be fulfilled. It morphs into a tacky sex scene played out in front of the tank and incest fantasies fuelled by shallow clichés about the 'Gothic menace' of German culture. Just as the film's setting is an Alpine sanatorium building implausibly located within the neo-Gothic Prussian castle, Verbinski's reading of *The Magic Mountain* is buried within an unconvincing mix of stereotypes about Germany.

5. Conclusion: For the Many, Not the Few?

Academic readers rarely ask how and why non-academic readers read a novel like *The Magic Mountain*. A systematic answer is impossible, so scholars usually do not attempt it at all. Instead, they take their own or other academic readers' experiences as the default reaction to literary texts, or the one that matters the most. In some cases, scholars also draw on contemporary reviews or famous readers' responses to texts recorded in essays, letters, or diary entries. But there are also many other types of data to draw on that can allow us to perform a closer reading of Mann's novel by revealing recurrent patterns in readers' responses to the text. In this chapter I have discussed one such pattern—readers who struggle to engage with *The Magic Mountain* because they are extremely critical of the economic structure that underpins it, or extremely uncritical of it—in that they want to monetize the experience of reading the novel.

Many different reading experiences and cultural uses of the book can be brought together under this heading. As a Soviet writer, Konstantin Fedin could not allow himself a full-on immersion in Mann's 'aquarium' of bourgeois decadence, and so his novel—and its reception in Soviet Russia—became a record of an impossible attraction to Mann's story-world. Many other Marxist and socially critical readers of the novel left behind traces of similar responses to *The Magic Mountain*. Bertolt Brecht, Georg Lukács, Hanns Eisler, Leszek Kołakowski, Peter Rühmkorf, Martin Walser, and Wolfgang Harich are just a few of such readers. To understand what attracted those readers to the novel, while simultaneously making them sceptical about it, I drew on Elif Batuman's account of Fredric Jameson's reading of Proust as presenting his 'only available "source of concrete images" of the classless Utopia'. *The Magic Mountain* similarly seems to portray people pursuing 'their education in the arts, sciences, etc., thanks to the free time and available means' that Marx had imagined in his vision of a fully realized communist society. But it is the part of his vision elided from the quote above that prevents Marxist-leaning readers from entering this Utopia: the time and means must be available 'to all'—for all individuals. Seen from this perspective, the question of conditions of entry into cultural education becomes the decisive theme of Mann's novel—a question that, as I argue, Mann was very much aware of. Who is culture for? Who is the enchanting 'Magic Mountain' experience aimed at—understood as both Hans's experience in Davos and the experience of reading about his experience? Who can afford to embark on this magical journey—to a luxurious sanatorium as well as into a 1000-page-long novel that chronicles a series of intellectual adventures?

Some readers of *The Magic Mountain* stay on the surface of the text by trying to evade this question, or giving a simplistic answer to it. They approach the novel in the manner of tourists who, to borrow Kästner's phrase, like to 'read and travel' in regions they know well. Kästner's novel raises important questions about what determines our cultural tastes and about the role of market forces in this process, and this allows him to reflect on his own book's conditions of production. Both the 'Davoser Hochschulkurse' and the World Economic Forum meetings mobilized the town's intellectual credentials established in and by *The Magic Mountain* to add splendour to their own attempts to make money from inviting people to Davos. Gore Verbinski's horror *A Cure for Wellness* set in an Alpine spa resort ultimately trades an original reading of Mann's novel for a set of familiar clichés about the 'Gothic menace' of German culture. In all these cases the desire to re-enact *The Magic Mountain* competes with a vested interest in monetizing this experience.

This is what enabled me to bring together in this chapter these different, sometimes contradictory readings and readers of Mann's novel: what unites them all is an interest in the conditions of entry into Mann's enchanted story-world. 'I have already made some 70,000 Marks on entry fees into my mystical-humorous aquarium', Mann had announced gleefully in 1925. Nearly a century on, we are still arguing about the price for admission into his immersive story-world. In Chapter 2, I look at one important reason why fictional stories are so valuable, even priceless, to us: the crucial role that they can play in our emotional lives.

2

Emotions

1. Introduction: (Not) Covering His Face with His Hands

In this chapter, I trace the consequences of the decision to enter the world of *The Magic Mountain*, whether with enthusiasm, diffidence, or reluctance. I consider one particular subset of readers who have found the novel uniquely engaging—readers, both real and fictional, who have suffered from tuberculosis or another long-term illness. The discussion will centre around the question of emotional expression, and in particular the culturally acceptable ways of expressing, managing, and coming to terms with physical and psychological suffering. I first look at how Hans Castorp deals with his feelings in *The Magic Mountain* at three different points in the novel: when he observes Clawdia Chauchat's departure from the sanatorium; when he interacts with Ferdinand Wehsal after her return; and when he listens to classical music after Joachim's death. These examples showcase the productive ambiguities surrounding the culturally contested issue of emotional expression in Mann's novel. I then move on to show how three very different responses to *The Magic Mountain* use Mann's novel, alongside various other cultural texts, to navigate psychological crises of their own. I intersperse my discussion with many other related records of readerly encounters with *The Magic Mountain*, including fan mail sent to Mann by tubercular readers, reviews of the novel written by medical professionals, and a recent art installation in a London hospital.

As in Chapter 1, here again a world literature lens will allow me to venture beyond Germany and chart the circulation and reception of Mann's novel across the boundaries of time, space, and language. The first novelistic response to *The Magic Mountain* considered in this chapter is *The Rack*, a largely forgotten English novel from the late 1950s written by A. E. Ellis, an Oxford graduate who never published another book. *The Rack* is set in a post-war tuberculosis sanatorium where most patients are young ex-soldiers taking a break from their universities due to ill health—a sort of 'Magic Mountain' populated by Oxbridge students.[1] The second text I analyse is *Norwegian Wood*, a global bestseller from the late 1980s written by Haruki Murakami, the most famous contemporary Japanese writer. The protagonist of *Norwegian Wood* reads *The Magic*

---

[1] A. E. Ellis, *The Rack* (London: Heinemann, 1958). Quotations given in the text are taken from this edition.

Mann's Magic Mountain: World Literature and Closer Reading Karolina Watroba, Oxford University Press.
© Karolina Watroba 2022. DOI: 10.1093/oso/9780192871794.003.0003

Mountain while his love interest leaves for an isolated sanatorium in the Japanese mountains during the 1968 student movement.[2] The third and final text I discuss here is 'Amundsen', a recent short story written by the Nobel laureate Alice Munro. 'Amundsen' is set during the Second World War in a tuberculosis sanatorium in rural Canada, and its two main characters navigate their strained relationship via competing readings of *The Magic Mountain*.[3]

It is therefore clear that I am dealing not just with authors who read *The Magic Mountain*, but also literary characters who do so, and always in moments of personal and social crisis. How do these readers engage with Mann's book? How does Mann's erudite novel about sickness and death fare when it is read in times of physical and psychological suffering? How can one be both an erudite and an emotional reader? And when readers turn into writers, how can emotional suffering be expressed without slipping into a melodramatic mode? What makes a text melodramatic, and why are some communities so invested in the idea that certain ways of representing human distress are distasteful? How to get beyond the restricting opposition between 'serious' and 'sentimental' art? These will be my guiding questions as I move through these different texts and probe the relationships between them to deepen my closer reading of *The Magic Mountain*.

*   *   *

A young man falls in love with a terminally sick woman and is diagnosed with the same illness—none other than tuberculosis, a staple of nineteenth-century melodramatic plots; one thinks of the innumerable Victorian novels in which the innocent heroine dies of consumption.[4] The hero and his beloved cannot be together due to social pressures, but they are granted one night together before her departure from the sanatorium. She later returns—but this time accompanied by another man. Although *The Magic Mountain* is not usually discussed in these terms, its basic plot premise is so melodramatic as to make it surprising that the novel does not wax sentimental. In fact, at one point Hans Castorp himself dismissively summarizes his own story in similar terms:

> es ist am Ende nichts Neues [...] an einem Badeort leben zwei Personen [...] wochenlang unter demselben Dach, in Distanz. Eines Tages machen sie Bekanntschaft, finden aufrichtiges Gefallen aneinander, und zugleich stellt sich heraus, daß der eine Teil im Begriffe ist, abzureisen. So ein Bedauern kommt häufig vor.   (p. 533)

---

[2] Haruki Murakami, *Norwegian Wood*, trans. Jay Rubin (London: Vintage, 2003). Quotations given in the text are taken from this edition.

[3] Alice Munro, 'Amundsen', in *Dear Life* (London: Chatto & Windus, 2012), pp. 31–66. Quotations given in the text are taken from this edition.

[4] See Katherine Byrne, *Tuberculosis and the Victorian Literary Imagination* (Cambridge: Cambridge University Press, 2011).

it's the old story […] two people […] spend weeks together under the same roof at a resort somewhere, always keeping their distance. And one day they become acquainted, find they like one another, but at the same time it turns out one party is about to leave. Regrettable things like that happen often.   (p. 419)

Rereading the book with an awareness of this potential for sentimental storytelling, I was struck by the sheer amount of narrative energy Mann spends on actively resisting a melodramatic mode. Before specific passages from *The Magic Mountain* that illustrate this are discussed, let me put more pressure on the notion of melodrama itself, a key concept in this chapter.[5]

Melodrama is one of those contested literary terms that seem either too narrow or too imprecise wherever they are used. Among other things, it is the name of a popular film genre that blossomed in the Golden Age of Hollywood. The director often cited as the greatest master of Hollywood melodrama was a German immigrant: Douglas Sirk, born in Hamburg as Hans Detlef Sierck, and known for films such as *All That Heaven Allows* (1955) and *Imitation of Life* (1959). Yet the term 'melodrama' was first used for a type of popular theatrical entertainment in France towards the end of the eighteenth century, which became particularly prevalent in Victorian Britain as a theatrical counterpart to the sentimental novel. Almost concurrently with the rise of theatrical melodrama, the story goes, critics began to undermine the genre, ultimately leading to its eclipse with the advent of modernism. But this does not ring true: sentimental and melodramatic effects have never gone out of fashion and remain widespread and readily recognizable in cultural texts to this day.

Why am I using the terms 'melodramatic' and 'sentimental' almost interchangeably, given that the sentimental novel has its own complex history? By the beginning of the twentieth century, melodrama and sentimentalism converged to form a joint aesthetic category that became one of the heaviest charges against literary value, as the epitome of aesthetic cliché and bad taste. When we say that something is sentimental, we are usually referring to affected, shallow, excessive, banal, and inauthentic emotion.[6] When we say that something is melodramatic, we usually are talking of 'heightening and sensation for their own sake, a dramaturgy of hyperbole, excess, excitement'.[7] Describing something as melodramatic or sentimental, then, is almost always pejorative: it is a value judgement insinuating that a text (or character, or scene, or piece of dialogue) is distastefully cheap, excessive, formulaic, or unrealistic, or that it tries to elicit an emotional response

---

[5] The following two paragraphs are primarily inspired by Peter Brooks's classic work: Peter Brooks, *The Melodramatic Imagination: Balzac, Henry James, Melodrama, and the Mode of Excess* (New Haven, CT: Yale University Press, 1995), as well as Robert C. Solomon, 'On Kitsch and Sentimentality', *The Journal of Aesthetics and Art Criticism*, 49.1 (1991), 1–14, and June Howard, 'What Is Sentimentality?', *American Literary History*, 11.1 (1999), 63–81.

[6] See ibid., pp. 65–66.   [7] Brooks, *The Melodramatic Imagination*, p. viii.

in a formulaic, predictable, overemphatic way; that it knows no other way of expressing emotional intensity than through hyperbole and stereotype—which, more often than not, involves a hysterical female body. Both the terms— melodrama and sentimentality—and their histories have been interestingly reappraised in recent decades,[8] but what I want to explore in this section is how Thomas Mann was working with the popular understanding of melodrama and sentimentality in the 1920s. Given that by then a great many ways of representing emotional intensity had become associated with cheap melodrama and sentimentality—and thus branded as unrefined, unsophisticated, and simply unacceptable in high modernist literature—how could an author like Mann circumvent these limitations and convey a sense of emotional intensity without falling back on melodramatic tropes?

The first passage that I will discuss in search of an answer to this question comes halfway through the novel and describes Hans Castorp's reaction to Clawdia's departure from the sanatorium. Our associations between certain ges- tures or movements and aesthetic evaluations are deeply entrenched—so how can Thomas Mann represent the parting of two lovers in a way that is as exciting and moving as melodrama, while also being decidedly free from melodrama and thereby not threatening our sense of decorum and taste?

> [...] denn am folgenden Tage hatte er kein Wort mehr mit Frau Chauchat gewechselt, sie kaum gesehen, sie zweimal von weitem gesehen: beim Mittagessen, als sie in blauem Tuchrock und weißer Wolljacke, unter dem Schmettern der Glastür und lieblich schleichend noch einmal zu Tische gegangen war, wobei ihm das Herz im Halse geschlagen und nur die scharfe Bewachung, die Fräulein Engelhart ihm zugewandt, ihn gehindert hatte, das Gesicht mit den Händen zu bedecken;—und dann nachmittags 3 Uhr, bei ihrer Abreise, der er nicht eigentlich beigewohnt, sondern der er von einem Korridorfenster aus, das den Blick auf die Anfahrt gewährte, zugesehen hatte.   (p. 526)

He did not, however, exchange a single word with Frau Chauchat the next day, hardly saw her—only twice, and then from some distance: at dinner, when she had appeared in her blue skirt and white wool sweater, slamming the glass door and gracefully slinking to her table one last time, which set his heart pounding in his throat and almost caused him to hide his face in his hands—only Fräulein Engelhart's sharp gaze had prevented that; and then again, at three that

---

[8] Examples include Suzanne Clark, *Sentimental Modernism: Women Writers and the Revolution of the Word* (Bloomington, IN: Indiana University Press, 1991) and Markman Ellis, *The Politics of Sensibility: Race, Gender and Commerce in the Sentimental Novel* (Cambridge: Cambridge University Press, 2004), alongside Brooks, Solomon, and Howard.

afternoon, as she was leaving, although he had not actually been present, but had merely watched from a hall window with a view to the driveway.   (p. 413)

All narrative energy in this passage is spent on avoiding a scene of melodramatic farewell, but the melodrama still shines through. We skip over the lover's depart-ure and only find out about it in retrospect: a little while earlier, we are told that six weeks have passed in the meantime. This creates a temporal distance. Mann also hides the description of Hans's bodily reaction to his lover's departure in a relative clause, as an addendum to what is already a very long sentence, making it sound like an unimportant aside. This creates a grammatical or syntactical distance. And as if these were not enough distancing techniques, Hans only sees Frau Chauchat from a distance ('von weitem') and through a window ('von einem Korridorfenster aus'). The detailed description of her outfit and movements, however, palpably suggests that Hans's gaze is fixed on Clawdia, even as the narrative denies him a chance to see her up close one more time.

While Hans can feel his heart pounding in his chest—a common trope of melodramatic bodily response—he is prevented from making a melodramatic gesture by the strict supervision of his neighbour at the table, a spinster keen on preserving social decorum, but also, crucially, doubling up as a guardian of narrative propriety. In social terms, Hans's bodily response must seem especially improper to Fräulein Engelhart: it perverts gender stereotypes of the day, with the woman cast in the role of a distanced and ruthless departing lover, and the man in the role of a feeble and excessively emotional partner left behind. As a 'Lehrerin an einer staatlichen höheren Töchterschule in Königsberg' ('teacher at a public school for well-bred young ladies in Königsberg') (p. 113/p. 84), Fräulein Engelhart will have had ample experience of chastising young women experien-cing and displaying too intense emotions. It is only ('nur') thanks to her 'scharfe Bewachung' ('sharp gaze') that Hans is stopped halfway through a melodramatic bodily response: he cannot prevent his heart from drumming against his chest, but he can control his arms. In the language of biology, which is so prominent in the novel, there is nothing that Hans and the narrator can do about the activity of the involuntary cardiac muscle, but the skeletal muscles of his arms can be, and are, controlled. The paradox is that even though the crucial movement of the arms is not carried out, it is still described; by saying that something did *not* happen, we nevertheless spell out the action. Thus, melodrama can be both palpably present in and decorously absent from this scene.

For a reader trained in conventional aesthetic judgements associated with Western art, the effectiveness of this passage from *The Magic Mountain*, and others like it, stems from the fact that they offer the guilty pleasures associated with sentimentality and melodrama while removing guilt from the equation. Mann's distancing techniques allow his readers to sidestep the accusation of excess emotionality, naivety, and bad taste. *The Magic Mountain* gives its readers the pleasures of melodramatic intensity, but also the tools for dealing with the shame that they might involuntarily feel because of how they have been culturally trained to react to it. Even though I find the passage about Clawdia's departure hauntingly beautiful, I cannot help but think of Rey Chow's pithy critique of nineteenth-century Anglo-German Romanticism, to which she traces back

> the assumption that literature should be about depth and interiority, that expression of emotional truth should be modest, if not altogether wordless, [...] that being cultured means being hostile toward any form of [...] exhibitionism, [and that] oppression and suffering should not be announced loudly or even mentioned too often by those who are undergoing it, for that would amount to poor taste and insincerity.[9]

Chow's critique provides an opportunity to flesh out the curious phrase 'scharfe Bewachung' which stands out in the passage from *The Magic Mountain*. Fräulein Engelhart's 'scharfe Bewachung' reveals the culturally specific politics of taste in the portrayal of emotional turmoil.

The counterpart to Fräulein Engelhart's sense of decorum is embodied in the character of another sanatorium patient—Ferdinand Wehsal, whose very surname 'has connotations of miserable whining' in German.[10] Not unlike Fräulein Engelhart, Wehsal becomes attached to Hans because he too is attracted to Clawdia Chauchat. But Hans finds Wehsal's behaviour distasteful, even repulsive:

> '[Sie] waren [doch einmal] im siebenten Himmel, allmächtiger Gott, und haben ihre Arme um Ihren Nacken gefühlt und all das, allmächtiger Gott, es brennt mir im Schlunde und in der Herzgrube, wenn ich dran denke,—und sehen im Vollbewußtsein dessen, was Ihnen zuteil geworden, auf meine bettelhaften Qualen hinab [...]
>
> 'Schön ist es nicht, wie Sie sich ausdrücken, Wehsal. Es ist sogar hochgradig abstoßend, das brauche ich Ihnen nicht zu verhehlen, da Sie mir Unverschämtheit vorwerfen, und abstoßend soll es auch wohl sein, Sie legen es geradezu darauf an, sich widrig zu machen und krümmen sich unausgesetzt. [...]'
>
> [...] 'Es ist aber ein Menschenbedürfnis,' sagte Wehsal kläglich, 'ein Menschenbedürfnis, lieber Castorp, zu reden und sich das Herz zu erleichtern, wenn man in solchen Schwulitäten sitzt wie ich.'

[9] Rey Chow, *Writing Diaspora: Tactics of Intervention in Contemporary Cultural Studies* (Bloomington, IN: Indiana University Press, 1993), p. 4.
[10] Michael Minden, *The German Bildungsroman: Incest and Inheritance* (Cambridge: Cambridge University Press, 1997), p. 228.

'Es ist sogar ein Menschenrecht, Wehsal, wenn Sie wollen. Aber es gibt Rechte, meiner Meinung nach, von denen man unter Umständen vernünftigerweise keinen Gebrauch macht.'   (pp. 932–36)

'[you] were [once] in seventh heaven, good God, and felt her arms around your neck—good God, just to think of it burns at my gut and tears at my heart—and, then, knowing full well all that was granted you, you look down on me in my wretched torment [. . .]

'You don't have a pretty way of expressing yourself, Wehsal. I find it really quite obnoxious—and I don't think I need to disguise the fact from you, since you've accused me of insulting you. I suppose you mean it to be repulsive, too; you quite deliberately attempt to make yourself disgusting, forever cringing and writhing. [. . .]'

[. . .] 'But it's an undeniable human urge,' Wehsal said piteously, 'a human necessity, dear Castorp, to speak, to ease your mind when you're in a mess like I'm in.'

'It is even a human *right*, Wehsal, if you like. But in my opinion, under certain circumstances, there are rights one does not exercise for good reason.'

(pp. 733–35)

In this passage Mann finds another ingenious way to inhabit the sentimental mode and mock it at the same time. Wehsal emerges as Hans's ridiculous 'Doppelgänger' who cannot control his emotions. The language he uses to express his devotion to Frau Chauchat is the language of the sentimental novel: effusive, mawkish, full of religious imagery, clichéd phrases, and hyperboles. Hans tries to contain Wehsal's profuse outpourings using the language of reason, propriety, and good taste. But the reader, of course, knows that Hans's own feelings are not too far removed from Wehsal's: it is just that his strict adherence to social conventions, deep shame, and repression do not allow him to express them. In this scene, then, Hans's internal policing of his thoughts and feelings—which has been seen so many times before in the novel, in so many different ways—is recast as a dialogue. Wehsal becomes the locus of Hans's repressed sentimentality, and Hans is terrified by just how repulsive melodrama is: it is 'abstoßend', says Hans twice, 'hochgradig abstoßend', 'widrig', and 'krumm'.

The critical vocabulary that Hans deploys here takes us back to a much earlier episode in the novel when, during a solitary mountain walk, he finds himself thinking of Clawdia and humming a popular love song:

> Wie berührt mich wundersam
> oft ein Wort von dir [. . .]
> das von deiner Lippe kam
> und zum Herzen mir!

(p. 214)

How oft it thrills me just to hear
You say some simple word, [...]
That spoken from your lips, my dear
Does leave my heart so stirred!

(p. 165)[11]

With a sudden shrug, however, Hans stops himself from singing the latter two lines: realizing that he has fallen prey to a bout of involuntary cultural memory, Hans tells himself that the song—'das zarte Liedchen' ('delicate little song'), 'das Gedichtchen' ('little poem')—note the diminutives!—is 'lächerlich' ('ridiculous'), 'abgeschmackt' ('tasteless'), 'läppisch empfindsam' ('insipidly sentimental'), 'albern' ('silly'); it is 'ein sanfter Unsinn' ('a gentle bit of nonsense'). Hans, 'hochnäsig gegen gewisse Ausdrucksmittel' ('very particular about how he did express himself'), passes 'das ästhetische Urteil' ('an aesthetic verdict') on the language of the song, 'indem er die Nase rümpfte' ('turning up his nose'), and rejects it 'mit einer gewissen Melancholie und Strenge' ('with a certain austere melancholy') (pp. 214–15/pp. 165–66). Hans's internalized 'scharfe Bewachung' strikes again, a form of cultural self-policing designed to ward off the impropriety of a spontaneous but socially unacceptable emotional attachment, as well as a spontaneous but aesthetically unacceptable cultural expression of it. Just as in the scene with Wehsal, one set of intense emotions is replaced by another: melodramatic intensity is replaced by an intense aversion to melodrama.

Wehsal's appeal to Hans resonates with Rey Chow's critique of Western aesthetics: both are attempts to reinstate the legitimacy of untethered emotional expression. But when Hans quips that there are 'human rights that one does not exercise for good reason', the heroic gesture of self-restraint he advocates (we are not far from the 'certain austere melancholy' with which Hans rejects 'the delicate little song' earlier on)—is far more appealing than Wehsal's effusions. Its appeal is to a great extent manufactured by very simple narrative means: the dialogue between the two men goes on for several pages, and Wehsal does most of the talking, so the reader, faced with a choice between lines upon lines of Wehsal's repetitive ideas and Hans's brief and concise responses, is likely to feel more sympathy towards the latter. In this scene it is Hans who exercises the 'scharfe Bewachung' earlier associated with Fräulein Engelhart. But just as in the scene of Clawdia's departure, the narrative retains the melodrama even as it distances itself from it. At this point, the dilemma of how to successfully and legitimately express intense emotions is still unresolved: we are shown failed attempts at doing so, but there is as yet no positive solution.

---

[11] The lyrics have been identified as Hermann Kletke's poem 'Mein und Dein'; see Michael Neumann, *Thomas Mann, 'Der Zauberberg': Kommentar*, GKFA (Frankfurt am Main: Fischer, 2002), p. 181.

It is in the famous section 'Fülle des Wohllauts' ('Fullness of Harmony') towards the very end of the novel that we first glimpse an experience of emotional intensity that is fully sanctioned by the narrative authority. At night, alone in the sanatorium's music room, Hans listens to his five favourite pieces of classical music: selected arias from Verdi's *Aida* (1871), Bizet's *Carmen* (1875), and Gounod's *Faust* (1859), as well as Debussy's 'Prélude à l'après-midi d'un faune' (1894) and Schubert's 'Lindenbaum' (1828). I will focus here on the three operas. As Hans listens to them, their plots are described from his point of view, with parallels drawn between the characters in the operas and Hans himself, as well as his cousin Joachim. This becomes increasingly clear as the narrator explicitly points out Hans's predilection for military themes in operas and suggests that Hans identifies Valentin from Gounod's *Faust* with Joachim.

This section of the novel has been extensively commented on, and most critics recognize the parallels between Hans Castorp's plot in *The Magic Mountain* and the dramatic situations represented in the music he listens to. Charles E. Passage made it the main tenet of his interpretation, in which he argues that the five pieces of music reflect a platonic yet deep-seated homoerotic attraction between Hans and Joachim.[12] Helmut Gutmann and Rodney Symington both discuss the parallels between Castorp's experiences in the novel and the music he listens to and show how the music played in the sanatorium relates to Hans's spiritual development.[13] Hans R. Vaget took this argument a step further and offered a political reading of the 'Fülle des Wohllauts' section.[14] But hardly any critic has discussed the significance of Hans's recognition of his own story in cultural texts, which is precisely the aspect of the text that interests me here. David Fuller comes close to it: he sees Hans as a 'model critic' who is 'professionally *amateur*' and can thus appreciate 'art as emotional knowledge'.[15] It is ironic that many academic readers admire Mann's portrayal of this experience *in* the novel, but at the same time do not pay any attention to non-academic readers who report undergoing this same experience, but *with* the novel.

To fully appreciate the cultural backlash against entrenched notions of aesthetic taste that Mann is countering here, it is instructive to consider the isolated

[12] Charles E. Passage, 'Hans Castorp's Musical Incantation', *Germanic Review*, 38 (1963), 238–56.

[13] Helmut Gutmann, 'Das Musikkapitel in Thomas Manns *Zauberberg*', *The German Quarterly*, 47 (1974), 415–31, and Rodney Symington, 'Music on Mann's Magic Mountain: "Fülle des Wohllauts" and Hans Castorp's "Selbstüberwindung"', in *Echoes and Influences of German Romanticism: Essays in Honour of Hans Eichner*, ed. Michael S. Batts, Anthony W. Riley, and Heinz Wetzel (New York: Peter Lang, 1987), pp. 155–82.

[14] Hans Rudolf Vaget, '"Politically Suspect": Music on the Magic Mountain', in *Thomas Mann's 'The Magic Mountain': A Casebook*, ed. Hans Rudolf Vaget (Frankfurt am Main: Fischer, 2006), pp. 123–41. On the importance of music in Thomas Mann's work more generally, see Hans Rudolf Vaget, *Seelenzauber. Thomas Mann und die Musik* (Frankfurt am Main: Fischer, 2006).

[15] David Fuller, 'A Kind of Loving: Hans Castorp as Model Critic', in *Thomas Mann and Shakespeare: Something Rich and Strange*, ed. Tobias Döring and Ewan Fernie (New York: Bloomsbury, 2015), pp. 207–28, p. 207.

instances when academic readers of *The Magic Mountain* have scolded him for providing (to their eyes) questionable kinds of cultural pleasure. For example, Martin Swales passed a harsh judgement on the famous section about the snow storm: 'in my view, the dream sequence is overwritten to the point of being a melodramatic scenario'.[16] Even more pertinent to my discussion here are Rodney Symington's dismissive words about Hans Castorp's response to the pieces he listens to in the music chapter: his interpretations of them are 'highly subjective', a 'wilful distortion [...] in order that the music fit the circumstances'; the fact that Mann does not specify the titles of the pieces discussed 'provid[es] the reader [...] merely with the chance to experience the pleasure of guessing the music correctly'.[17] Swales, Symington, and many other academic readers of *The Magic Mountain* have a rather narrow view of what might and should be pleasurable in our encounters with culture.

Meanwhile, in *Uses of Literature*, Rita Felski usefully theorized the significance of the readerly experience of recognition, both as depicted in fiction (Thomas Buddenbrook's reading of Schopenhauer is one of her examples) and as undergone by real-life readers:

> what does it mean to recognize oneself in a book? The experience seems at once utterly mundane yet singularly mysterious. While turning a page I am arrested by a compelling description, a constellation of events, a conversation between characters, an interior monologue. Suddenly and without warning, a flash of connection leaps across the gap between text and reader; an affinity or an attunement is brought to light [...] I cannot help seeing traces of myself in the pages I am reading [...] Such episodes show readers becoming absorbed in scripts that confound their sense of who and what they are. They come to see themselves differently by gazing outward rather than inward, by deciphering ink marks on a page.[18]

Felski also argues that some of the most eloquent descriptions of enchantment have come from critics writing about opera.[19] Mann's description of Hans's relationship with music is a case in point—to use Felski's terms, it blends recognition and enchantment.

Most of the recordings that Hans listens to are in foreign languages, and we are told that Hans 'verstand nicht jedes Wort' ('understood [...] not every word'),

[16] Martin Swales, *The German Bildungsroman from Wieland to Hesse* (Princeton, NJ: Princeton University Press, 1978), p. 114.

[17] Symington, 'Music on Mann's Magic Mountain', pp. 165–66.

[18] Rita Felski, *Uses of Literature* (Oxford: Blackwell, 2008), p. 23.   [19] Ibid., p. 71.

but intuitively grasps the overall meaning of each piece 'mit Hilfe [...] seiner Sympathie für diese Situationen, einer vertraulichen Anteilnahme, die wuchs, je öfter er die [...] Platten laufen ließ' ('given [...] his sympathy for its situations, a personal empathy that had increased each time he played the [...] records') (p. 975/p. 766). The operatic plots are recounted in highly melodramatic terms; *Aida* is explicitly called a 'Melodrama' (p. 977). Hans's attitude towards this music is aptly summarized in the following comment about an aria from *Carmen*: 'es war inhaltlich nicht weit her mit der Arie, aber ihr flehender Gefühlsausdruck war im höchsten Grade rührend' ('the content of the aria was not much, but the way it pleaded with such emotion touched him profoundly') (p. 983/p. 772). The aria conveys 'den Schmerz, die Sehnsucht, die verlorene Zärtlichkeit, die süße Verzweiflung' ('anguish and longing, [...] forlorn tenderness and sweet despair') experienced by José, the soldier torn between a sense of military duty and his passionate love for Carmen: '"Dein ist mein Herz", beteuerte er abgeschmackter, aber allerzärtlichster Weise zum Überfluß' ('"My heart is yours," he assured her in trite, but tenderest excess') (p. 983/p. 772). José's outpouring of emotions, then, is characterized as melodramatic, distasteful, and excessive; and yet the cultural value of this music is entirely sanctioned by the narrative at this point. How is this possible? The melodramatic operas to which Hans is listening afford him a sense of resolution:

> was er [...] letztlich empfand, verstand und genoß, [...] das war die siegende Idealität der Musik, der Kunst, des menschlichen Gemüts, die hohe und unwiderlegliche Beschönigung, die sie der gemeinen Gräßlichkeit der wirklichen Dinge angedeihen ließ. [...] Die tröstliche Kraft dieser Beschönigung tat dem Zuhörer außerordentlich wohl [...]   (pp. 978–79)

> ultimately what he felt, understood, and relished was the victorious ideality of music, of art, of human emotions, their sublime and incontrovertible ability to gloss over the crude horrors of reality. [...] The consoling power of beauty to gloss things over did its listener a great deal of good [...]   (pp. 768–69)

Listening to operas that Hans associates with Joachim's fate helps him manage the difficult emotions he is experiencing after his cousin's death. It allows Hans to experience his emotions as an external, objective truth, rather than an internal, subjective experience. This time, emotions are not externalized as a futile bodily gesture or Wehsal's purposeless logorrhoea; this time, suffering is transformed into beauty, and this process makes suffering more bearable for Hans. It is a deeply contentious attitude, and I will soon discuss how various readers of *The Magic Mountain*, most notably A. E. Ellis, have reacted against it. Another reason why listening to *Carmen*, *Aida*, and *Faust* gives Hans solace is that it reassures him that he is not alone. He might be alone in the music room, but he is surrounded by other people's voices. On a more figurative level, Hans recognizes his own experience, as well as Joachim's fate, in a series of cultural texts. Again, I will show how all three responses to *The Magic Mountain* discussed in this chapter stage similar moments of recognition, or lack thereof, when readers recognize their own experiences depicted in culture, or fail to do so.

Taken together, Hans Castorp's various encounters with melodrama—in his own bodily responses to intense emotions, in Ferdinand Wehsal's tortured monologues, and in operatic arias—suggest a more nuanced understanding of what melodrama is and what it entails. It is a confrontation with cultural norms of emotional expression, which is less about the emotions themselves and more about the cultural policing of who can or should experience what, and how. In *The Magic Mountain* not only do we see different ways of dealing with intense emotions as depicted in a literary narrative, but we can also identify a range of possible aesthetic and ethical responses to literary depictions of suffering. This, too, is a theme which I will further explore in *The Rack*, *Norwegian Wood*, and 'Amundsen'.

2. 'Is This the Promised End?'

'I have known more than one reader to take up the book and lay it down again, for fear of contracting tuberculosis through suggestion', wrote Hermann J. Weigand in his 1933 study of *The Magic Mountain*; he went on: 'if a hundred Anglo-Saxon readers of the *Zauberberg*, selected at random, were asked to tell in one sentence what impressed them as its most extraordinary feature, a majority of them would point, I dare say, to the author's infatuation with so macabre a subject'.[20] In this early example of the speculative branch of Thomas Mann reception studies, Weigand goes on to juxtapose 'the German national temperament' and its attitude towards illness with 'the Anglo-Saxon world's' ideas about it, which he summarizes by quoting Bernard Shaw: 'disease is not interesting: it is something to be done away with by general consent, and that is all about it'. Whether Weigand's grasp of the 'Anglo-Saxon character' was faulty, or whether the 'national temperament' is more subject to change than he imagined, the reception of *The Magic Mountain* in Britain after the Second World War tells a different story of the reading public's attitudes towards illness.

A handful of reviews (including one on a dubious right-wing website), a fifty-word note in *The Oxford Companion to English Literature*, and a few mentions in critical studies of literary representations of tuberculosis: that is all that a reader

---

[20] Hermann J. Weigand, '*The Magic Mountain*': *A Study of Thomas Mann's Novel 'Der Zauberberg'* (Chapel Hill, NC: University of North Carolina Press, 1964), p. 39.

who stumbles across *The Rack*, Derek Lindsay's only and nowadays largely forgotten novel, is likely to discover. Lindsay (1920–2000) published *The Rack* in 1958 under the pseudonym A. E. Ellis, and the book is largely inspired by his own youth. Having fought in the Second World War, Lindsay received a scholarship to study at Oxford, but was soon diagnosed with tuberculosis and sent to a tuberculosis sanatorium in the Alps.

The Rack tells a similar story: Paul Davenant, an ex-soldier studying at Cambridge, discovers that he has contracted tuberculosis during the war and ends up in a tuberculosis sanatorium in the French Alps, alongside dozens of other students funded through the same public scheme. The novel tells the story of their struggle to regain health. After their war experience the students suffer not only from tuberculosis but also from shell shock (now known as posttraumatic stress disorder); the latter condition, though not formally acknowledged at any point, seeps into the narrative at every turn. Paul's illness is particularly severe and he must stay in the sanatorium long after other students have left, which pushes him into an existential crisis. A glimmer of hope appears when Paul falls in love with another patient, Michèle, a 17-year-old from Belgium. But their love affair has no future: both are sick and impoverished. *The Rack* ends when Paul and Michèle are forced to part and Paul is on the verge of suicide. The book records Paul's physical and psychological torment with melodramatic intensity, and yet Paul angrily rejects all available cultural narratives of suffering which he encounters, including *The Magic Mountain*. It is only in *King Lear* that Paul ultimately finds some solace in the last pages of the novel, when it is also revealed that the titular 'rack' is a metaphor borrowed from Shakespeare's play: Lear is described as being stretched out 'upon the rack of this rough world'.

Upon its publication, *The Rack* garnered positive reviews and was even included in the Penguin Modern Classics series. Among its most enthusiastic readers were Graham Greene and Sylvia Plath, undoubtedly attracted to its unflinching, detailed descriptions of physical and mental suffering. Edwin Muir, who reviewed the novel for *The Observer*, confessed: 'I cannot think of another novel so filled with distinct impressions of various kinds and degrees of pain, brought on by piercings, gashings, scrapings and pumpings of the animate flesh. The book has the smell of places where diseased bodies are tortured'; the text 'draws us into the vortex of physical suffering'.[21] Sylvia Plath was inspired to write *The Bell Jar*, which was published in the early 1960s shortly before she died by suicide, after reading *The Rack*.[22] One of Greene's most successful novels, *The End of the Affair*, which came out just a few years earlier, features another fated affair that only fully ends after one lover's harrowing death from a lung infection. All

---

[21] Edwin Muir, 'Endurance Point: *The Rack* by A. E. Ellis', *The Observer*, 9 November 1958, 21.

[22] See Robin Peel, *Writing Back: Sylvia Plath and Cold War Politics* (London: Associated University Presses, 2002), p. 47.

editions of *The Rack* bear Greene's endorsement on the front cover: 'there are certain books we call great for want of a better term, that rise like monuments above the cemeteries of literature: *Clarissa Harlowe, Great Expectations, Ulysses. The Rack* to my mind is one of this company.' But despite Greene's enthusiasm, and even though two new editions of *The Rack* appeared in 2014 and 2016, the novel has been almost entirely forgotten since the 1950s and 1960s; the only substantial discussion of it in literary scholarship is a chapter in Jeffrey Meyers's monograph on disease in literature, which also features a chapter on *The Magic Mountain*.[23]

It is indeed fitting for *The Rack* to be discussed alongside *The Magic Mountain*. Meyers interprets the former as a sombre response to the latter. His conclusion is that 'the greatness of *The Rack* lies in Ellis's rejection of illusory consolations about the grandeur and dignity of "meaningful death", and his courageous recognition that suffering is the inevitable fate of mankind'.[24] This interpretation implicitly places *The Rack* in opposition to *The Magic Mountain* and its frivolous infatuation with death and decay. The novel's reviewers in the late 1950s felt the same way. Muir writes that Ellis 'describes [the] final states of agony with wonderful truth';[25] the review in *The Spectator*, entitled 'Back to the Mountain', commends *The Rack* for 'treat[ing] tuberculosis as a physical malady, not as a mystical experience' and for 'present[ing] the clinical details starkly [. . . but] not for morbid or sensational reasons'.[26] Maureen Howard's review explicitly compares and contrasts *The Magic Mountain* and *The Rack*, as well as contemporary French existentialist writing. She argues that '*The Rack* tries to be both a novel of ideas [. . .] and a novel of feeling', with the former micro-genre developing through a series of explicit metaphysical statements, and the latter working 'implicitly by evoking an extended mood of anguish and absurdity'. Howard ultimately concludes that, unlike in Mann's novel, the characters' viewpoints in *The Rack* 'don't develop into any system of ideas'; rather, the book is successful as 'a striking mood-piece' whose main character gradually becomes 'an expert in suffering'.[27]

For all these critics, the value of *The Rack* lies in its perceived honesty and directness in the portrayal of physical and emotional suffering. They welcome *The Rack* as a valuable antidote to Mann's highly stylized and over-intellectualized portrayal of illness as an elevating spiritual force. In 1975, Graham Greene reminisced about his experience of reading *The Magic Mountain* as a young man: the novel 'beeindruckte mich wie der Anblick des Montblanc—ich empfand keinen Wunsch, damit zu leben' ('impressed me like the view of Mont Blanc—I

---

[23] Jeffrey Meyers, *Disease and the Novel 1880–1960* (London: Macmillan, 1985), pp. 93–107.
[24] Ibid., p. 107.   [25] Muir, 'Endurance Point', p. 21.
[26] Geoffrey Nicholson, 'Back to the Mountain', *The Spectator*, 31 October 1958, 592.
[27] Maureen Howard, 'This Long Disease, My Life', *The Kenyon Review*, 22.1 (1960), 156–59.

felt no desire to live with it').[28] But is this a fair reading of Mann? Is there really such a clear-cut opposition between *The Magic Mountain*, a 'novel of ideas', and *The Rack*, a 'novel of feeling'? The relationship between the narrative strategies in these two texts is much more complex than this, and in the process of destabilizing the binary opposition between 'novels of ideas' and 'novels of feeling', we can learn a lot not only about Mann's and Ellis's writing but also, more generally, about the uses of literary imagination in the face of suffering.

Though many doctors harshly criticized Mann's novel upon its publication, some medical professionals were much more sympathetic to it, and praised it in terms that are exactly the opposite of those used by reviewers in 1950s Britain. One doctor wrote in the *Deutsche Medizinische Wochenschrift*:

> Die medizinische Literatur über den Zusammenhang von Psyche und Lungentuberkulose ist bisher nur sehr spärlich, während Laien schon seit langer Zeit dieses Problem mit größtem Interesse verfolgt haben [...] Hier sollte die Arbeit der Ärzte, eine vernünftige Psychotherapie, neben und mit der eigentlichen medizinischen Therapie einsetzen. Dazu fordert der Roman von Thomas Mann geradezu heraus, und deshalb sollten die Ärzte ihn nicht als einen gegen sich gerichteten Angriff betrachten, sondern als Mahnung zur Erkenntnis und Einsicht.

> There is at present very little medical literature about the relation between tuberculosis of the lungs and psychological phenomena, whereas laymen have for a long time shown great interest in this problem [...] This is where the doctor's work, a sensible psychotherapy alongside and together with the actual medical therapy, ought to start. Thomas Mann's novel challenges us to do just that, and that is why doctors should see it not as an attack on them, but as a stimulus to reflection and understanding.[29]

This doctor is sensitive to the difference between 'illness as defined by the medical profession' and 'illness as experienced by the patient', and argues that *The Magic Mountain* fills an important cultural gap in articulating the latter facet of the disease.[30] A few years later another doctor coined the term 'die Zauberberg-Krankheit' ('Magic Mountain Malady') to refer to the psychological toll that tuberculosis takes on those who suffer from it.[31] Many decades on, a South African doctor and amateur musician, whose daughter shared an office with me in Oxford for a time, was so taken by Mann's portrayal of illness that he composed

---

[28] Marcel Reich-Ranicki, ed., *Was halten Sie von Thomas Mann?* (Frankfurt am Main: Fischer, 1988), p. 27.
[29] Quoted in Malte Herwig, 'The "Magic Mountain Malady": *The Magic Mountain* and the Medical Community, 1924–2006', in *Thomas Mann's 'The Magic Mountain': A Casebook*, ed. Hans Rudolf Vaget (Oxford: Oxford University Press, 2008), pp. 245–64, pp. 261–62 and p. 253.
[30] Ibid., p. 255.   [31] See ibid.

an entire musical adaptation of the novel. But in *The Rack*, Ellis suggests that Mann in fact misrepresented patients' experience of tuberculosis.

To begin fleshing out the relationship between *The Magic Mountain* and *The Rack*, it is worth considering how Ellis's novel acknowledges its debt to Thomas Mann. The text contains numerous subtle allusions to *The Magic Mountain*. For example, Paul is 27 years old upon his arrival, and Michèle is 17; their sanatorium has seven floors, and Paul's illness goes through seven distinct stages which are explicitly counted out in the novel by another patient, an engineer called Hans. This character clearly alludes to Hans Castorp, and the number seven is a structural device famously employed by Mann throughout *The Magic Mountain*: the novel is divided into seven chapters, Hans arrives in Davos in 1907 and stays in the sanatorium for seven years, and so on.[32] When Paul first arrives in the sanatorium in *The Rack* and asks his doctor how long he will have to stay there, the doctor responds: 'you should know, *monsieur*, that this is not the sort of place to which you come for three weeks' (p. 31). Not only does this line hark back to how long Hans Castorp originally planned to stay in Davos, but it also posits the existence of shared cultural knowledge about stories of tuberculosis ('you should know, *monsieur*'). Indeed, *The Rack* is set on dissecting the cultural topos of tuberculosis. When Paul relates the course of his illness to another patient, it is described as 'a story which adhered to an all too familiar pattern' (p. 22). This pattern is mainly associated with *The Magic Mountain*—the book that effectively monopolized cultural narratives of tuberculosis by the mid-twentieth century, and to which *The Rack* was compared in virtually every review upon its publication.

The Rack is deeply metafictional: it is acutely aware of its own literary lineage and full of various literary allusions. At several points in the novel, different characters compare real life with literary scenarios. 'Life, alas, is not a novel in which things somehow contrive to come all right in the end', writes Michèle's mother to Paul at the end of the book, entreating him to end his relationship with her daughter (p. 413). Much earlier on, the head doctor in the sanatorium teases Paul, who repeatedly loses all hope and declines further treatment: 'this is our stock conversation. If you were writing a novel about our relationship you would have difficulty in sustaining much interest in the dialogue' (p. 208). Some pages later, Paul observes in a conversation with Michèle that sanatorium patients tend to grow so used to their new lives with tuberculosis that 'it's as though one's past life were something one had once read in a half-forgotten novel' (p. 262). What connects all these passages is the suggestion that Paul's experiences at the sana-torium are distinctly unlike conventional literary scenarios: his conversations with others are repetitive and inconclusive, a good ending in the future is not in sight,

---

[32] For more examples, see Oskar Seidlin, 'The Lofty Game of Numbers: The Mynheer Peeperkorn Episode in Thomas Mann's *Der Zauberberg*', *PMLA*, 86 (1971), 924–39.

and it is only his past life, before he contracted tuberculosis, that sounds like material for a novel.

The idea that Paul's life at the sanatorium does not lend itself to a novelistic treatment is, of course, deeply ironic: after all, it furnishes *The Rack* with its plot. One might be tempted to assume, then, that the novel merely registers the ultimate dilemma of representation: how does one convey innermost feelings and the harrowing experience of physical and psychological suffering in an authentic way, given that all literary representation is necessarily constructed and mediated? But Ellis's project seems to be more nuanced than this. In his novel the bedridden sanatorium patients, including Paul, read prodigiously to kill time, which prompts the sanatorium authorities to produce a leaflet containing the official recommendations on the subject:

> READING MATTER: Reading can play a therapeutic role in the recovery of the patient, and patients should endeavour to use their enforced leisure profitably. The reading of textbooks and books potentially of use in the patient's civil occupation is whole-heartedly recommended, whilst, for diversion, novels of adventurous, humorous or romantic interest are advised. Books of a pessimistic nature, or which reflect a gloomy or morbid view of life, will not, in the best interests of the patient, be tolerated.   (p. 364)

We have already encountered this attitude in another Swiss doctor from another novel written by another tubercular writer—Doctor Klebe from Konstantin Fedin's *Sanatorium Arktur*, who tried to stop his patients from reading *The Magic Mountain* and recommended Edgar Wallace's adventure stories instead. According to these official rules of the cure in Paul's sanatorium, *The Magic Mountain* is clearly detrimental to the treatment of tuberculosis, and so is *The Rack* itself, for that matter; but both books ironically denounce the idea that mindlessness and a sense of denial are helpful for those faced with terminal illness.

What is the alternative presented in *The Rack*? The first clue appears on the novel's very first page, in the epigraph taken from Henry de Montherlant's essay 'Mors et Vita' published in *La Revue des deux mondes* in 1932. Montherlant rejects all attempts to appear heroic in the face of death, the artificial and dishonest self-stylization of

> tous ces gens qui font des mots historiques en mourant, [...] qui dans trois jours n'existeront plus, et qui veulent encore se faire admirer, qui posent, qui mentent jusqu'au dernier souffle.

> a lot of people [who], on the verge of death, utter famous last words [..., who] will have ceased to exist three days' hence, yet [...] still want to arouse admiration and adopt a pose and tell a lie with their last gasp.

He goes on to declare that 'l'admiration du monde vous couvre de bave comme une limace qui se traîne' ('the admiration of the world covers you with slime like the trail of a slug').[33] Several examples of such pseudo-heroic, attention-grabbing deaths occur in *The Rack*. One of Paul's best friends at the sanatorium, John Cotterell, dies following a strange, highly dramatic episode, which takes place in the final stages of his illness, the morning after the induction of his pneumothorax. Cotterell slips out of the sanatorium and ventures forth into the mountains, overcome by the obsessive idea that he must pick gentians for Paul—'little blue flowers that it is strictly forbidden to pick' (p. 185). Cotterell's strange, delirious quest is densely intertextual: it calls to mind the 'blaue Blume' in *Heinrich von Ofterdingen*, but also the heliotropes (another species of blue flower) that Hans Castorp picks in *The Magic Mountain* in an episode that itself alludes to Novalis.

Cotterell's attempt at a grand, heroic gesture is an utter failure. He is found on a mountain pass, 'half-suffocated', 'wearing flannel trousers, a pyjama jacket and stockings which were shredded and stiff with blood'; 'his pockets were filled with gentians' (p. 185). He is brought back to the sanatorium, but it turns out that his lung has perforated, and he dies a few hours later. The medical staff and patients at the sanatorium find Cotterell's fit of terminal, drug-induced obsession unintelligible and grotesque. Paul's doctor, who tells him what has happened to his friend, finishes the story thus:

> but let us never forget that the main drift goes on, less spectacular but more significant—the reclaiming of dying men and women. And this brings me to my purpose in visiting you this evening. I wish to speak about your condition and your prospects for the future [...]   (pp. 185–86)

The doctor contrasts Cotterell's spectacular but insignificant outburst with the uneventful and protracted course of convalescence which awaits Paul. John Cotterell's fate seems to be an extreme version of the pointless and inauthentic heroism in the face of death decried by Montherlant. But the doctor's alternative—accepting the prolonged convalescence with no promise that it is ever going to be effective—is not appealing to Paul either. Throughout the novel Paul struggles to find any narrative that would adequately address his suffering and grant him a sense of resolution.

The Magic Mountain has been shown to be an important implicit intertext for *The Rack*, even though Hans Castorp's story was flatly rejected as a model for Paul's ordeal. But there are other narratives of suffering which are offered to Ellis's hero at the sanatorium. The first one addresses the fact that his affliction is part

---

[33] Henry de Montherlant, *Selected Essays*, trans. John Weightman (London: Weidenfeld & Nicholson, 1960), pp. 92–93.

tuberculosis, part ill-fated love; both reside in the chest, and they are strangely interrelated. Paul's breath might be taken away by the sight of Michèle to whom he is attracted, but he might also be out of breath because his lungs do not function properly. His final relapse—'like claws dividing tissue, pain tore his chest' (p. 312)—ensues while a couple reminiscent of 'das schlechte Russenpaar' ('the bad Russian couple'), Castorp's neighbours in *The Magic Mountain*, is making love next door, so that Paul can hear 'the creaking of the bed, [...] the distinct and unremitting accompaniment of a hand patting bare flesh [...] alternate, raucous gasps' (p. 312). The parallel between an all-consuming physical passion and the intense suffering of a tubercular body resonates with Doktor Krokowski's Freudian lectures in *The Magic Mountain* on 'das Krankheitssymptom [als] verkappte Liebesbetätigung und alle Krankheit [als] verwandelte Liebe' ('any symptom of illness [as] a masked form of love in action, and illness [as] merely transformed love') (p. 196/p. 151).

In *The Rack*, disease is not just a cover for fervent love: love itself is often described in clinical terms, too. The nurses at the sanatorium gossip about 'the actual clinical limits of [Paul and Michèle's] affair' (p. 229). Described in harsh, medical terms, their sexual relations are made to sound like a surgical intervention analogous to pneumothorax or thoracoplasty. Conversely, while Michèle is undergoing a chest operation, thoracoscopy, Paul envisages her 'nude to the waist, strapped to the operating table, instruments protruding from her side, her whole slender body' (p. 219). This erotically tinted, almost sadistic vision further links love and lovemaking to tuberculosis and its surgical treatment. Even the couple's first kiss turns out to be unexpectedly violent and painful: Paul 'clasped her desperately, held her face in his hands, covered her features with kisses, pressed his lips against her lips until the pain made her gasp, and under his teeth thin fillets of blood spread from her lips to his mouth' (p. 217). When Paul later declares his love for Michèle, he 'explained himself in tortuous, stilted phrases' (p. 231), and gradually these types of phrases begin to permeate the text of the novel itself. The narrative of suffering which blends tuberculosis and love gives way to the narrative which blends tuberculosis and mental illness.

The Rack is also suffused with ballistic metaphors for the experience of tuberculosis, influenced by the memory of war. It is hinted that Paul suffers from bouts of shell shock and depression, and his own perception of himself is that 'the whole of his life had been the attempt, sometimes more, usually less, successful of concealing the true nature of his feelings from those about him' (p. 332). Perhaps that is why Paul is so ill-disposed towards X-ray plates—they strike him as a token of intimacy, as a way of giving others access to one's innermost self, something that Hans Castorp also perceives in *The Magic Mountain*. When an intrusive English girl at the sanatorium assails Paul in his room with 'a brief-case filled with a representative selection of her X-ray plates' (p. 191), Paul is perturbed and irritated. Then, faced with the prospect of Michèle's departure from the sanatorium, Paul feels 'as if the pressure of his emotions had produced a spontaneous pre-frontal leucotomy' (p. 285). This brutal procedure involved removing the connections between the frontal lobes and the rest of the brain. It was intended to treat psychiatric disorders but was discredited just a few years after it was first performed in the 1930s. Paul fantasizes about this invasive, violent procedure as a way of releasing the unbearable emotional tension that is gradually getting the better of him. This emotional tension at least partly stems from Paul's experience of the war. Nowhere in the book is there any suggestion that *The Magic Mountain* might help him confront it, or indeed A. E. Ellis, his creator, who also fought in the British Army during the Second World War.

However, other responses to Mann's novel were possible. In *49th Parallel*, a British film directed in 1941 by Michael Powell in collaboration with Emeric Pressburger, a Nazi officer burns a cherished possession of a Canadian anti-Nazi—a copy of *The Magic Mountain*. Conceived as a propaganda film to help sway opinions in the still neutral United States, *49th Parallel* features *The Magic Mountain* to allude both to Nazi book burnings and to Thomas Mann's position as the voice of liberal Germany. In the film, his novel functions as an emblem of civilization that is worth preserving even in the times of war.

Even more tellingly, in 1945, the US War Department ordered 10,000 copies of a special German-language edition of *The Magic Mountain*, which, alongside other German books vetted by the War Department, were distributed to German prisoners of war interned in more than 500 camps in the United States.[34] The aim of the 'Bücherreihe Neue Welt' ('Book Series New World'), as this initiative was called, was to re-educate the prisoners who had served under Hitler; Mann's works were seen as an appropriate medium for this re-education due to his 'efforts to create a democratic mythology to rival that of fascism'.[35] Tobias Boes has analysed letters to the editor of the POW newspaper *Der Ruf* to show how robust and perhaps unexpected the response to the 'Bücherreihe Neue Welt' was. One POW, signed as Dr Wolfgang Hildebrandt, reminisced in an open letter to Thomas Mann published in *Der Ruf*: '*Der Zauberberg* hat mich in der Dünndruckausgabe von 1926 durch alle Kommandos des Krieges begleitet' ('*The Magic Mountain* in the thin-paper edition of 1926 accompanied me wherever I went during the war').[36] His copy of the book was the affordable edition which, as discussed in Chapter 1, Mann had insisted on with an eye to broadening his readership. The 'Bücherreihe Neue Welt' edition of the novel was now 'in allen Kriegsgefangenenlagern zu haben' ('available in all POW camps'), and 'die wahrhaft zauberhafte Wirkung des Romans besteht darin, dass der deutsche Kriegsgefangene

[34] See Tobias Boes, *Thomas Mann's War* (Ithaca, NY: Cornell University Press, 2019), pp. 212–20.
[35] Ibid., p. 216.
[36] Wolfgang Hildebrandt, 'Zauberberg und Kriegsgefangenschaft: Offener Brief an Thomas Mann', *Der Ruf*, 1 October 1945, 4.

sein eigenes Schicksal, seine eigene Geschichte in ihm erzählt findet' ('the truly magical effect of the novel is this: German prisoners of war find in it their own fate, their own story'), Hildebrandt added.

He went on to compare both his participation in the war and his stay in the internment camp to Hans Castorp's intellectual adventures in the Berghof sanatorium. Like many other young German men of his generation, he experimented with the Nazi ideology in the same way that Castorp experimented with Naphta's 'terroristische Propaganda' ('terrorist propaganda'), but now he can hear again 'die Stimme Settembrinis, die Stimme der Demokratie' ('Settembrini's voice, the voice of democracy'). Like Castorp, he experiences intellectual freedom while in physical confinement, but is not immune to occasional bouts of 'Lethargie und seelische Niedergeschlagenheit' ('lethargy and psychological despondency'); and the 'Zeiterlebnis des deutschen Kriegsgefangenen' ('the way that a prisoner of war experiences time') is similar to Castorp's. These parallels are drawn with ample use of relevant quotations from *The Magic Mountain* and presented as applicable to thousands of German POWs. There is only one 'Hans Castorp der Dichtung' ('fictional Hans Castorp'), but there are thousands of 'Castorps der Wirklichkeit' ('real-life Castorps')—the '"Sorgenkinder des Lebens" und "problem children" der AMG' ('the "problem children" of life and of the AMG' [Allied Military Government for Occupied Territories]).[37] Hildebrandt's desire to exculpate himself, not least in the eyes of the Americans who were soon to begin issuing denazification directives in Germany, was undoubtedly a large motivation behind his open letter to Mann. Even so, his extraordinary intellectual and emotional investment in *The Magic Mountain* clearly shines through.

In *The Rack*, Paul does not find this kind of comfort in *The Magic Mountain* at all. But then, finally, at the very end of the novel, when he has lost all hope of recovery, Paul does find a source of solace: he picks up on a line from *King Lear* to describe his physical and psychological pain. He chances upon the journal of a nineteenth-century English painter, Benjamin Robert Haydon, who died by suicide. Haydon's suicide note ended with the following words: 'stretch me no more on this rough world—Lear' (p. 413). Paul realizes that this is a misquotation, so he consults his copy of *King Lear* and finds the correct quote in the last scene of the last act of the play:

> O, let him pass! He hates him
> That would upon the rack of this rough world
> Stretch him out longer.

There are two important differences between the lines from Shakespeare and Haydon's misquotation. First, Haydon has changed the quote from the third

[37] Ibid., p. 4.

person—in Shakespeare's play, it is Kent's commentary on Lear's suffering—to the first person, as though it were Lear who is repining over his own situation. Haydon's self-dramatization aligns him with 'tous ces gens qui font des mots historiques en mourant' decried by Montherlant. In contrast, Paul—and Ellis—see Shakespeare's Lear as a figure who confronts the reality of his own suffering, rather than putting on a mask of heroism. The second difference between Shakespeare's original and Haydon's misquotation is that, as Paul realizes, Haydon 'forgot the rack' (p. 414)—which allows the reader of *The Rack* to finally make sense of the novel's title.

A meta-narrative frame emerges at this point, linking 'the rack' on the novel's cover with 'the rack' on its last page, quoted from the last page of *King Lear*. Ellis's novel reaches its conclusion with intimations of Paul's impending death, be it suicide or a lethal bout of tuberculosis, thus connecting the end of the narrative with the end of Paul's life. The text has been preparing us for Paul's death from the very beginning, and with each severe relapse the reader has been led to ask herself, like Kent in *King Lear*, 'is this the promised end?'[38] But then each time Paul survived: to quote Kent again, 'the wonder is he hath endured so long'.[39] The effect of a painfully deferred ending, which tortures the reader nearly as much as it tortures the protagonist, is present in both *The Rack* and *King Lear*: in his famous interpretation of Shakespeare's play Stephen Booth argued that 'not ending is a primary characteristic of *King Lear*', and that the last lines of the play 'come close to pointing out the audience's parallel ordeal: *King Lear* is too long, almost unendurably so'.[40] *The Rack* thus ends with an evocation of Shakespeare's most dramatic enactment of protracted suffering, which retrospectively legitimizes the novel's own obsessive focus on Paul's torment by identifying its source at the heart of the English—or even, as for Harold Bloom—Western literary canon.[41]

Just as Hans finds solace in *Aida*, *Carmen*, and *Faust*, Paul finds it in *King Lear*. But neither Paul nor the narrator of *The Rack* seems to realize that the cultural text Paul feels drawn to is just one possibility among many. Paul is particularly receptive towards *King Lear* because he is a young man educated at Cambridge in the 1940s, and as such is trained to appreciate and revere Shakespeare. It is telling that Paul, even on the verge of suicide, is so invested in correcting a misquotation of the Bard's words: he treats Shakespeare's play as a sacred text, a grounding cultural convention that one can rely on in the face of death. One

[38] William Shakespeare, *King Lear*, in *The New Oxford Shakespeare: The Complete Works*, ed. Gary Taylor and others (Oxford: Oxford University Press, 2016), pp. 2347–433, p. 2431.
[39] Ibid., p. 2433.
[40] Stephen Booth, *'King Lear', 'Macbeth', Indefinition, and Tragedy* (New Haven, CT: Yale University Press, 1983), pp. 15–16.
[41] Jeffrey Meyers additionally points out several other allusions to Shakespeare—to *Hamlet* as well as *King Lear*—made earlier on in the novel; see Meyers, *Disease and the Novel*, p. 100. See also Harold Bloom, *The Western Canon* (London: Macmillan, 1995); for a contrasting view on the source of literary value, see Barbara Herrnstein Smith, 'Contingencies of Value', *Critical Inquiry*, 10 (1983), 1–35.

thinks here of Aldous Huxley's *Brave New World* (1932), another twentieth-century British novel that borrowed its title from Shakespeare; John, one of the main characters, is brought up in a 'Reservation' away from the dystopian, highly controlled European society, and his entire worldview is based on the complete works of Shakespeare, the only literature that was available to read at the Reservation, and which he knows by heart.

But in an ironic twist, Paul's unwavering belief in an authoritative and faithful rendering of Shakespeare's words is somewhat undermined by the fact that the supposedly correct quotation from *King Lear* supplied in the novel contains a mistake. All editions of *King Lear* based on the seventeenth-century prints of the play—for example, *The New Oxford Shakespeare*—have 'tough' in place of 'rough';[42] the latter seems to have been taken from one of the eighteenth-century editions of the play, which were influential and widespread, but sometimes unreliable.[43] *The Rack* postulates the existence of a fixed cultural canon, but in fact reveals that it is a malleable construct, ceaselessly shaped and reshaped by its readers. Shakespeare is read and reread both literally—editors make out the individual letters of the text, and figuratively—readers interpret its meaning and establish its value.

While in *The Magic Mountain* the narrator makes it clear that Hans finds a 'tröstliche Kraft' in certain operas due to his 'sympathy for its situations, a personal empathy', the narrator of *The Rack* does not reflect on the reason why *King Lear* exercises such an enormous influence over Paul. In Ellis's novel it is a given that Shakespeare's portrayal of suffering is authentic and legitimate. A comparison between *The Rack* and *The Magic Mountain* brings out a productive ambiguity in Mann's novel: while Hans constantly finds himself caught up in orthodox cultural hierarchies and feels impelled to stop himself from humming a popular love song and covering his face with his hands in a moment of strong emotion, the cultural authority of classical opera is not taken for granted. Instead, it is up for discussion.

Haydon's liberal use of Shakespeare's words to suit his own personal situation is frowned upon in *The Rack*; meanwhile, the value of the arias from *Aida*, *Carmen*, and *Faust* in *The Magic Mountain* rests on Hans being able to apply them to his own life, the fact that he can imagine Joachim in place of Valentin in Gounod's *Faust*. The operas appeal to Hans because they respond to his individual situation at a given point in time, and this is more important than their hypothetical eternal and universal relevance and abstract aesthetic value. *The Rack* demonstrates the concern that a misquotation of Shakespeare might make the Bard appear excessively melodramatic, but Hans and the narrator of *The Magic Mountain* are not at all concerned about the operas being melodramatic and sentimental. As long as it works for Hans in the moment when he needs it, the arias can sound 'trite, in tenderest excess'. At the

---

[42] Shakespeare, 'King Lear', p. 2432.   [43] I am indebted to Rachael Hodge for this observation.

same time, however, a popular love song perceived to be 'trite' or 'tasteless' is not a viable site of cultural identification and release of emotions for Hans, even though he feels instinctively drawn to it. *The Rack* is permeated with an anxiety about excessive self-dramatization and pompousness which can only be assuaged by the ultimate authority of Shakespeare, whose reputation pre-emptively rebuts any accusations of melodramatic excess. *The Magic Mountain* is more liberal in its approach to the value of what is perceived to be high culture, but it grants its protagonist less agency in his own approach to what is categorized as popular culture. In other words, Hans Castorp is allowed to have a deeply individual aesthetic response to a classical opera, but not to a popular song. The rigidity of this distinction is a potential blind spot in the novel: while the narrative voice in *The Magic Mountain* relentlessly exposes the formulaic processes of the cultural policing of emotions, the novel is not as hyper-aware of its own embeddedness in conservative cultural hierarchies and received sets of aesthetic judgements.

In the next text I am going to look at, the cultural landscape is dramatically different. Not all that dissimilar to Paul Davenant, Toru Watanabe—the protagonist of Haruki Murakami's global bestseller *Norwegian Wood*—is a young Japanese student confronted with a series of personal traumas: the illness and death of several of the people closest to him. In *Norwegian Wood*, however, canonical works of Western culture are available as useful tools rather than monumental obstacles which prevent one from expressing one's suffering, or unquestioned sources of authority that legitimize it. In this way, Murakami's novel can serve as a useful counterpart to both *The Rack* and *The Magic Mountain*. It puts more pressure on the idea that the cultural field can be neatly divided into discrete parts: the 'lowbrow' and the 'highbrow', the 'serious' and the 'sentimental', 'novels of feeling' and 'novels of ideas'.

3. 'Word-Searching Sickness'

Toru Watanabe, the protagonist and first-person narrator of *Noruwei no mori* (*Norwegian Wood*), is an avid reader. At the age of 20, in 1968, Toru is a university student in Tokyo. He studies drama and takes German language classes, but what he most enjoys reading are iconic American novels of the preceding few decades, such as F. Scott Fitzgerald's *The Great Gatsby* (1925) and J. D. Salinger's *The Catcher in the Rye* (1951).[44] Toru's favourite books serve many different functions in his life. His literary tastes set him apart from most other Japanese students, who, in the heat of the protest movement, favour contemporary political French and

---

[44] Toru never quite admits to being a fan of *The Catcher in the Rye*, but when another character comments that he has 'this funny way of talking' and suggests that he is 'trying to imitate that boy in *Catcher in the Rye*', Toru just says 'no way!', 'with a smile' (p. 131).

Japanese writers. When Toru meets another student who also likes *The Great Gatsby*, the two quickly become friends. On that basis, they could have easily made friends with Haruki Murakami (b. 1949) himself, too: Toru's taste in books is aligned with Murakami's own aesthetic preferences. *The Great Gatsby* is reportedly Murakami's favourite novel, one that he claims led him to become a writer in the first place; he has even translated it into Japanese, alongside books by many others among Toru's favourite authors.

Not only do books win Toru friends, but on several occasions he also manages to impress women with his pensive posture at a bar, a thick book in one hand and a cigarette in the other. And when on his own, 'with [his] eyes closed, [he] would touch a familiar book and draw its fragrance deep inside [him]. This was enough to make [him] happy' (p. 37). Books provide Toru with a sense of identity, comfort, and reassurance, not unlike Hans Castorp's 'Vorzugsplatten' ('favourite records') and Paul Davenant's personal edition of Shakespeare ('he opened his Shakespeare', reads the line at the end of *The Rack*).

Some of Toru's books also serve an important function on a meta-literary level. As critics have noted, in *Norwegian Wood* Murakami was inspired by the narrative structure of *The Great Gatsby* and *The Catcher in the Rye*—novels that became famous for their insecure first-person narrators, ridden with self-doubt and dealing with personal traumas.[45] These two books appear alongside references to many other literary texts, films, and both classical and popular music. Murakami's strategy is to pit against each other a whole cast of competing narrative voices, different storytelling strategies, and artistic registers that are often perceived as diametrically opposed, from Bach to the Beatles, and from Salinger's deeply personal and iconoclastic first-person narration to Thomas Mann's erudite novel of ideas. Murakami is playing with the perception that literature and art can be neatly divided into the 'lowbrow' and the 'highbrow'. In *Norwegian Wood* these supposedly competing artistic models are mobilized together in response to one fundamental dilemma, which we have already encountered in both Mann's and Ellis's novels: how to express emotional truth, emotional suffering, through language, and, in particular, literary language.

The connection between *Norwegian Wood* and *The Magic Mountain* has been noted in passing in several discussions of Murakami's novel, but has not yet been extensively discussed. Jay Rubin—Murakami's English translator and a scholar of Japanese literature—mentions it briefly in his book on Murakami, but does not go into much detail.[46] Yasumasa Oguro lists various similarities between the two texts, but without discussing their larger significance, which is my goal in this

---

[45] See William Marling, *Gatekeepers: The Emergence of World Literature and the 1960s* (Oxford: Oxford University Press, 2016), p. 127.

[46] Jay Rubin, *Haruki Murakami and the Music of Words* (London: Vintage, 2005), p. 155.

section.[47] A copy of *The Magic Mountain* makes its first appearance a quarter of the way into *Norwegian Wood*. Toru is 'absorbed' in it the day he gets a letter from Naoko, his love interest, who lives in a mountain sanatorium called Ami Hostel: 'a place in the hills outside Kyoto [...] not exactly a hospital, more a sanatorium kind of thing with a far freer style of treatment [...] a quiet place cut off from the world', where she can 'rest her nerves' (p. 56). The precise nature of the ailments treated at Ami Hostel, the type of patients who stay there, the credentials of the doctors at the sanatorium, the character of the therapy they practise, and finally the course of convalescence and recovery, all remain shrouded in mystery and are never quite explained in the novel. Broadly speaking, Ami Hostel seems to be a liberally minded mental institution that is following unorthodox methods. In her letter, Naoko invites Toru to visit her there. The following morning, Toru sets off by train and soon arrives in the sanatorium.

He has taken his copy of *The Magic Mountain* with him. Reiko, Naoko's roommate in the sanatorium, finds it inappropriate: 'how could you bring a book like that to a place like this?' she asks—and Toru concedes: 'she was right, of course' (p. 138). Reiko's accusation and Toru's self-consciousness clearly suggest that there is something problematic about *The Magic Mountain* making its way into the story-world. The characters in Murakami's novel are troubled by its presence. Do they fear that Mann's iconic sanatorium novel may become an unwelcome commentary on their own fate? Will they too become fascinated by sickness and death and never leave the sanatorium, never return to the world of the living? Unbeknown to Toru, the 20-year-old student, the spectre of Mann's novel hangs over his own story, as told in retrospect by Toru, the nearly 40-year-old journalist, from page one. At 37, Toru is overcome by an unstoppable flood of painful memories while on a plane landing in Hamburg. This is, of course, the city from which Hans Castorp sets off by train to visit his cousin in a mountain tuberculosis sanatorium. The story has come full circle: for Toru, reading *The Magic Mountain* was a way to deal with his difficult emotions when visiting Naoko in a sanatorium, and nearly twenty years later, arriving at the place where Mann's story had begun, he feels the urge to write his own story, to cope with the return of these same difficult emotions.

The Magic Mountain is a tale of a visitor to a sanatorium who discovers dormant sickness in himself. Hans Castorp stays on the 'Magic Mountain'; Toru reads the story of Hans's stay on the 'Magic Mountain' and then writes his own version of it. Toru's story, narrated in the first person, is permeated with tropes and motifs borrowed from *The Magic Mountain*. Towards the beginning of the

[47] See Yasumasa Oguro, 'Die Brechungen der modernen japanischen Literatur: Thomas Mann bei Yukio Mishima, Kunio Tsuji und Haruki Murakami', *Neue Beiträge zur Germanistik*, 2.4 (2003), 107–21. I am grateful to Professor Motohiro Kojima, who researches European intertexts in Murakami's writing, for confirming that this topic had not been discussed in Japanese-language scholarship either.

novel, when Toru recounts the suicide of his 17-year-old friend Kizuki, he describes his emotional state in the aftermath of Kizuki's death:

> I tried hard to forget, but there remained inside me a vague knot of air. And as time went by, the knot began to take on a clear and simple form, a form that I am able to put into words, like this: *Death exists, not as the opposite but as a part of life.* It's a cliché translated into words, but at the time I felt it not as words but as that knot of air inside me. Death exists [. . .] and we go on living and breathing it into our lungs like fine dust [. . .] in the midst of life, everything revolved around death.   (p. 30)

Toru asserts that he 'lost the ability to see death and life in [. . .] simple terms'—as opposites, separate from and independent of each other—'the night Kizuki died', and went on to turn 18 'with that knot of air in [his] chest', stuck inside the 'suffocating contradiction' of death and life (pp. 30–31). Yet the language and imagery used to describe Toru's feelings suggest the strong influence of a book that he will only read three years after Kizuki's death—Thomas Mann's *The Magic Mountain*.

Toru's insight that 'death exists not as the opposite but as a part of life' is also a central element of Hans Castorp's seven-year-long fascination with death as recounted in *The Magic Mountain*. Hans reaches this insight at a tuberculosis sanatorium full of patients with sick lungs. In Hans's chest, a 'petite tache humide' ('a little moist spot') is also discovered, and it becomes metaphorically connected with Hans's proximity to and fascination with death. Toru's description of a suffocating 'knot of air' in his chest following the realization that 'we go on living and breathing [death] into our lungs like fine dust' is clearly inspired by Murakami's reading of Mann—and Toru's own reading too. This preoccupation with death, which Toru shares with Hans Castorp, will persist throughout. As Toru says, for a long time his 'memory remained fixed on the dead rather than the living' (p. 363), which is also Hans's predicament in the sanatorium. Toru states that he and Naoko 'were bound together at the border between life and death' (p. 379). But just as Hans, fascinated by death as he is, comes under the influence of life-affirming forces in the sanatorium, Toru also encounters them—embodied in Midori, his second love interest in the novel. It is for her that he will call out 'again and again [. . .] from the dead centre of this place that was no place' after Naoko's death at the very end of the book (p. 386).

There are more parallels between *The Magic Mountain* and *Norwegian Wood*. Toru compares his student dorm to Naoko's sanatorium: 'aside from the variety in people's ages, the scene looked pretty much like that of the dining hall in my dormitory' (p. 139). His dorm is 'located on a hill' (p. 11), and since the year is 1968, the students never cease to discuss political issues, but they are strangely passive—bold political speeches never quite translate into successful action, and 'in terms of everyday life, it made no practical difference [. . .] whether the place was right wing or left wing or anything else' (p. 13). All this mirrors Hans's impressions of his Swiss sanatorium, and especially of the endless disputes between Settembrini and Naphta, which are often perceived as constituting the bulk of Mann's novel. Moreover, even before Naoko ends up at an institution that resembles Mann's mountain sanatorium for tubercular patients, Toru talks about her condition in terms that seem to foreshadow the way her fate relates to Mann's story. Toru describes Naoko's voice as trembling, 'as though she were speaking on a windy hilltop' (p. 3), and as her mental health gradually deteriorates, Toru focuses on the fact that she 'lost much weight' but became 'a lot prettier' (p. 22) and started frequently 'dabbing at her mouth with a handkerchief' (pp. 32 and 140), as though wiping invisible phlegm off her lips: a stereotypical, romanticized description of a female tuberculosis sufferer. We also find out that when Naoko was younger, when Kizuki was still alive, she was in a hospital and had a 'chest operation' (p. 166). All these memories seem gently refracted through *The Magic Mountain*, as though Toru found it hard to face the reality of Naoko's mental illness and chose to recast her condition as tuberculosis—a more tangible, physical ailment known to him from Mann's novel.

With this point we get to the crux of the matter: why is it significant in the larger scheme of the book that Murakami peppers it with allusions to *The Magic Mountain*? It matters because Murakami's novel is about the struggle for expression. Naoko's mental health problems first manifest themselves as a failure to express herself verbally: 'she seemed to be trying—and failing—to find exactly the right word or expression', observes Toru towards the beginning of the novel (p. 22). 'I can never say what I want to say', Naoko tries to explain a few pages later: 'I try to say something, but all I get are the wrong words—the wrong words or the exact *opposite* words from what I mean. I try to correct myself, and that only makes it worse. I lose track of what I was trying to say to begin with' (p. 25). 'Everybody feels like that to some extent', replies Toru. 'They're trying to express themselves and it bothers them when they can't get it right.' But Naoko looks 'disappointed with [his] answer': 'no, that's not it either', she says 'without further explanation' (p. 25). Later on, Reiko writes to Toru that the first symptom of Naoko's final decline was 'her loss of the ability to write letters' (p. 318).

But Toru often feels at a loss for words, too. He insists that at first he couldn't articulate in words his insight into the relationship between life and death that he reached after Kizuki's death—he only felt it as a 'knot of air inside [him]'. Crystallized into words, it would turn into a 'cliché', claims Toru. A few years later he feels that he shares Naoko's condition, her inability to express herself verbally: 'I could never find the words to express myself. Strange, I seemed to have caught her word-searching sickness' (p. 37). Naoko's sickness is characterized as an inability to express her feelings, as a failure of communication, a loss for words. Toru suggests that her sickness is contagious and that he has caught it too. But the very metaphor of sickness is one which he is already borrowing from its cure: *The Magic Mountain*, the novel that will help him work through his difficult emotions by articulating them.

Toru reads *The Magic Mountain*, Naoko lives it. But when the sickness is being at a loss for words, reading is a more powerful form of living. 'The only real problem with this place is that once you're here you don't want to leave—or you're afraid to leave', writes Naoko in her letter about the sanatorium (p. 115). This is exactly what happens to Hans Castorp in *The Magic Mountain*. Naoko herself will die by suicide when faced with the prospect of leaving the sanatorium for the 'outside world'. Toru is more cautious: 'if I stayed around too long, I might end up living here', he says jokingly when Reiko invites him to stay at the sanatorium a little longer (p. 195). Reading *The Magic Mountain* is more salutary than living on the 'Magic Mountain'. For a while, Naoko manages to write Toru letters from the sanatorium. But Toru is better at this, too: when events take a particularly fateful turn towards the end of the novel, he writes 'a huge number of letters [...] it was as if I were writing letters to hold together the pieces of my crumbling life' (p. 341). Toru will go even further: eventually, he will become the narrator of his own story in *Norwegian Wood*—an entire book modelled on *The Magic Mountain*. This was also Thomas Mann's strategy: when he accompanied his wife to Davos in 1912 and a doctor suggested that he too could use a mountain cure, Mann '[hat] es vorgezogen, den *Zauberberg* zu schreiben' ('chose to write *The Magic Mountain* instead').[48]

Meanwhile, Naoko makes a failed attempt to work through her grief with books, reading several volumes from her sister's library after her death: 'it was so sad. They had her comments in the margins and flowers pressed between the pages and letters from boyfriends, and every time I came across something like that I'd cry. I cried a lot' (p. 190). Unlike Naoko, Toru manages to deal with painful memories by arranging them into a meaningful narrative—one of the most important functions of storytelling and literature—and he does so by structuring it as a version of *The Magic Mountain*, a classic work he had read at the time of the traumatic events surrounding Kizuki's and Naoko's deaths, and drawing inspiration from many other texts, including *The Great Gatsby* and *The Catcher in the Rye*. It seems that the hidden desire to become a writer has been dormant in him since his student days: 'the others in the dorm thought I wanted to be a writer because I was always alone with a book' (p. 36). In a brief side remark in the novel, it is revealed that Toru's job in middle age is as a journalist. He must have overcome the 'word-searching sickness' that ostensibly killed Naoko, and *The Magic Mountain* has played a key role in this healing process.

---

[48] Thomas Mann, *Selbstkommentare: 'Der Zauberberg'*, ed. Hans Wysling and Marianne Eich-Fischer (Frankfurt am Main: Fischer, 1993), p. 133.

Toru Watanabe is receptive to cultural texts that he finds useful at any given moment, unlike Paul Davenant with his 'cultural monogamy'—his fixation on Shakespeare as the centre of the canon which cannot ever be displaced. Toru is not as constrained as Hans Castorp, either: he is not restricted by social perceptions of what counts as 'serious' or 'sentimental' literature. One might be tempted to assume that this is simply a function of the different historical moments in which Hans and Toru grow up: Wilhelmine Germany and 1960s Tokyo, respectively. But in *Norwegian Wood* it is made clear that the student protests of 1968, just like any other political or social movement, have produced their own cultural orthodoxies. Toru differs from other students because he is not interested in reading contemporary French existentialist novels like everybody else. He is much more interested in seeking out books that are not the cultural norm in his social circle: in contrast to *The Rack*, where the process of re-appropriating the canon embodied by Shakespeare's oeuvre is never reflected on, *Norwegian Wood* is a much more self-aware, creative, and critical engagement with the Western canon.

Murakami's references to Western culture in *Norwegian Wood* are neither hollow nor facile, as his detractors often claim,[49] but deeply ingrained in the novel's plot and structure. Just as Western novels serve a variety of functions in Toru's life, they are also important to Murakami in how he structures his work. *Norwegian Wood* is a version of *The Magic Mountain* that is full of nods to numerous other cultural texts: it is an ode to literature's healing power in the face of death, to literature's life-sustaining force, and to the creative possibilities inherent in an act of reading—both for Toru and for Murakami. This approach to literature is reflected in the adoption of a first-person narrative voice. Critics often point out Murakami's commitment to creating an identity narrative for his characters as a healing process, as a form of therapy.[50] And so it turns out that while Thomas Mann's literary sanatorium might not quite cure tuberculosis, it does have the potential to administer healing language and narrative structure to somebody who is at a loss for words.

We have already seen that at least some doctors in the 1920s praised *The Magic Mountain* for inventing a language that could articulate the psychological consequences of tuberculosis for its sufferers. Murakami perceived a similar therapeutic potential in Mann's novel, and was not the only later reader to do so. Roland Barthes, an avid reader of *The Magic Mountain* and a tuberculosis sufferer

---

[49] I analyse the critical debates surrounding contemporary novels with a global reach, especially those written by non-Western authors, but highly successful on the Western literary market, such as Haruki Murakami's works, in Karolina Watroba, 'World Literature and Literary Value: Is "Global" the New "Lowbrow"?', *The Cambridge Journal of Postcolonial Literary Inquiry*, 5 (2018), 53–68. See also Betiel Wasihun, 'The Name "Kafka": Evocation and Resistance in Haruki Murakami's *Kafka on the Shore*', *MLN*, 129.5 (2014), 1199–216.

[50] Matthew Carl Strecher, 'At the Critical Stage: A Report on the State of Murakami Haruki Studies', *Literature Compass*, 8.11 (2011), 856–69, pp. 863–64.

himself, thought that his symptoms aligned more closely with Mann's descriptions in the novel than any medical descriptions; he experienced his illness through the lens of one of his favourite books.[51] In a similar vein, one recent reader recounted in an online review how she read *The Magic Mountain* while 'recovering from orthopaedic surgery', and explained how she found this choice 'so perfect' that she thought 'a copy should be handed out with every preadmission packet given to surgical patients': 'the last thing I wanted to do was lie around the apartment, and yet, it was the only thing I could do. And here was *The Magic Mountain*, with writing so slow that it forced me to luxuriate in my recovery.'[52] A review in *The Guardian* from 2011 said:

> [Mann's book] is many things: a modernist classic, a traditional bildungsroman, a comedy of manners, an allegory of pre-war bourgeois Europe, and—perhaps most importantly this time of year—the ideal book to keep you company on the long winter nights, when whichever flu bug is doing the rounds has gained the upper hand and forced you into a sneezing retreat to your sickbed.

It's 'an essential purchase for every sickbed this winter', the reviewer concluded.[53] But the reader recovering from orthopaedic surgery adopted a more serious tone: 'surgery brings you frighteningly close to your own human-ness, your own body, your own mortality', and so she wanted to read 'about characters thinking about these matters'. Another reader wrote in a blog post that she picked up *The Magic Mountain* because her father-in-law, diagnosed with multiple myeloma, was reading it during his stay in the hospital.[54]

This particular cultural use of Mann's novel has the potential to appeal to readers on a larger scale too. 'Mountain', a permanent art installation by Karel Martens which transformed the lobby of the Cancer Centre at Guy's and St Thomas' Hospital in London in 2017, was inspired by *The Magic Mountain*—'a novel which depicts a place of healing, relaxation and contemplation which is cut off from everyday life'.[55] 'Mountain' is part of a prize-winning project which aims to 'transform the experience of those undergoing cancer treatment through high-quality, specially commissioned culture', drawing on 'a large body of evidence

---

[51] Kate Briggs, *This Little Art* (London: Fitzcarraldo, 2017), p. 15.

[52] Sarah Van Arsdale, 'Hobbling Up the Magic Mountain', *Fiction Writers Review*, 20 September 2009 <https://fictionwritersreview.com/essay/hobbling-up-the-magic-mountain-with-illustrations-by-the-author/> [accessed 10 June 2019].

[53] W. B. Gooderham, 'Winter Reads: *The Magic Mountain* by Thomas Mann', *The Guardian*, 14 December 2011 <http://www.theguardian.com/books/2011/dec/14/winter-reads-thomas-mann-magic-mountain> [accessed 10 May 2019].

[54] Maud Newton, 'Pulling Thomas Mann's *The Magic Mountain* Off the Shelf', 28 June 2009 <http://maudnewton.com/blog/pulling-thomas-manns-the-magic-mountain-off-the-shelf/> [accessed 10 June 2019].

[55] Anon., '"Mountain" at Guy's and St Thomas' Hospital' <https://www.pentagram.com/work/mountain-at-guys-and-st-thomas-hospital/story> [accessed 10 June 2019].

suggesting that art can contribute to better health and wellbeing; helping reduce stress, aid recovery and reduce the length of hospital stays'.[56]

While not as unambiguously positive in their tone, several letters that Mann received from readers who encountered *The Magic Mountain* in tuberculosis sanatoria show how an experience of illness might change and deepen readers' engagement with the novel. In December 1924, just a month after the novel's publication, Jakob Wassermann wrote to Mann from Davos, where he was recovering from a metabolic disease: 'es wird Sie amüsieren, zu erfahren, daß ich das ganze Buch in vier Tagen—in Davos gelesen habe, also sozusagen an der Quelle' ('it will amuse you to hear that I read the whole book in four days, in Davos—at the source, as it were').[57] In 1947, another reader wrote Mann a letter from a sanatorium in the Swiss town. Mann wrote back to him: 'Ihre Entdeckung meiner und anderer Bücher in der Freiheit, die Ihnen die Krankheit gewährte, hat etwas Packendes für mich, und sie erinnert auch an die berauschende Horizonterweiterung, die der junge Castorp "bei uns hier oben" erfuhr' ('there is something thrilling in your discovery of my book, and other books, in the freedom that your sickness has granted you; it reminds me of the intoxicating broadening of Hans Castorp's horizons that he experienced "with us up here"'). He went on to point out that 'an Ihnen hat [das Buch] offenbar einen ausnehmend disponierten Leser' ('clearly you are an exceptionally suitable reader for this book'), but then promptly added: 'aber wollte Gott, diese Disposition wäre nicht so spezifischer Art!' ('but by God, if only your suitability were not quite so specific in nature!').[58] Mann recognized that tuberculosis sufferers formed a group of readers uniquely attuned to *The Magic Mountain* but was also conscious of the human suffering that was the cost of this particular brand of immersive reading.

4. 'I Know. I Know. You've Read *The Magic Mountain*'

In the final text discussed in this chapter, Alice Munro's short story 'Amundsen', canonical European texts—*The Magic Mountain* and Leo Tolstoy's *War and Peace* (1869)—also take on a crucial role. But unlike in *The Rack*, where the protagonist's one and only 'correct' interpretation of Shakespeare is never called into question, and unlike in *Norwegian Wood*, where a young man is at liberty to make use of cultural texts as he pleases while his girlfriend wastes away in a sanatorium, 'Amundsen' is a story of a young woman caught up in an

[56] Anon., 'Arts Programme at New Cancer Centre at Guy's Wins Design Award', 22 June 2017 <https://futurecity.co.uk/arts-programme-at-new-cancer-centre-at-guys-wins-design-award/> [accessed 10 June 2019].

[57] Thomas Mann, *Briefwechsel mit Autoren*, ed. Hans Wysling (Frankfurt am Main: Fischer, 1988), pp. 481–82.

[58] Mann, *Selbstkommentare*, pp. 147–48.

interpretative war with an older man, with both cultural authority and happiness in love at stake. By thematizing and staging the act of choosing one's cultural allegiances, 'Amundsen' is a powerful response to *The Magic Mountain*. It throws into sharp relief the extent to which Mann's book relies on unquestioned ideas about who and what culture is for, but also points to the immense possibilities opened up by a reading of the novel that is at once deeply immersive and sharply critical.

Alice Munro (b. 1931) first published 'Amundsen' in 2012 in *The New Yorker* and then included a lightly edited version in the collection *Dear Life*, which came out a few months later—less than a year before Munro was awarded the 2013 Nobel Prize in Literature.[59] In *Dear Life*, 'Amundsen' features alongside several other tales of young women travelling on trains across Canada in search of a better life, adventure, and romance. Amundsen is a small town in the icy countryside of Ontario, where a young woman—Vivien Hyde, the first-person narrator of the story—arrives by train in 1945, during the last months of the war, to take up a job as a teacher in a sanatorium for tubercular children. There she meets Dr Alister Fox, a cold and emotionally unavailable surgeon and director of the sanatorium. They strike up a relationship and Dr Fox decides they should get married; however, when they drive to Huntsville, a larger nearby town, where they are to have a simple civil ceremony, he changes his mind and breaks up with Vivien. He drops her off at the train station the very same day and buys her a ticket to Toronto, her hometown. In a short epilogue we find out that Vivien makes a life for herself there, and ten years later runs into Fox on the street, but—despite her tacit hopes—they do not resume their relationship.

'Amundsen' has not yet been discussed much in literary criticism. Ronja Söldenwagner's first brief and rather unadventurous discussion[60] and Ailsa Cox's tenuous reading of Dr Fox as a spectral figure[61] were followed by Cristiana Pugliese's intriguing (if at times a little strained) psychoanalytical interpretation of the story, focusing on the significance of food and meals.[62] None of these critics discussed 'Amundsen' in the specific context of its relationship to *The Magic Mountain*. However, Vivien and Dr Fox explicitly compare

[59] The *New Yorker* version is available at <https://www.newyorker.com/magazine/2012/08/27/amundsen> [accessed 5 February 2018]. In the *Dear Life* version, there are changes in punctuation, and the order of some paragraphs is rearranged. A few sentences are added in various places, mainly to create a richer sense of Vivien's past—her life with her grandparents in Toronto, before she moved to Amundsen.

[60] Ronja Söldenwagner, 'Love, Gender and Social Pressure in "Amundsen"', in *For (Dear) Life: Close Readings of Alice Munro's Ultimate Fiction*, ed. Eva-Sabine Zehelein (Münster: LIT, 2014), pp. 13–19.

[61] Ailsa Cox, '"Almost Like a Ghost": Spectral Figures in Alice Munro's Short Fiction', in *Liminality and the Short Story: Boundary Crossings in American, Canadian, and British Writing*, ed. Jochen Achilles and Ina Bergmann (Abingdon: Routledge, 2014), pp. 238–50, pp. 246–49.

[62] Cristiana Pugliese, 'Dangerous Appetites: Food and Deception in "Amundsen"', in *Alice Munro and the Anatomy of the Short Story*, ed. Oriana Palusci (Newcastle upon Tyne: Cambridge Scholars Publishing, 2017), pp. 129–38.

their sanatorium to Mann's setting and discuss his novel at a pivotal point in the plot. As with other texts in my corpus, my interest in this story is twofold. What work does *The Magic Mountain* do in 'Amundsen'? And what can Munro's use of Mann's text reveal about *The Magic Mountain* and its cultural appeal? Read alongside *The Rack* and *Norwegian Wood*, 'Amundsen' can help us better understand the significance of encounters with canonical culture, this time in the story of a young, lonely, vulnerable woman, left heartbroken at the end of the war.

In 'Dear Life', the autobiographical story that closes Munro's book and lends its title to the collection, the author mentions reading *The Magic Mountain* as a young girl, and being deeply impressed by it:

> I sat down with my feet in the warming oven, which had lost its door, and read the big novels I borrowed from the town library: *Independent People*, which was about life in Iceland, harder than ours by far, but with a hopeless grandeur to it, or *Remembrance of Things Past*, which was about nothing I could understand at all but which I would not give up just because of that, or *The Magic Mountain*, about tuberculosis and a great argument between what on one side seemed to be a genial and progressive notion of life and, on the other, a dark but somehow thrilling despair.[63]

Like Vivien in 'Amundsen', Munro presents herself reading 'big novels'—by Mann, Proust, and Halldór Laxness, an Icelandic Nobel laureate—on her own rather than 'in school' (p. 49). Vivien is vulnerable but more independent than her peers, and she uses Mann to prove her intellectual worth, to prove that she is cultured enough to be taken seriously by the head doctor in the sanatorium.

But this is not easy: her first attempt ends in humiliation. Here is Vivien's first encounter with Dr Fox:

> He struck me as between ten and fifteen years older than myself and at first he talked to me just in the way an older man would do. A preoccupied future employer. He asked about my trip, about the arrangements for my suitcase. He wanted to know how I thought I would like living up here in the woods, after Toronto, whether I would be bored.
> Not in the least, I said, and added that it was beautiful.
> 'It's like—it's like being inside a Russian novel.'
> He looked at me attentively for the first time.
> 'Is it really? Which Russian novel?'

---

[63] Alice Munro, 'Dear Life', in *Dear Life* (London: Chatto & Windus, 2012), pp. 299–319, pp. 309–10.

His eyes were a light, bright grayish blue. One eyebrow had risen, like a little peaked cap.

It was not that I hadn't read Russian novels. I had read some all through and some partway. But because of that eyebrow, and his amused but confrontational expression, I could not remember any title except *War and Peace*. I did not want to say that because it was what anybody would remember.

'*War and Peace*.'

'Well, it's only the Peace we've got here, I'd say. But if it was the War you were hankering after I suppose you would have joined one of those women's outfits and got yourself overseas.'

I was angry and humiliated because I had not really been showing off. Or not only showing off. I had wanted to say what a wonderful effect this scenery had on me.

He was evidently the sort of person who posed questions that were traps for you to fall into.

[. . .]'I don't suppose you have any experience with tuberculosis?'

'Well I've read—'

'I know. I know. You've read *The Magic Mountain*.' Another trap sprung, and he seemed restored. 'Things have moved on a bit from that, I hope.'   (pp. 36–37)

In this brilliantly understated yet evocative scene, Vivien and Fox clash because they evidently make different uses of literature. Fox is interested in establishing his intellectual superiority and creating a sense of hierarchy between Vivien and himself. He takes steps to demonstrate that he is the master of the literary canon: his prodding questions and sly answers suggest a deep familiarity with Russian novels and *The Magic Mountain* and put Vivien in the position of an intellectual imposter who is making claims to a canon that is not hers.

Vivien is startled and baffled: for her, talking about books serves altogether different purposes, not all that different from those perceived by Hans Castorp and Toru Watanabe. First, it is a way to articulate emotions: 'I had wanted to say what a wonderful effect this scenery had on me', she says. Second, it is a way to forge interpersonal connections: she wants to talk about Russian novels and *The Magic Mountain* to indicate that she and Fox share cultural knowledge. Third, talking about books is her way of dealing with a tough new situation: Vivien tries to decode her new, unfamiliar surroundings by drawing comparisons with fictional landscapes she knows from books, be they Russian forests or a Swiss sanatorium.

The relationship between Vivien and Fox develops as they change their opinions of each other's reading habits. In the course of the story they gradually establish who has read what, how many books each of them owns, and where and how they read them. Dr Fox invites Vivien to have dinner at his place—'a stucco-covered house with a dormer window over the front door, books stacked on the sill of that window', as she observes from the street (p. 43). His books are displayed in the front window of his house for everybody in the town to be in no doubt of his bookish credentials. Fox's strategy is effective: soon after her arrival in Amundsen, Vivien finds out that other female employees at the sanatorium 'were in awe of Dr Fox partly because he had read so many books' (p. 39).

And yet upon closer investigation, Dr Fox's collection of books turns out to be eclectic, even random. While preparing dinner, Fox invites Vivien to have a look at his books, and what she sees emboldens her to revisit their first conversation, and question him on his interpretation of *The Magic Mountain*:

> There were quantities of books to look at. Not just on bookshelves but on tables and chairs and windowsills and piled on the floor. After I had examined several of them I concluded that he favored buying books in batches and probably belonged to several book clubs. The Harvard Classics. The histories of Will and Ariel Durant—the very same that could be found on my grandfather's shelves. Fiction and poetry seemed in short supply, though there were a few surprising children's classics.
>
> Books on the American Civil War, the South African War, the Napoleonic Wars, the Peloponnesian War, the campaigns of Julius Caesar. *Explorations of the Amazon and the Arctic. Shackleton Caught in the Ice. Franklin's Doom, the Donner Party and the Lost Tribes, Buried Cities of Central Africa, Newton and Alchemy, Secrets of the Hindu Kush.* Books suggesting someone anxious to know, to possess great scattered lumps of knowledge. Perhaps not someone whose tastes were firm and exacting.
>
> So when he had asked me, 'Which Russian novel?' it was possible that he had not had so firm a platform as I had thought.
>
> When he called 'Ready,' and I opened the door, I was armed with this new skepticism.
>
> I said, 'Who do you agree with, Naphta or Settembrini?'
>
> 'I beg your pardon?'
>
> 'In *The Magic Mountain*. Do you like Naphta best or Settembrini?'
>
> 'To be honest, I've always thought they were a pair of windbags. You?'
>
> 'Settembrini is more humane but Naphta is more interesting.'
>
> 'They tell you that in school?'
>
> 'I never read it in school,' I said coolly.
>
> He gave me a quick look, that eyebrow raised.
>
> 'Pardon me. If there's anything in there that interests you, feel free. Feel free to come down here and read in your time off. There's an electric heater I could set

up, since I imagine you are not experienced with woodstoves. Shall we think
about that? I can rustle you up an extra key.'

'Thank you.'   (pp. 48–49)

Having taken a closer look at Dr Fox's books, Vivien realizes that he has misled
her as to how well read he really is. He buys books 'in batches', relying on the
offerings of book clubs, he does not read much fiction or poetry at all, and Vivien
is familiar with some of his books because she has seen them in her family library
as well. By now, Vivien has seen that, in Dr Fox's case, 'reading a lot of books' goes
hand in hand with 'tearing a strip off'—a tendency to scold others (p. 39). She
decides that her own upbringing and education are not inferior to Dr Fox's, and
this gives her the courage to approach him about Thomas Mann again.

Vivien's philosophical interest in Settembrini and Naphta resembles Alice
Munro's own recollection of what moved her as a young reader: 'a great argument
between what on one side seemed to be a genial and progressive notion of life and,
on the other, a dark but somehow thrilling despair'. In 'Amundsen', Munro
reconstructs a version of that 'great argument'; the conflict between Vivien and
Fox, between two different readers of The Magic Mountain, is modelled on that
between Settembrini and Naphta in Mann's novel. Perhaps this aspect of the text
is signalled in its title as well, evoking as it does Amundsen's and Scott's race to the
South Pole, another competition in which cultural prestige was at stake. Vivien's
bold demonstration of intellectual independence—she is a young woman who
reads a 'big novel' on her own, not 'in school', and is attuned to the philosophical
debates played out in it—wins her Dr Fox's respect. As a token of this respect, he
offers her access to his books; in other circumstances she 'would have jumped at
the chance' (p. 52), but Vivien feels unable to accept. She realizes she would be so
agitated about being in his apartment that she would not be able to 'read a word'.
Books and reading have taken on a new tinge: they are now a vehicle for romance.

The romance commences when the dinner date at Dr Fox's house culminates in
a strange variation on the chest examination scene, a staple in narratives of
tuberculosis, including The Magic Mountain itself. Similar scenes feature in
many other fictional responses to The Magic Mountain, including André de
Toth's film The Other Love (1947) based on a story written by Erich Maria
Remarque, Remarque's novel Der Himmel kennt keine Günstlinge (Heaven Has
No Favourites) (1959), and Vittorio De Sica's film A Brief Vacation. Vivien and
Fox are doing the dishes and chatting about his medical practice (lungs, thoracoplasty, streptomycin) when he lays 'his hands against [her] upper back. Such firm
pressure, fingers separated—he might almost have been taking stock of [her] body
in a professional way.' Vivien 'could still feel the pressure' when she 'went to bed
that night' (p. 51). This is a familiar scenario: a young, vulnerable woman meets an
older doctor, an authority figure, who chooses to assert his power by touching her

body in a way that blurs boundaries between a detached medical examination and an erotic encounter.

Later on in the story, as Vivien and Fox are driving to Huntsville to get married, Vivien thinks to herself that she 'find[s] it exciting that he is a surgeon though [she] would never admit that' (p. 59). Part of Fox's appeal to Vivien is precisely his cold, detached authority as a doctor, and a man in power. But this also means that he is emotionally unavailable; in some situations he strikes Vivien as 'brutal' (p. 56). He is not romantic at all, and if Vivien wants to keep him, she must play along. She must give up all fantasies about her wedding: when she does, Fox says approvingly that 'he had known that [she] was not that idiotic conventional sort of girl' (p. 57). Theirs is going to be 'a bare-bones wedding', he declares.

And yet Vivien does indulge in romantic fantasies. She tries to control them as long as she is with Fox. She knows she 'must keep these feelings to [her]self' (p. 59), but they break free once he breaks up with her. The last few pages of the story are filled to the brim with imaginary melodramatic scenarios that Vivien conjures up, unable to deal with the thought of Dr Fox abandoning her forever: him coming back, telling her that 'this was all a joke', 'or a test, as in some medieval drama', or undergoing 'a change of mind', 'struck by a realization of his folly he turns in the middle of the road and comes speeding back' (p. 63). Even as she is getting on the train, 'fantasies are running through [her] mind' (p. 64): 'it might not be too late for me to jump from the train. Jump free and run through the station to the street where he would just have parked the car and is running up the steps thinking not too late, pray not too late.' Then, passing by Amundsen on the train, she imagines herself 'jumping up and leaving the train and running to his house and demanding to know why, why' (p. 65). Once in Toronto, she says that 'for years I thought I might run into him' (p. 65), and when she does eventually run into him, ten years later, it 'seemed as if we could make our way out of that crowd, that in a moment we would be together' (p. 66). And even when, after a short exchange, they walk past each other and go off in opposite directions, Vivien keeps thinking about the things that have not happened, the scenarios that have not come to pass: 'no breathless cry, no hand on my shoulder when I reached the sidewalk' (p. 66). In her abandonment by Fox, Vivien finds solace in coming up with melodramatic scenarios about his return.

But melodramatic scenarios have been at play since the story's beginning. Vivien's initial reaction to the frozen landscape around the sanatorium—'so still, so immense an enchantment' (p. 33)—and her notion of 'being inside a Russian novel' (mocked by Fox) both indicate that she tries to imaginatively transform the drab reality of her life into something infinitely more appealing and exciting—her own 'Magic Mountain' or, to render the German title of Mann's novel more precisely, 'enchanted mountain'. Vivien seeks solace in imagining her life as a re-enactment of her favourite novels. Her desire to translate the disappointing reality of her life into more appealing literary scenarios closely corresponds to Hans Castorp's recognition of 'die hohe und unwiderlegliche Beschönigung, die sie [die Kunst] der gemeinen Gräßlichkeit der wirklichen Dinge angedeihen ließ,' a recognition shared by Toru Watanabe, who reads *The Magic Mountain* during his visit in Naoko's sanatorium. But Paul Davenant from *The Rack* would condemn Vivien's attitude as contemptible and embarrassing self-dramatization, which is exactly how Fox sees it.

The most sensitive area of Vivien's life where her ideas, hopes, and expectations clash with Fox's in this way is their lovemaking. When Vivien describes their first sexual encounter, she juxtaposes his cold, calculated approach—'my state of virginity [...] did not appear to be a surprise—he provided a towel as well as a condom'—with her passion and imagination: 'my passion could have been the surprise to us both. Imagination, as it turned out, might be as good a preparation as experience' (p. 56).[64] This is Vivien's subtle way of suggesting to the reader that she has been indulging in passionate erotic fantasies all along. We soon get a glimpse of one of these fantasies when Vivien is in the car with Fox, on their way to get married in Huntsville: 'right now I believe I could lie down for him in any bog or mucky hole, or feel my spine crushed against any roadside rock, should he require an upright encounter' (p. 59). It is this erotic fantasy that is held in check by her knowledge that she 'must keep these feelings to [her]self'. Once again, we encounter a censoring of emotions that takes us back to Fräulein Engelhart's 'scharfe Bewachung' of Hans Castorp's feelings.

Vivien's involvement with an emotionally unavailable man corresponds to the exploration of polar regions implied in the story's title, and the name of the town where the story is set: Roald Amundsen was a Norwegian explorer of polar regions, including the northern shores of Canada. Vivien brings the heat of melodrama to the polar regions. For her, icy landscapes evoke the romance of Russian novels, even if Fox undermines this association instantly with his emotional coldness. But there is even more to the title than this. Amundsen was a European exploring Canada: Vivien is a Canadian exploring European culture. While she is fascinated by big European novels, her own tale is told within the economy of the short story, a genre of which Alice Munro is a contemporary master. *The Magic Mountain* and *War and Peace*—two big, sprawling, expansive novels about war, love, upper-class life, and philosophy—are juxtaposed with Vivien's restrained, humble, and sparse account of her brief stay in the icy regions of Ontario, of wartime poverty, a drab and decaying sanatorium for tubercular children, her fiancé's emotional unavailability, and her 'bare-bones wedding', which does not even take place. The plot that Munro is dealing with seems to organically shrink to the size of the short story when considered alongside the expansive and lush plots of the kind of literature that Vivien and Fox discuss.

---

[64] This passage is much less developed in the *New Yorker* version: 'my passion was the surprise, to us both', it says, and the sentence about Vivien's imagination is not there at all.

While Germans and Russians wage wars (news of Russians entering Berlin is heard on the radio as Vivien and Fox are driving to Huntsville) and write great novels about them, Canadians are left to observe events from afar, and their lives do not measure up to these great European plots, as Vivien discovers.

And yet Vivien turns out to be an engaged reader of European classics, one who finds a way to use imagination to enhance her life, deal with rejection, and vindicate herself by telling her story with just as much passion and feeling as she sees fit, in the first person—which Paul Davenant finds so inappropriate in Haydon's misquotation of *King Lear*, and which Toru Watanabe inhabits so effortlessly in imitation of Holden Caulfield in *The Catcher in the Rye* and Nick Carraway in *The Great Gatsby*. Vivien does not inhabit the first-person narration as easily: in 'Amundsen' the choice of one's own position vis-à-vis canonical culture is much more contested than in *Norwegian Wood*. All cultural choices are up for debate; nothing is taken for granted. In *The Rack*, the authority of the canon remains unchallenged; *The Magic Mountain* thematizes Hans Castorp's growing engagement with culture, but the underlying politics of taste is a blind spot in this otherwise highly self-aware novel; in *Norwegian Wood*, Toru constantly asserts his varied cultural allegiances—he chooses to speak like Holden Caulfield and to structure his narrative as a version of *The Magic Mountain*—but the novel does not stage the fraught drama of making these choices in the first place. It is in 'Amundsen' that we finally see this theme taking centre stage in the plot and narrative structure of the text.

5. Conclusion: Real-Life Castorps

Aristotle argued that literature wields mysterious power of 'catharsis', or cleansing of our emotions, by confronting us with different scenarios of human fate. This understanding of literature's function is shared by many critics, ranging from narratologists like Wayne C. Booth to cognitive psychologists like Keith Oatley.[65] In recent years many academic readers have found themselves arguing with renewed intensity that literature is good for us. But as these arguments are usually propelled by the necessity to justify our work to sceptics inside and outside academia, and particularly to funding bodies, they often end up sounding vague, defensive, or even insincere—especially if they are wholly detached from our actual scholarly practice.[66] A focus on a selection of case studies organized around a common theme—encounters with *The Magic Mountain*—might prove more

---

[65] See Wayne Booth, *The Company We Keep* (Berkeley, CA: University of California Press, 1988), and Keith Oatley, *Such Stuff as Dreams: The Psychology of Fiction* (Chichester: Wiley-Blackwell, 2011).
[66] For a lucid summary of recent debates about the relevance of the humanities, and especially literary studies, see Helen Small, *The Value of the Humanities* (Oxford: Oxford University Press, 2013).

powerful than an abstract theoretical account, or one based on anecdotal evidence predominantly informed by one person's experience.

In line with my methodology throughout this study of world literature and closer reading, in this chapter I focused on compelling accounts of various fictional and real-life readers around the world to show how they use books in moments of personal and political crises to make life more bearable for themselves. Why do academic readers so often struggle to acknowledge, articulate, and analyse this important aspect of the experience of reading? In his study of the cultural reception of Mignon, a character from Goethe's *Wilhelm Meister*, Terence Cave pointed out that 'the advent of modernism in the twentieth century has [...] created a powerful critical suspicion of emotional response unless it can be grounded in ways that are perceived as intellectually respectable'.[67] As my study of everyday reading practices demonstrates, however, anxiety about 'intellectual respectability' is not external to our emotional responses to culture, but part and parcel of them. Most readers are self-aware enough to realize that it is possible to make different uses of books, and so these different uses themselves, pitted against each other, become a contested issue that touches on crucial questions of cultural authority and legitimacy.

Differing levels of engagement with *The Magic Mountain* often derive from implicit judgements about the emotional impact of literature and the cultural policing of emotions. In *The Magic Mountain*, listening to classic operas helps Hans Castorp deal with Joachim's death. A. E. Ellis and his reviewers, however, perceived *The Magic Mountain* to be a novel that does not adequately deal with suffering, and Paul Davenant finds solace in *King Lear* instead. Meanwhile, other tubercular and wartime readers of Mann's book responded to his writing more strongly, and *The Magic Mountain* even inspired a recent art project in a London hospital. In *Norwegian Wood*, Mann's novel helps Toru Watanabe deal with the deaths of his young friends, read alongside other cultural texts, ranging from *The Great Gatsby* and *The Catcher in the Rye* to Bach's music and 'Norwegian Wood', a song by the Beatles. It is a cultural landscape that Hans Castorp would find deeply troubling, ashamed as he is of humming a popular song about love. In 'Amundsen', Vivien Hyde, a young and vulnerable woman, deals with her loneliness and her fiancé's betrayal by imagining herself to be a heroine of a grand European novel. Dr Fox is sceptical of her ability to be both an emotional and intellectually independent reader, but she proves that emotional engagement and critical awareness can go hand in hand. This recognition is the subject of my next—and final—chapter.

To draw the first two chapters of this book together, responses to and critiques of *The Magic Mountain* motivated by economic concerns and focused on emotional engagement with literature might at first glance seem to lead us away from

---

[67] Terence Cave, *Mignon's Afterlives: Crossing Cultures from Goethe to the Twenty-First Century* (Oxford: Oxford University Press, 2011), p. 30.

the kind of old-fashioned high culture that many associate with Mann's novel, but in fact they cut to its very core. The greatest anxiety surrounding this kind of culture is being considered 'cheap', in its double meaning of 'affordable' and 'affected'. The texts in my corpus—Fedin's *Sanatorium Arktur*, Kästner's *Der Zauberlehrling*, Verbinski's *A Cure for Wellness*, Ellis's *The Rack*, Murakami's *Norwegian Wood*, and Munro's 'Amundsen'—all put more pressure on high European culture's anxiety of affluence. If Hans Castorp's experience in *The Magic Mountain* is supposed to embody the human condition, then these texts are interested in the ambiguities inherent in Mann's novel, in aspects of experience that Mann's novel potentially leaves out, glosses over, misrepresents, or does not fully resolve, whether economic concerns or intense emotions. These texts are written and populated by readers of *The Magic Mountain* who feel both drawn to and excluded from the novel's narrative, and by writing themselves into Mann's monumental book, they ultimately enlarge its meaning and extend its cultural pull. It is this mechanism, in its different facets, that I explore in this study of world literature and closer reading: through case studies of different responses to *The Magic Mountain* around the world, I ask what it means to participate in culture, and argue that this is precisely what the novel is all about.

3

Erudition

1. Introduction: Intellectual Table Tennis

At the end of Chapter 2, I discussed a fictional reader of *The Magic Mountain*—Vivien Hyde, the protagonist of 'Amundsen'—who, much like Alice Munro, the real-life reader of Mann's novel who invented her, tries to reconcile the pleasure of immersion and the pleasure of reflection in her reading of *The Magic Mountain*. Vivien's antagonist, Dr Fox, a very self-assured man, is set on shaming Vivien into accepting that there is a strict boundary between these two modes of reading. But in the story it is Vivien who ultimately proves to be a more engaged reader of Mann—precisely because she does not shy away from melding both her intellectual and emotional capacities in the encounter with *The Magic Mountain*.

Fox and Vivien thereby represent two diametrically opposed approaches to reading. The first approach, which in the Western tradition goes back at least to Plato, sees immersion as 'inaccessible to analytical thought' and therefore 'dangerous and intellectually void'.[1] Similarly, in 1920s Germany Bertolt Brecht famously insisted that modern theatre should prevent the spectator from emotionally engaging with the events of a play (being 'in eine Bühnenaktion verwickelt' or 'hineinversetzt') and instead turn her into a critical observer, and early film theory painted a chilling picture of an impressionable, defenceless spectator who surrenders herself to the spectacle ('sich [dem] Schauspiel hingibt').[2] According to Plato, Brecht, early film theory and many other critics over the centuries, emotionally engaged reading is dangerous and stultifying; the opposite of such readerly immersion, which snaps the reader or spectator out of it, is critical reflection.

But many others have instinctively felt that this is a false opposition. Thomas Mann, for one, had his doubts. In 1937, he wrote of Wagner's music that it is questionable 'ob gerade hier Reflexion und Begeisterung, Reflexion und *Gefühl*

---

[1] Jean-Marie Schaeffer and Ioana Vultur, 'Immersion', in *Routledge Handbook of Narrative Theory*, ed. David Herman, Manfred Jahn, and Marie-Laure Ryan (Abingdon: Routledge, 2010), pp. 237–39, p. 237.

[2] Bertolt Brecht, 'Anmerkungen zur Oper *Aufstieg und Fall der Stadt Mahagonny*', in *Werke: Große Kommentierte Berliner und Frankfurter Ausgabe*, ed. Werner Hecht and others (Frankfurt am Main: Suhrkamp, 1988–98), xxiv: *Schriften 4: Texte zu Stücken*, ed. Peter Kraft (1991), pp. 74–86, pp. 78 and 85; Hugo von Hofmannsthal, 'Der Ersatz für die Träume', in *Gesammelte Werke*, ed. Bernd Schoeller (Frankfurt am Main: Fischer, 1979–80), ix: *Reden und Aufsätze II: 1914–1924* (1979), pp. 141–45, p. 144. For more similar examples from early film theory, see Frank Kessler, '"Spellbound in Darkness": Narrative Absorption Discussed by Film Theory', in *Narrative Absorption*, ed. Frank Hakemulder and others (Amsterdam: John Benjamins, 2017), pp. 119–32.

scharf zu trennen sind' ('whether reflection and fascination, reflection and *feeling* should be sharply distinguished in this particular case'); in fact, he argued, both are at play in the creation as well as reception of Wagner's works.³ Mann was disappointed whenever readers of *The Magic Mountain* described it as 'ein Werk des Verstandes und der Kritik' ('a work of intellect and critique')⁴ and pleased whenever they recognized his narrative strategy as 'die wechselseitige Durchdringung von Plastik und Kritik' ('mutual penetration of vividness and critique'):⁵ for narrative literature to be effective, Mann thought, intellectual reflection had to be embedded in an engaging story-world. In *Uses of Literature*, Rita Felski argues persuasively that 'the history of modern art is poorly explained as a story of intellectualization, a developmental arc away from affect and immersion toward ever greater levels of analytical self-consciousness';⁶ instead, both the intellect and the emotions are at play in every reading experience.

Drawing on John Guillory's work on academic reading, Felski identifies a common attitude among literary scholars—professional readers—who stand back from the pleasure of engaged reading to encourage critical reflection. And yet, she writes, '[The fact] that one person immerses herself in the joys of *Jane Eyre*, while another views it as a symptomatic expression of Victorian imperialism, often has less to do with the political beliefs of those involved than their position in different scenes of reading.'⁷ Felski identifies one of the crucial ethical dilemmas in academic scholarship on literature: is it morally wrong to enjoy reading a text whose ideological premises, conditions of production, or implicit value judgements are problematic to us? An extreme answer to this question was famously given in 1973 by Laura Mulvey, a feminist film critic who posited that the goal of film criticism should be to destroy the pleasure of film, a medium predicated on the objectification of the female body by the 'male gaze' of the camera: 'it is said that analyzing pleasure, or beauty, destroys it', she wrote; 'that is the intention of this article'.⁸ But does the pleasure of emotionally engaged reading need to be uncritical and unreflective? Is such pleasure indeed uncritical and unreflective? In this chapter, I discuss examples of real-life and fictional readers of *The Magic Mountain* whose experiences of reading clearly show that emotional engagement and critical reflection can coexist and even depend on each other.

* * *

To develop this final stage of my closer reading of Mann's novel, I start by challenging the widely held view that *The Magic Mountain* privileges critical

³ Thomas Mann, 'Richard Wagner und *Der Ring des Nibelungen*', in *Gesammelte Werke*, ed. Hans Bürgin (Frankfurt am Main: Fischer, 1960–1974), ix: *Reden und Aufsätze 1* (1960), pp. 505–27, p. 519.
⁴ Thomas Mann, *Selbstkommentare*: '*Der Zauberberg*', ed. Hans Wysling and Marianne Eich-Fischer (Frankfurt am Main: Fischer, 1993), p. 105.
⁵ Ibid., p. 50.   ⁶ Rita Felski, *Uses of Literature* (Oxford: Blackwell, 2008), p. 74.
⁷ Ibid., p. 12.
⁸ Laura Mulvey, 'Visual Pleasure and Narrative Cinema', *Screen*, 16.3 (1975), 6–18, p. 7.

reflection over emotional engagement and thus appeals only to highly erudite and intellectual readers, drawing on Mann's own conception of his work, the metaphorical connotations of the novel's title and their impact on readers, advertising campaigns and marketing strategies deployed by Mann's German and American publishers, and various records of reading encounters with the novel. This will allow me to rebut a frequently made assumption: that 'highbrow' culture privileges critical reflection, while 'lowbrow' culture privileges emotional engagement. A key resource that I draw on here is Goodreads, a website where readers form online book clubs, reading books together and discussing them in real time over the course of a few months. I analyse the forum devoted to debates between Settembrini and Naphta and argue that *The Magic Mountain* was designed to make its reader feel like an intellectual imposter, but in the process, the reader gets an exciting opportunity to dissect the cultural politics of erudition.

Thanks to adopting a world literature lens, I am able to develop this argument by considering three recent international afterlives of *The Magic Mountain* that are sensitive to this issue: Paweł Huelle's Polish novel *Castorp* (2004),[9] Hayao Miyazaki's Japanese animated film *The Wind Rises* (2013),[10] and Paolo Sorrentino's British/Italian film *Youth* (2015).[11] These examples will help refute the idea that immersion in fictional worlds is a barrier to critical reflection. *Castorp* and *The Wind Rises*—a prequel and a sequel to *The Magic Mountain*, respectively—both feature Hans Castorp as a figure who is at once uniquely immersed in and reflective about his cultural environment. In Huelle's novel, Castorp—a young student in Danzig—rereads *Effi Briest* and finds the novel uniquely engaging, but this engaged reading experience teaches him about the reality of German imperial expansion in Eastern Europe. In Miyazaki's film, Castorp—a dissident who has escaped from Nazi Germany to Japan—sings a German song about the attraction of immersion, but at the same time is the only character in the film fully aware of the fraught political situation in the run-up to the Second World War. Sorrentino's film, while a much more distant relative of Mann's novel, stages cultural anxiety about the relative merits of intellectualism and levity in art in a similar way, suggesting that it is one of the most powerful cultural tropes activated by *The Magic Mountain*. All three texts enter into a playful dialogue with Mann's novel, probing the tension between emotional engagement and critical reflection, and ultimately demonstrating that the two are often much more entwined than critics usually assume.

*   *   *

[9] Quotations from the novel in the text are taken from the following edition: Paweł Huelle, *Castorp* (Cracow: Znak, 2009). English translations are taken from the following edition: Paweł Huelle, *Castorp*, trans. Antonia Lloyd-Jones (London: Serpent's Tail, 2007).

[10] *The Wind Rises*, dir. by Hayao Miyazaki (StudioCanal, 2014).

[11] *Youth*, dir. by Paolo Sorrentino (StudioCanal, 2016).

The Magic Mountain is often described—by both its academic and non-academic readers—as an intellectual novel, a philosophical novel, a novel of ideas, or an encyclopaedic panorama of European culture.[12] Disciplines that Hans comes into contact with in the course of the novel include philosophy, sociology, economics, history, politics, classics, linguistics, rhetoric, literature, music, painting, sculpture, photography, cinema, psychology, psychoanalysis, theology, anatomy, biology, botany, astrology, astronomy, engineering, ecology, physics, mathematics, meteorology, medicine, pathology, geography, alchemy, pharmacology, chemistry—and even the making of encyclopaedias themselves, since Settembrini is working on one. This 'informational overload' led Geoffrey Winthrop-Young to call *The Magic Mountain* 'the first epic of modern information'.[13]

It may therefore come as a surprise to some readers that the author of this extraordinarily erudite novel had no formal university education, did not read the primary sources on most of the intellectual matters that the novel discusses, knew philosophy almost exclusively from reading Nietzsche and Schopenhauer, did not systematically read Goethe until years after he had published *The Magic Mountain*, and unscrupulously paraphrased whole paragraphs from popular books on science, medicine, politics, music, and other topics—in some cases so closely that it could be considered plagiarism.[14] 'Für den *Zauberberg* habe ich freilich mancherlei gelesen, aber [...] ich [vergesse] diese Hilfsmittel, ja auch die Kenntnisse selbst, die sie vermittelten, merkwürdig rasch' ('I did read quite a lot for *The Magic Mountain*, but I forget such aids, indeed the things I learn themselves, remarkably quickly'), Mann admitted in a letter in 1937.[15] Against all appearances, 'die philosophischen Kenntnisse Thomas Manns sind gering' ('Thomas Mann's philosophical knowledge [was] scant'), claims Helmut Koopmann.[16]

Koopmann's assessment that Mann's knowledge of philosophy was 'gering' sounds like an absolute judgement, but surely what is implied here is a judgement that is deeply relative. In a culture extremely anxious about intellectual standards,

---

[12] See, for example, Helmut Koopmann, *Die Entwicklung des intellektualen Romans bei Thomas Mann* (Bonn: Bouvier, 1980); Theodore Ziolkowski, *Dimensions of the Modern Novel: German Texts and European Contexts* (Princeton, NJ: Princeton University Press, 1969), pp. 68–69, and Italo Calvino, *Six Memos for the Next Millennium*, trans. Patrick Creagh (Cambridge, MA: Harvard University Press, 1988), p. 116.

[13] Geoffrey Winthrop-Young, 'Magic Media Mountain: Technology and the Umbildungsroman', in *Reading Matters: Narrative in the New Media Ecology*, ed. Joseph Tabbi and Michael Wutz (Ithaca, NY: Cornell University Press, 1997), pp. 29–52, p. 50. Parts of this section were first published in Karolina Watroba, 'The Anxiety of Difficulty: Trying to Read Thomas Mann', *The Point*, 27 (2022) <https://thepointmag.com/criticism/the-anxiety-of-difficulty/> [accessed 25 May 2022].

[14] See, for example, Erkme Joseph, 'Hans Castorps biologische Phantasie in der Frostnacht', *Wirkendes Wort*, 46 (1996), 393–411.

[15] Mann, *Selbstkommentare*, p. 124.

[16] Helmut Koopmann (ed.), *Thomas-Mann-Handbuch* (Stuttgart: A. Kröner, 2001), p. 259.

Mann both exceeded these standards and yet did not quite live up to them. His study of Nietzsche and Schopenhauer was detailed and extensive and is on display in the overall design and many specific passages of *The Magic Mountain*, as well as in many of his other texts, from *Buddenbrooks* to the Joseph tetralogy. He read very widely and assimilated what he read with ease, ready to employ his battery of cultural references in convincing, often original and thought-provoking ways. But his knowledge tended to be second-hand and rather patchy; he would often read up on whatever material he needed in a given moment before swiftly moving on.

In other words, the real-life Thomas Mann was not erudite in the same way as the implied author of *The Magic Mountain*, who tends to strike his readers as 'almost intimidatingly cultivated'[17] or 'ostentatiously knowledgeable'.[18] The omniscient narrator of the novel with his elegant, stylish German powerfully evokes the traditions of old-fashioned European learning and, more specifically, German 'Bildung'. *The Magic Mountain*'s successful self-fashioning as a symbol of erudition and cultural sophistication can be traced in its cultural afterlives.[19] I have discussed many examples of this, ranging from the reverence with which students at the Davoser 'Hochschulkurse' in the late 1920s compared Heidegger and Cassirer's discussion to the plot of *The Magic Mountain* to Klaus Schwab's decision to choose Davos as the location for the World Economic Forum.

The air of erudition and the sense of belonging to canonical high culture are produced in *The Magic Mountain* through a variety of stylistic and structural choices. These include a carefully crafted ironic narrative perspective, an abundance of rhetorical tropes associated with philosophical writings, a broad range of references to canonical works of German and European high culture, and lively descriptions of intellectual discussions, where the impression of intellectualism rests less on the actual contents of the discussions and more on a persuasive portrayal of the discussants' rhetorical skills, gesticulation, facial expressions, and body language. What follows is a typical example:

'Was Sie bürgerliche Lebensbejahung zu nennen belieben', entgegnete Herr Settembrini mit dem vorderen Teil der Lippen, während seine Mundwinkel unter dem geschwungenen Schnurrbart sich straff in die Breite zogen und sein Hals sich auf ganz eigentümliche Art schräg und ruckweise aus dem Kragen herausschraubte, 'wird immer bereit gefunden werden, für die Ideen der Vernunft und Sittlichkeit und für ihren rechtmäßigen Einfluß auf junge schwankende Seelen in jeder beliebigen Form einzutreten.'   (p. 572)

---

[17] W. H. Bruford, *The German Tradition of Self-Cultivation: 'Bildung' from Humboldt to Thomas Mann* (Cambridge: Cambridge University Press, 1975), p. 206.

[18] Erich Heller, *Thomas Mann: The Ironic German* (London: Secker & Warburg, 1958), p. 15.

[19] See also Rebecca Braun, 'Cultural Impact and the Power of Myth in Popular Public Constructions of Authorship', in *Cultural Impact in the German Context*, ed. Rebecca Braun and Lyn Marven (Rochester, NY: Camden House, 2010), pp. 78–96.

'What you like to call the "bourgeois affirmation of life," Herr Settembrini replied—setting the corners of his mouth in a taut line under the sweep of his moustache, so that only the front of his lips moved, and screwing his neck up out of his collar at an odd backward slant—'will always be found ready to advocate ideals of reason and morality and to impress them on young, wavering minds by whatever means available.' (pp. 449–50)

Wedged in between two halves of Settembrini's reply, Mann's witty and vivid description of the movement of his lips and neck as he delivers his riposte to Naphta literally tears it apart—and on the figurative level, it tears apart the illusion that the impact of their discussion relies on the quality of their ideas rather than their delivery.

Hermann Kurzke argued that this narrative strategy, which he dubbed 'Regieanweisungen' ('stage directions'), is mainly used to discredit Settembrini's ideas, 'weil es das Gedankliche aufs Körperliche reduziert' ('because it reduces the intellectual content to bodily gestures').[20] But most readers perceive this effect in both interlocutors. In Huelle's *Castorp* there is a scene in which Hans observes a heated discussion between two elderly men taking the waters at a 'Kurhaus', clearly modelled on Settembrini and Naphta: 'jakże śmieszni byli ci dwaj nadzy panowie [...] przypominali postacie z iluzjonu, jak gdyby w przesadnej gestyku-lacji i horrendalnych minach wyczerpywała się cała ich energia oraz istota sporu' ('how comical these two naked gentlemen were [...] they reminded him of characters from a silent film, as if all their energy and the heart of their dispute were being spent on their exaggerated gesticulation and horrendous facial expres-sions' (p. 149/pp. 161–62). Mann's novel is a brilliant exercise in the performance of erudition and sophistication, but this self-indulgent spectacle of intellectual and cultural superiority ultimately draws so much attention to itself that *The Magic Mountain* ends up laying bare its own pretence.

But what happens when readers encounter this combination of erudite content and erudite form? They are likely to feel intimated and overwhelmed—simply not erudite enough to handle it. *The Magic Mountain*, perhaps the greatest novel ever written by somebody who often felt like an intellectual imposter, is designed to make its reader feel like an intellectual imposter, too. This strategy raises import-ant questions about the cultural construction of erudition. A good starting point from which to explore these issues is presented by the conversations between Settembrini and Naphta, two tubercular patients who act as Hans Castorp's mentors. The intellectual landscape of *The Magic Mountain* is often reduced to these conversations, but this is not quite right. For one thing, Naphta only makes an appearance in the second half of the book. There are also many other

[20] Hermann Kurzke, *Thomas Mann: Epoche, Werk, Wirkung* (Munich: Beck, 2010), p. 205.

characters who contribute important ideas to the overall purport of the novel, including Mynheer Peeperkorn, who makes the two 'diskutierende Philosophen' ('philosophers engaged in discussion') appear as 'belanglose Intellektuellen' ('irrelevant intellectuals');[21] he was modelled on Gerhart Hauptmann, perceived by Mann as the embodiment of 'the anti-intellectual type of "Dichter"'.[22] Mann's portrayal of Settembrini and Naphta is also much more differentiated than the suggestive set of dichotomies often associated with them, according to which Settembrini stands for the forces of human reason, the values of the Enlightenment, and a humanist outlook on life, while Naphta represents the illicit allure of mysticism, the threat of religious terror, and an obsession with death and decay.

From here, scholarship on *The Magic Mountain* usually takes one of two routes. The first route is the so-called 'Quellenforschung': the study of the sources of, or influences upon, a literary work. Large passages in Settembrini's and Naphta's speeches are made up of approximate quotations of Nietzsche, Schopenhauer, and various popular historians and thinkers of the turn of the century, including Thomas Mann himself—in the novel he recycled some of his own earlier essays. The aim of the 'Quellenforschung' is to uncover as many such sources as possible. While the 'Quellenforschung' has led to many interesting discoveries, most of the time it lacks explanatory power. A good example of this is the following critical annotation to a Latin phrase that Settembrini uses in one of his disputes with Naphta, 'Roma locuta':

> Aus (lat.) Roma locuta est, causa finita est: Rom (= der Papst) hat gesprochen, die Angelegenheit ist entschieden. Lateinische Übersetzung von Vers 784 (Rome a parlé, l'affaire est terminée) aus der Satire *Philotanus*, die der Abbé Grécourt 1720 gegen die Jesuiten geschrieben hat. (Ob Thomas Mann diese Herkunft des unter Gebildeten redensartlichen Wortes kannte, ist allerdings sehr fraglich.)

> From the Latin 'Roma locuta est, causa finita est': Rome (= the Pope) has spoken, the case is closed. Latin translation of verse 784 (Rome a parlé, l'affaire est terminée) from the satire *Philotanus* written by Abbé Grécourt against the Jesuits in 1720. (However, it is doubtful whether Thomas Mann knew the origin of this phrase, commonly used among well-educated men.)[23]

---

[21] Hans Wysling, 'Der Zauberberg', in *Thomas-Mann-Handbuch*, ed. Helmut Koopmann (Stuttgart: A. Kröner, 2001), pp. 397–422, p. 416.
[22] Hans Rudolf Vaget, 'The Making of *The Magic Mountain*', in *Thomas Mann's* The Magic Mountain: *A Casebook*, ed. Hans Rudolf Vaget (Oxford: Oxford University Press, 2008), pp. 13–30, p. 26.
[23] Michael Neumann, *Thomas Mann, 'Der Zauberberg': Kommentar*, GKFA (Frankfurt am Main: Fischer, 2002), p. 288.

The tracing back of this phrase to a Latin translation of an eighteenth-century French treatise against the Jesuits seems fitting, given that Settembrini uses it to scold Naphta, who is a Jesuit himself. But as the author of this critical note admits, it is highly unlikely that Mann knew the origin of this phrase, 'commonly used among well-educated men'. No attempt is made here to explore the implications of Mann's predilection for erudite phrases whose origins he did not even know.

There are many similar examples to be found in Thomas Mann's correspondence. In 1930, Mann was asked about the source of a quote from Virgil which he had used in The Magic Mountain, but he could not remember it at all.[24] He also famously confessed to not having read any of Freud's works at the time of writing The Magic Mountain; 'however, one could be influenced in this sphere without any direct contact with his work, because for a long time the air had been filled with the thoughts and results of the psychoanalytic school',[25] he wrote to another correspondent; 'man atmete sie [die psychoanalytischen Theorien] ein, auch ohne sie ausdrücklich zu studieren' ('you breathed in psychoanalytic theories without explicitly studying them');[26] 'wahrscheinlich sollte man denken, dass ich zur Zeit des Zauberbergs diese Dinge studiert haben müsse. Manches darin [...] ist auch studiert. Aber das meiste ist "aus der Luft" gegriffen' ('presumably one would assume that I must have studied these things while at work on The Magic Mountain. I did study some of it. But most of it was just "in the air"').[27] A short note in Euphorion explains how Mann came up with the phrase 'placet experiri', which Hans borrows from Settembrini to describe the spirit of intellectual adventurousness that he embraces in the sanatorium—it was a misunderstanding of a line from Petrarch, which Mann had come across in a magazine.[28]

And yet Mann's carefully cultivated public persona was rather different. At the time of his lectures at Princeton in the late 1930s, Mann was often portrayed as 'somebody able to summon at a moment's notice centuries' worth of interdisciplinary humanistic knowledge'.[29] In the early 1940s, Brecht commented on his occasional meetings with Mann in Los Angeles: 'dann schauen 3000 Jahre auf mich hinab' ('then 3000 years look down on me').[30] Around the same time, Mann's daughter Erika advised him jokingly to 'remain as godlike [...] as possible' in his BBC broadcasts in occupied Germany.[31] Meanwhile, Mann

---

[24] Mann, Selbstkommentare, p. 107.   [25] Ibid., p. 142.
[26] Ibid., p. 165.   [27] Ibid., p. 168.
[28] Ludwig Völker, 'Ein Mißverständnis und seine Folgen: "placet experiri" als Wahlspruch Petrarcas in Thomas Manns Roman Der Zauberberg', Euphorion, 67 (1973), 383–85.
[29] Tobias Boes, Thomas Mann's War: Literature, Politics, and the World Republic of Letters (Ithaca, NY: Cornell University Press, 2019), p. 110.
[30] See Johannes Roskothen, '"Der Stehkragen sprach": Die unproduktive Spannung zwischen Thomas Mann und Bertolt Brecht—eine Rekonstruktion', Düsseldorfer Beiträge zur Thomas Mann-Forschung, 2 (2013), 61–78, p. 70.
[31] J. F. Slattery, 'Thomas Mann und die B.B.C.: Die Bedingungen ihrer Zusammenarbeit 1940–1945', Thomas Mann Jahrbuch, 5 (1992), 142–70, p. 161.

would pick up and sometimes misquote bits from magazines, would often work with widespread ideas about texts rather than the texts themselves, and was being actively stylized as a cultural symbol through carefully orchestrated book tours and advertisement campaigns run by savvy German and American marketers. My point here is not that Mann was a fraud—rather, that a closer look at how he acquired, constructed, and performed his erudition, and how it was received by his readers, brings out very clearly the contrast between what erudition actually consists in and how we usually imagine and portray it.

In *Thomas Mann: The Uses of Tradition*, T. J. Reed wrote:

> [despite] all appearances to the contrary, *Der Zauberberg* is not the creation of a brooding philosophical polymath, nor a paean to 'Bildung' in its secondary sense of the inert materials of education, what Nietzsche once called the stony bits of knowledge that rattled loosely inside 'cultivated' nineteenth-century Man. It is rather the work of one who, as a humanist and a humorist, is concerned to put the materials of culture where they belong: in the perspective of human purposes. Once this is understood, the demands that *Der Zauberberg* makes on its readers prove less formidable than is usually supposed.[32]

Other academic readers of Thomas Mann know this to be true. In a literature review following the publication of Reed's influential study, Hermann Kurzke summarized Reed's challenge to traditional studies of Mann, saying that he

> kritisiert [...] die Vorstellung von Thomas Mann als einem universal belesenen Repräsentanten der ganzen abendländischen Kultur und von seinem Werk als dem Résumé Jahrtausende durchlaufender Traditionslinien; kritisiert also die implizite Voraussetzung vieler Einflußforschungen.
>
> criticizes the view of Thomas Mann as an encyclopaedically well-read representative of the entire Western culture, and of his work as a summa of thousands of years of tradition; in other words, he criticizes the implicit starting point of many influential studies of Mann.[33]

And yet a misleading understanding of Mann's erudition, together with the kind of reader that his writing demands, have persisted and dominated his perception in Germany and beyond, resulting in a relative loss of popularity with readers put off by his formidable reputation (when I tell German friends that I study Mann, they almost invariably go 'uff!')—a fact that conservative Mann scholars, who are at least partially to blame for this state of affairs, then bemoan.

[32] T. J. Reed, *Thomas Mann: The Uses of Tradition* (Oxford: Clarendon Press, 1996), p. 248.
[33] Hermann Kurzke, ed., *Stationen der Thomas-Mann-Forschung: Aufsätze seit 1970* (Würzburg: Königshausen & Neumann, 1985), pp. 102–03.

The 'Quellenforschung' is one possible approach to the debates between Settembrini and Naphta. Another popular approach is to try and decide who wins these debates. The most common way of doing this is by scrutinizing the author's intentions. Did Mann ultimately support Settembrini's views? Or Naphta's views? Or neither? A similar question is to ask whether the novel is ultimately more dependent on Schopenhauer or on Nietzsche.[34] However, this tends to be inconclusive, since novels are not philosophical treatises which prove or disprove a thesis by way of logical argumentation. The question that interests me instead is this: why did Mann choose to write a novel about philosophy rather than a philosophical treatise? Both the 'Quellenforschung' and the scholarship that reads *The Magic Mountain* as committed to specific philosophical arguments leave this important question unanswered, and they do not offer a persuasive account of Mann's strategies in shaping the philosophical debates in the novel either. If academic readers cannot give a good answer to these questions, it might be more instructive to take a broader view of readerly encounters with philosophy in *The Magic Mountain*.

Many scholars of *The Magic Mountain* assume that an old-fashioned kind of German 'Bildung' is a prerequisite for a fruitful reading of the novel. As I have shown in the Introduction, this assumption is the starting point of Kurzke's authoritative monograph on Mann. But perceived deficiencies in humanist learning are already thematized in *The Magic Mountain* itself. In the figure of Hans Castorp, a young engineer, the novel provides a model of how to approach philosophical debates between Settembrini and Naphta without much philosophical training at all. Most of the time these debates are way over Hans's head, and yet he still finds ways to enjoy them, and even participate in them. Michael Beddow wrote that Hans Castorp 'finds it all "hörenswert" [worth hearing], although not every reader will agree'.[35] Non-academic readers of *The Magic Mountain* often find themselves in a similar position.

Even though academic readers rarely reflect on it explicitly when writing about the novel, the fact is that very few readers will feel at ease when confronted with a thirty-page-long conversation between Settembrini and Naphta that covers topics ranging from Plotinus to Voltaire, from medieval Church history to nineteenth-century nationalist movements in Europe, and from John Stuart Mill to Chinese Daoism. And yet this is precisely what readers are confronted with in 'Vom Gottesstaat und von übler Erlösung' ('The City of God and Evil Deliverance'), a section in the sixth chapter—roughly halfway through the novel's 1000 pages—which recounts the first long discussion between Settembrini and Naphta. The acquired ease with which academic readers, after years of careful study of *The*

Magic Mountain, are able to confront passages like this is in fact a distortion of the text—and a prime example of the situation recently described by Tom Lutz: 'the scholar and the critic pretend to have already ingested it all [the entire cultural archive], pretend to a comprehension that we know—that we even explicitly argue—is unachievable.'[36]

To explain what I mean by this, I turn to readers of *The Magic Mountain* whose experiences routinely go unreported and unaccounted for in the academic scholarship on the novel. How do they respond to the philosophical discussions between Settembrini and Naphta? Here is one such unreported example, taken from a recent online review of *The Magic Mountain*: 'as a reader [. . .], you don't have to penetrate these conversations; it's enough to sit back and nod, turning the pages, letting the thoughts of Thomas Mann as expressed through Herr Settembrini or Herr Naphta wash over you.'[37] The effect this reader describes is similar to Roland Barthes's concept of 'l'effet de réel', or 'the reality effect'. Referring to realist novels, Barthes pointed out that literary descriptions not only tell readers about the specific details of what a given object looks like but also give them the general impression that it is a *real* object.[38] Similarly, we can talk about 'the erudition effect': a philosophical discussion represented in a literary text does not matter just because of its content, but also because of the impression readers get that they are witnessing an erudite exchange. Rendering this phrase in French—as 'l'effet de l'érudition'—might be even more effective, not just because it is closer to Barthes's original term, but also because French terms often carry a whiff of intellectuality in the English-speaking world. This seems to correspond to the point that this reviewer made. It is also interesting to note that the verb the reviewer used—'to wash over'—is very much within the figurative realm of the immersion metaphor, suggesting that varieties of immersive reading are possible not just with texts that are simple and accessible, like detective novels, but also with texts that are more difficult and less accessible.

In one of the greatest bestsellers of the last few years, Karl Ove Knausgaard's series of autobiographical novels *Min Kamp* (*My Struggle*) (2009–11), the narrator gradually reads almost all of Mann's books and comes to similar conclusions. He enjoys *Doktor Faustus* even though he 'was unable to grasp the bit about music and musical theory'; 'but I was used to that in this kind of novel', he continues, 'there were always great expanses I just skimmed without understanding, more or less like the French dialogue that could suddenly crop up in some books.'[39] The

---

[36] Tom Lutz, 'In the Shadow of the Archive', in *The Critic as Amateur*, ed. Saikat Majumdar and Aarthi Vadde (New York: Bloomsbury, 2020), pp. 49–61, p. 59.

[37] Sarah Van Arsdale, 'Hobbling Up the Magic Mountain', *Fiction Writers Review*, 20 September 2009 <https://fictionwritersreview.com/essay/hobbling-up-the-magic-mountain-with-illustrations-by-the-author/> [accessed 10 June 2019].

[38] See Roland Barthes, 'L'effet de réel', *Communications*, 11 (1968), 84–89.

[39] Karl Ove Knausgaard, *Dancing in the Dark*, trans. Don Bartlett (London: Vintage, 2015), p. 398. I am indebted to Colton Valentine for this and the next reference.

example of the French dialogue makes one think of Hans Castorp's long-awaited conversation with Clawdia Chauchat, which takes place almost entirely in French over the course of several pages. It comes as no surprise, then, that in the next volume Knausgaard's narrator goes on to report on his experience of reading *The Magic Mountain*—which he also enjoys tremendously, even though he 'was unfamiliar with the frame of reference within which the discussions [between Settembrini and Naphta] unfolded'.[40]

It is worth pointing out here that Mann was not entirely fluent in French and had to consult a dictionary when working on the French conversation, and in the end asked a friend whose French was much better than his to edit it[41]—not unlike Hans Castorp himself, who anxiously asks Joachim after his very first, brief attempt at speaking French in the sanatorium: 'hoffentlich habe ich keinen Fehler im Französischen gemacht bei dem, was ich sagte?' ('I hope there weren't any mistakes in my French when I answered—were there?') (p. 168/p. 129). But any extra work or consultation that Mann felt he needed to write the French conversation is elided from the text. The surface of the novel is made to look like an effortless individual performance even though it actually involved consulting reference works and getting help from others. Yet again, the reader implied by the text—one who can effortlessly switch from German to French—is more cultured than Mann himself.

Some particularly peevish readers were much exercised by this. Franz Josef Scheuren analysed the marginal notes left in his copy of *The Magic Mountain* by Ernst Bertram, a writer, university professor, and later Nazi sympathizer, whom Mann counted among his close friends in the 1920s. Scheuren lists numerous snide comments made by Bertram about Mann's spelling mistakes in foreign language phrases, especially in French. One such mistake is accompanied by the following comment: 'aber am Schluß tust du, als könntest du seitenlang französisch schreiben' ('but in the end you pretend to be able to write pages and pages of French').[42] Another comment reads: 'das kommt davon, wenn man tut, als könne man Französisch...' ('that's what happens when you pretend to be fluent in French...').[43] Bertram finds Mann's use of French pretentious; next to the word 'Crayon', used to describe Clawdia Chauchat's pencil, Bertram notes in the margin: 'Bleistift wäre auch zu ungebildet' ('pencil would be just too uneducated').[44] A little later he notes sarcastically: 'die deutsche Sprache empfiehlt sich denen, die Französisch zu können vorgeben' ('the German language commends

[40] Karl Ove Knausgaard, *Some Rain Must Fall*, trans. Don Bartlett (London: Vintage, 2016), p. 262.
[41] Peter De Mendelssohn, *Nachbemerkungen zu Thomas Mann* (Frankfurt am Main: Fischer, 1982), vol. i, pp. 78–80.
[42] Franz Josef Scheuren, 'Ernst Bertrams Lesespuren im Widmungsexemplar von Thomas Manns *Der Zauberberg*', *Thomas Mann Jahrbuch*, 16 (2003), 55–65, p. 60.
[43] Ibid., p. 61.   [44] Ibid., p. 60.

itself to those who pretend to be fluent in French').[45] He goes as far as to compare what he perceived as Mann's attempts to appear more cultured than he really was with the frequent 'Bildungsschnitzer' ('uneducated blunders') of the character Frau Stöhr in *The Magic Mountain*. Bertram takes malicious pleasure in pointing out Mann's linguistic slips in the same way that Mann's narrator fixates on mocking Stöhr's mistakes. At one point, Bertram explicitly notes in the margin: 'wer machte sich über Frau Stöhr lustig?' ('who made fun of Frau Stöhr?').[46] Of course, all this tells us rather more about Ernst Bertram than Thomas Mann—but it also shows how sensitive at least some readers have been to Mann's intimations of erudition, and how fraught the cultural performance of erudition can be.

Many readers do not respond to Mann's narrative with Bertram's sense of peevish superiority or accept the inaccessibility of the text as easily as Knausgaard's narrator: instead, they are unsettled by it. On the Goodreads forum from 2013, discussing the section 'The City of God', one reader confessed:

> I will be perfectly honest, this was my least favorite chapter because of the endless debates between Naphta and Settembrini. I quote Hans, who I agree with here: 'Hans Castorp stood with bent head and burrowed with his stick in the snow, pondering the vast confusion of it all.' Can someone help me find their discussions interesting?[47]

This last plea should make every scholar of literature stop in their tracks. Does this reader's question not sum up one of the most important functions of literary scholarship? Should critics not be helping readers find Thomas Mann interesting and enjoyable? Is this not the perfect opportunity to 'forge a bridge between the great writers and the general reader', as Philip Swallow postulated in David Lodge's *Small World*? But there were no literary scholars on hand on the online forum. Fortunately, other non-academic readers came to the rescue.

One of them responded by arguing that Mann had anticipated that reader's reaction to the endless philosophical debates and put in ironical meta-comments to acknowledge it, just like the one about Hans Castorp's great confusion. The reader goes on: 'I'm sure that we would've enjoyed the Settembrini-Naphta exchanges a lot more had we been in on all the details—it's our limitations as readers that we are not able to enjoy the text.'[48] The text makes the readers feel inadequate: not sufficiently erudite to follow it. But being able or unable to follow a text is not a binary opposition; it is a spectrum. These readers were not able to concentrate on the details of the philosophical discussions, but they picked up on

---

[45]   Ibid., p. 61.   [46]   Ibid., p. 61.
[47]   'Thomas Mann's The Magic Mountain Discussion, Chapter VI [October 7 to 27]' <https://www.goodreads.com/topic/show/1406735-4-chapter-vi-october-7-to-27> [accessed 15 March 2019].
[48]   Ibid.

other aspects of the text. The first reader started noticing the emotional tensions in the chapter, as well as an interesting facet of the theme of time and its passage in the novel: Settembrini and Naphta 'have a life sentence—they are dying—this is it for them. This adds a real poignance to their debates because of the way they conduct themselves with this full knowledge of their impending doom as if they have all the time in the world.'[49] Then another reader chimed in: 'I found [the Settembrini-Naphta debates] fascinating, from an intellectual Ping-Pong PoV. I like this kind of debate in the same way that other people like watching a game of tennis.'[50] This is yet another possible way to approach the philosophical debates in *The Magic Mountain*.

It is worth dwelling on the metaphor of 'intellectual table tennis' a little longer. The following passage from 'The City of God' illustrates what this reader had in mind:

Die Zuhörer atmeten aus, denn sie hatten die Luft angehalten bei Herrn Settembrinis großer Replik. Hans Castorp konnte sogar nicht umhin, mit der Hand, wenn auch zurückhaltenderweise, auf den Tischrand zu schlagen. 'Brillant!' sagte er zwischen den Zähnen [...] Dann aber wandten sich beide dem eben zurückgeschlagenen Interlokutor zu [...].   (pp. 602–03)

His listeners, who held their breath during Herr Settembrini's grand rejoinder, breathed out again now. Hans Castorp could not help slamming his hand, though with restraint, on the edge of the table. 'Brillant!' he said with clenched teeth. [...] But then they both turned back to the other disputant, who had just been rebuffed [...].   (p. 473)

This performance of erudition is the counterpart to the performance of emotion in melodrama: an exaggerated, can't-miss-it representation of something that is recognizable to readers from their lives, but never encountered in quite so distilled a form outside the covers of books.[51] Hans and his cousin Joachim really do behave as if they were watching a tennis match: looking from one opponent to the other, holding their breath when one of them strikes, letting out a cry of applause, and then observing how the other strikes back. Ludwig Englert, the student who attended the 'Davoser Disputation' between Heidegger and Cassirer, compared their debate to 'einem Boxkampf' ('a boxing match').[52] Closer to home, a recent debate between philosophers Jordan Peterson and Slavoj Žižek was also said to 'have the feel of a heavyweight boxing match'.[53] This, we are told, is how all conversations between Settembrini and Naphta come across:

---

[49] Ibid.   [50] Ibid.   [51] I am indebted to Conor Brennan for this remark.
[52] Ludwig Englert, 'Als Student bei den Zweiten Davoser Hochschulkursen März 1929', in *Nachlese zu Heidegger*, ed. Guido Schneeberger (Bern: [n. pub.], 1962), pp. 1–6, p. 4.
[53] Stephen Marche, 'The "Debate of the Century": What Happened When Jordan Peterson Debated Slavoj Žižek', 20 April 2019 <https://www.theguardian.com/world/2019/apr/20/jordan-peterson-slavoj-zizek-happiness-capitalism-marxism> [accessed 20 June 2019].

Ein Streit, der geführt wird, als ob es ums Leben ginge, außerdem aber mit einem Witz und Schliff, als ob es nicht ums Leben, sondern nur um ein elegantes Wettspiel ginge—und so wurden alle Dispute zwischen Settembrini und Naphta geführt:—ein solcher Streit ist selbstverständlich und an und für sich unterhaltend anzuhören, auch für den, der wenig davon versteht und seine Tragweite nur undeutlich absieht.   (p. 782)

an argument carried on as if it were a matter of life and death, and with such wit and polish as if it were *not*, but merely an elegant competition—and that was how all disputes were carried on between Settembrini and Naphta—such an argument is, in and of itself, quite naturally entertaining to listen to, even for someone who understands little of it and only vaguely comprehends its significance.   (p. 615)

In order to be fully attuned to this game of 'intellectual table tennis' or 'boxing match', readers need to renounce their agency, to let themselves be overwhelmed by the text, to submit to it—in other words, to immerse themselves in it and let it wash over them.

The notion of letting the difficulty just 'wash over' you is a typical example in a body of reviews of another novel on Goodreads analysed by Emmett Stinson and Beth Driscoll.[54] While their chosen novel, *The Swan Book* (2013) by the Indigenous Australian author Alexis Wright, is certainly different from *The Magic Mountain* in many ways, they nevertheless associate its difficulty with the techniques of literary modernism. Indeed, many responses to *The Swan Book* discussed by Stinson and Driscoll are strikingly similar to the comments on *The Magic Mountain* discussed in this section. While some readers were happy for the difficulty to 'wash over them', others wanted to have the book explained to them;[55] difficulty was seen to 'refuse reader expectations, generate anger, shame or delight, or position readers in a perceived cultural hierarchy'.[56] The goal of Stinson and Driscoll's study was to understand 'how difficulty is "used" by readers, authors, and mediators (such as publishers) within literary networks, rather than returning again to questions of inclusivity and exclusivity or prestige and pretension, which have often shadowed discussions of difficulty'.[57] The authors concluded that 'Goodreads should be considered a twenty-first-century forum for middlebrow practices that negotiate between prestige and accessibility'.[58] Interestingly, Catherine Turner and Tobias Boes have both argued that *The Magic Mountain* was originally marketed and received in the United States as a distinctly middle-brow text. Mann's American publisher produced advertisements that 'both

---

[54] Emmett Stinson and Beth Driscoll, 'Difficult Literature on Goodreads: Reading Alexis Wright's *The Swan Book*', *Textual Practice*, 26 June 2020 [pre-print] <https://doi.org/10.1080/0950236X.2020.1786718> [accessed 1 May 2021], 1–22, p. 13.

[55] Ibid., p. 16.   [56] Ibid., p. 7.   [57] Ibid., p. 5.   [58] Ibid., p. 15.

assured readers that they ought to be able to read these novels on their own and confirmed their fears that they could not'.[59]

It therefore comes as no surprise that, in the case of *The Magic Mountain*, immersion in the text is necessary to understand 'l'effet de l'érudition', to understand that it depends less on the details of argumentation and more on the performative display of knowingness, that to participate in Settembrini's and Naphta's discussions one needs to learn to imitate their rhetorical strategies, tone of voice, and body language. A critical reflection on the internal laws of critical reflection as it is practised by Settembrini and Naphta is only possible through immersion. Mann might have got the idea for staging 'l'effet de l'érudition' in this way from listening to Georg Lukács, whom he met during the last phase of work on *The Magic Mountain*: 'Lukács hat mir einmal in Wien eine Stunde lang seine Theorien entwickelt. Solange er sprach, hatte er recht. [Nachher blieb] der Eindruck fast unheimlicher Abstraktheit zurück' ('In Vienna I once heard Lukács hold forth about his theories for a solid hour. As long as he was speaking, he was right. All that remained afterwards was an impression of almost uncanny abstractness').[60] What a great way to describe the intellectual habitus of many a philosopher! It suggests the kind of impression that Mann was hoping to recreate for his readers: the impression of witnessing a performance of erudition which one cannot hope to penetrate.

This is certainly how many readers on the Goodreads forum felt. The reader who first wrote about readers' limitations in enjoying *The Magic Mountain* went on to reach a more nuanced view: 'I think the problem is that Mann has given us "too much" & most readers end up feeling that they've bitten off more than they can chew. In other words, they feel out of their depth & blame the writer for that unsavoury feeling. Me? I feel humbled by this book.'[61] The vocabulary that this reader uses to describe their encounter with *The Magic Mountain*—'feeling out of one's depth', 'feeling humbled', 'an unsavoury feeling'—suggests a full-on emotional response to a perceived lack of cultural capital. *The Magic Mountain* makes you feel inadequate as a reader. You do not have the kind of learning that the book requires of you. But there is a decisive twist: has this kind of learning ever existed? Did Hans Castorp have it? Did anybody other than Settembrini and Naphta have it? Thomas Mann, for one, did not, given that he had composed many of the philosophical debates in *The Magic Mountain* by paraphrasing whole passages from other books and promptly forgot the details of his sources once he was finished with his writing.

[59] Catherine Turner, *Marketing Modernism Between the Two World Wars* (Amherst, MA: University of Massachusetts Press, 2003), p. 222.
[60] Quoted in Georg Lukács, *Thomas Mann* (Berlin: Aufbau, 1949), p. 6.
[61] 'Thomas Mann's *The Magic Mountain* Discussion'.

The idea of learning and erudition that emerges out of *The Magic Mountain* is that it always exists somewhere else. In a different book, in a different time, in a different place. It is accessible to somebody else, just not you. Especially towards the beginning of the novel, the words 'Bildung' and 'gebildet', indicating the possession of cultural education and refinement, appear far less often than their opposites. 'Unbildung', 'ungebildet', and 'Bildungsschnitzer' are used with reference to Frau Stöhr more than twenty times (seven, twelve, and three times, respectively). Meanwhile, Frau Stöhr herself takes pleasure in describing another patient as 'ein Mensch ohne all und jede Bildung', a man sorely lacking in 'Bildung' (p. 117). As much as the novel is about the pursuit of 'Bildung', it is also about the anxiety that one might in fact be 'ungebildet'. The reader is invited to make fun of Frau Stöhr, but might also feel anxious about being like her. As we have seen, even Thomas Mann was not immune from being compared to Stöhr, the object of his own parodistic efforts. Sara Danius wrote that *The Magic Mountain* is 'a novel about knowledge—its conditions, its processes, its consequences';[62] it is also about its anxieties, myths, fantasies, and phantoms. *The Magic Mountain* creates the phantom of an impossibly erudite 'ideal reader' so that it can make its actual readers feel inferior to the task of reading it. This is, in essence, how the novel works: it forces readers to confront their anxieties about not being a good enough reader.

Here is how Susan Sontag put it, reminiscing about her first encounter with Thomas Mann: 'everything that surrounds my meeting with him has the colour of shame'.[63] Sontag read *The Magic Mountain* as a teenager in the 1940s and was captivated, but also intimidated. She soon found out that Mann was living very close to her, in Pacific Palisades, just outside Los Angeles. Sontag and a friend of hers managed to get themselves invited to pay a visit to Mann's house (the meeting she described in the quote above). As Kai Sina has shown, Sontag in fact modified several aspects of her meeting with Mann to engineer a sense of 'heightened alienation and [. . .] exaggerated contrast' between herself and the famous author.[64] This is because she was also describing a more symbolical meeting between two cultural traditions—between the old German writer who seems to embody pre-war European culture and a young American girl who reads his book and loves it, but feels that she does not have a chance to ever measure up to him. We saw much the same configuration in Alice Munro's 'Amundsen' and 'Dear Life'. Carlos Fuentes also told a similar story of his encounter with Mann, whom he saw towards the end of his life in Switzerland:

---

[62] Sara Danius, *The Senses of Modernism: Technology, Perception, and Aesthetics* (Ithaca, NY: Cornell University Press, 2002), p. 58.

[63] Susan Sontag, 'Pilgrimage', in *A Companion to Thomas Mann's 'The Magic Mountain'*, ed. Stephen D. Dowden (Columbia, SC: Camden House, 1999), pp. 221–39, p. 221.

[64] Kai Sina, 'Reading *The Magic Mountain* in Arizona: Susan Sontag's Reflections on Thomas Mann', *Naharaim*, 9 (2015), 89–107, p. 102.

I was curious, I was impertinent. Dare I approach Thomas Mann—I, a 21-year-old Mexican student with a lot of reading behind me, true, but with all the gaucherie of one still ignorant of social and intellectual sophistication? Susan Sontag, in a memorable piece, has recalled how she, even younger than I, entered the inner sanctum of Thomas Mann's house in Los Angeles in the 1940s, and found precious little to say, but much to observe. I had nothing to say but, like Sontag, a lot to observe.[65]

Sontag's memory of her meeting with Mann seems to have become its own micro-genre: a report of an acute case of intellectual imposter syndrome inflicted by an encounter with Thomas Mann's writing. This is precisely the effect engineered by *The Magic Mountain*.

But what if a reader refuses to be shamed into submission? Then she might be in for a treat. Quite literally: a piece of cake is going to be involved. Another reader on Goodreads wrote:

I'm reading slowly. Actually enjoyed the City of God chapter, better read very slowly. All the philosophical disagreements take place over tea and Baumkuchen. My very favorite German cake, made over a turning spit with layer after thin layer of batter poured on. Then baked, the resulting tall 'tree' is sliced in horizontal layers that reveal the tree 'rings' sometimes highlighted with chocolate powder. It's divine. Settembrini finally says enough arguing, but only pushes himself from the table once his cup and plate are empty.[66]

For this reader, the main tension in 'The City of God' is *not* between Settembrini's humanist vision of a world republic and Naphta's vision of a totalitarian regime, but rather between Settembrini's moral indignation at Naphta and his failure to resist Naphta's delicious 'Baumkuchen'—despite his criticism of Naphta's opulent lifestyle. Here is the relevant passage from the novel:

Herr Settembrini hatte eine gewaltige Art, zu fragen. Hochaufgerichtet saß er und ließ seine ehrenhaften Worte auf den kleinen Herrn Naphta niedersausen, am Ende die Stimme so mächtig hochziehend, daß man wohl hörte, wie sicher er war, daß des Gegners Antwort hierauf nur in beschämtem Schweigen bestehen könne. Er hatte ein Stück Baumkuchen zwischen den Fingern gehalten, während er sprach, legte es aber nun auf den Teller zurück, da er nach dieser Fragestellung nicht hineinbeißen mochte. [. . .] 'Nun, es ist genug', erklärte Herr Settembrini

---

[65] Carlos Fuentes, 'How Zurich Invented the Modern World', *Salon*, 30 September 1997 <https://www.salon.com/1997/09/30/zurich> [accessed 10 May 2019].

[66] 'The Thomas Mann Group Discussion, Week 7 – September 23–29' <https://www.goodreads.com/topic/show/1410475-week-7——september-23-29-read-from-the-city-of-god-an-evil-delive> [accessed 15 March 2019].

> mit leicht bebender Stimme, indem er Tasse und Teller von sich schob, die
> übrigens leer waren, und sich vom seidenen Sofa erhob.   (pp. 599, 611)

> Herr Settembrini had a forceful way of posing questions. He sat up straight and
> pelted little Herr Naphta with righteous words, his voice swelling so powerfully
> toward the end that you could hear just how certain he was that his opponent's
> answer could take only one form—embarrassed silence. He had been holding a
> piece of cake between his fingers as he spoke, but now he laid it back on his plate,
> unwilling to take a bite after such questions. [...] 'Well, then, enough,' Herr
> Settembrini declared with a slight quiver in his voice, pushing his plate and cup
> away—both empty now—and getting up from the silk sofa.   (pp. 470, 480)

The reader from the online forum who picked up on this was immersed in the
narrative—highly attuned to Settembrini's body language and Mann's humour,
which so often gets lost in overly serious treatments of the philosophical content
of the novel.

In another subforum on *The Magic Mountain*, Goodreads readers exchanged
links to academic articles and books, including an article by Jeffrey Meyers about
Mann's humour in *The Magic Mountain*,[67] in which he writes that 'Thomas
Mann's reputation as a difficult, ponderous, heavyweight novelist, and the erudite
allusions, serious subject matter, and philosophical themes of *The Magic
Mountain* [...] have led readers to ignore the comic and satiric tone that enlivens
his morbid novel.'[68] This account of Mann's novel seemed particularly appealing
to the readers on Goodreads—once they found a way to get around the paywall. In
her introduction to John E. Woods's translation of the novel, A.S. Byatt wrote that
her 'early readings of *The Magic Mountain*, impeded by scholarly earnestness,
trying to get [her] bearings in an ocean of unfamiliar words, [...] quite failed to
see how *funny*, as well as ironic and subtle, much of the argumentation and debate
is'.[69] For a reader attuned to the language of immersion, Byatt's dilemma was that
she denied herself the pleasure of immersion in this 'ocean', trained to only value
the 'scholarly earnestness' of critical reflection in encounters with books like *The
Magic Mountain*.

But immersion can *lead to* critical reflection. As Felski points out, 'academics
have a tendency to overintellectualize knowledge, which can also be a matter of
practice, habituation, flair, or "feel"';[70] 'reflective thought is not like acetone or
nail-polish remover, an unsticking agent that miraculously dissolves all ties'.[71]

---

[67] 'Journal articles about The Magic Mountain' <https://www.goodreads.com/topic/show/
1404552-journal-articles-about-the-magic-mountain> [accessed 15 March 2019].

[68] Jeffrey Meyers, 'Comedy in *The Magic Mountain*', *The New Criterion*, 30.2 (2011), 1–6, p. 1.

[69] A. S. Byatt, 'Introduction', in Thomas Mann, *The Magic Mountain* (New York: A. A. Knopf,
2005), trans. John E. Woods, pp. vii–xxi, p. xiii.

[70] Rita Felski, *Hooked: Art and Attachment* (Chicago: The University of Chicago Press, 2020), p. 72.

[71] Ibid., p. 129.

And so the reader who picked up on the 'Baumkuchen' scene did not stop there. A few days later she wrote another comment, wondering about the rings of the 'Baumkuchen'. The reader concluded that Settembrini's and Naphta's arguments 'are circular and intricate just like the cake'. A full-on immersion in the story-world, complete with vivid impressions of the kind of food that the characters are eating, has not precluded this reader's 'reflective thought', but rather enabled it.

What adds strength to this interpretation is that other passages in the novel tell us that food can function as a bite-sized introduction to philosophy for Hans Castorp. In a passage about hermetic philosophy, Naphta tells Hans about this esoteric science in the context of Freemasonry (and Settembrini is a mason), to which Hans responds:

> '"Hermetik" ist gut gesagt, Herr Naphta. "Hermetisch"—das Wort hat mir immer gefallen. Es ist ein richtiges Zauberwort mit weitläufigen Assoziationen. Entschuldigen Sie, aber ich muß immer dabei an unsere Weckgläser denken, die unsere Hamburger Hausdame [...] in ihrer Speisekammer [...] stehen hat,— hermetisch verschlossene Gläser mit Früchten und Fleisch und allem möglichen darin.'   (p. 770)

> '"Hermetism"—that's well put, Herr Naphta. "Hermetic"—I've always liked that word. It's a magic word with vague, vast associations. Forgive me, but I can't help thinking about our old canning jars, the ones our housekeeper in Hamburg [...] has standing in rows on shelves in her pantry: hermetically sealed jars, with fruit and meat and all sorts of other things inside.   (p. 605)

Hans is talking about 'Weckgläser'—canning jars or mason jars with a hermetic (airtight) seal. He goes on to reflect on how time stops inside a jar like this: you put in food, and when you take it out months or even years later, it is still perfectly preserved. Many important connections are being made here: between the secluded life in a sanatorium and a tightly sealed jar of jam, between the title of the novel—'Zauberberg'—and the 'Zauberwort' 'hermeticism' that so fascinates Hans, and between life and death and their interrelatedness in Naphta's esoteric philosophy. A little later the narrator will characterize the treatment of time in Castorp's story as a 'hermetische[r] Zauber' (p. 817). Hans instinctively does exactly what Byatt struggled to do: he immerses himself in 'an ocean of unfamiliar words' with pleasure, and in this way arrives at critical reflection.

But this is exactly the sort of conversation between Hans and Naphta that Settembrini strictly condemns. Settembrini believes that you need a certain type of erudition to safely face Naphta and his ideas; otherwise it can be dangerous. To put it in more general terms, Settembrini thinks that Hans should not be at liberty to participate in the cultural debates that surround him. This sounds rather dubious coming from a spokesman for the powers of the human intellect, and yet here it is: 'Sie sind ungewappnet gegen intellektuelles Blendwerk, Sie sind der Gefahr ausgesetzt, unter den Einwirkungen dieser halb fanatischen und halb boshaften Rabulistik Schaden zu nehmen an Geist und Seele' ('you enter the fray unarmed against such intellectual chicanery. If exposed to the influences of this half-fanatic, half-malicious humbug, both your mind and souls are in danger') (p. 615/p. 483). But Hans is not as clueless as Settembrini assumes. In the passage about hermetic jars, Hans comes up with an unlikely association that turns out to shed some light on the deeper philosophical themes running through the novel, just as the reader on the online forum picked up on the type of cake that Settembrini and Naphta eat, unlocking a new perspective on the dynamic of their philosophical debate.

Settembrini would not approve of it. He addresses Hans again in 'The City of God': 'unterrichten Sie sich, aber produzieren Sie nicht' ('you may learn, but please do not perform') (p. 610/p. 479). This could be a tagline for Settembrini's model of cultural participation. If he does not find you clever enough, he will consign you to the role of a disengaged observer—which is paradoxical given his condemnation of passive behaviour elsewhere in the novel. But *The Magic Mountain* as a whole is all about feeling consigned to intellectual inferiority and passivity, and nevertheless trying to become intellectually independent and active, albeit with varying results. For one thing, this describes Hans Castorp's trajectory, and accounts for his joy and excitement at throwing in a word about hermetically sealed jars when Naphta discusses esoteric science. But the joy of participating in culture is also a driving force behind all the different types of encounters with *The Magic Mountain* discussed in this section. There is the 'Quellenforscher' who takes pleasure in identifying the source of a line in *The Magic Mountain* that has hitherto been considered obscure. There is the reader on an online forum who wrestles with the complexities of Mann's novel together with other readers. There is the writer who writes an essay about her encounter with Thomas Mann and his books. And there is me, tracing the reception of *The Magic Mountain* in all these fascinating texts and contexts, intrigued to see which other readers have responded to my favourite novel, and how, and why.

I have discussed many readers striving to become worthy of Mann's book, a process for which the very title of the novel provides the perfect metaphor: the metaphor of a mountain ascent. Many non-academic reviewers compare the process of reading *The Magic Mountain* to climbing up a high mountain.[72] It is such an apt metaphor because it captures both the effort that this book requires of its reader, and its self-stylization as the pinnacle of high culture. The title captures perfectly, to use Fredric Jameson's phrase, the 'mid-cult pride in getting through

---

[72] See, for example, [Anon.], 'Der Zauberberg (The Magic Mountain) by Thomas Mann (Review)', 1 August 2013 <https://tonysreadinglist.wordpress.com/2013/08/01/der-zauberberg-the-magic-mountain-by-thomas-mann-review> [accessed 15 March 2019].

long and difficult books'.[73] When the novel was first published in English, its American advertising tagline was short and pithy: 'it still towers.'[74] Presumably meaning that it towers intellectually over you, American reader. No wonder that Susan Sontag's predominant response upon encountering Thomas Mann was shame!

Jenny Erpenbeck, in her acceptance speech for the Thomas Mann Prize of the Hanseatic City of Lübeck and the Bavarian Academy of Fine Arts, reminisced about her early encounters with Mann's work. These were strikingly similar to other examples discussed here, even though she later developed a deep appreciation of his writing. Erpenbeck begins thus:

Nachdem ich als Halbwüchsige meinen Vater Jahr um Jahr gefragt hatte, ob ich denn nicht endlich einmal den *Zauberberg* lesen dürfe, mir mein Vater aber Jahr um Jahr zwar Adalbert Stifter oder Laurence Sterne zu lesen gab, bei dem Titel *Zauberberg* jedoch immer befand, das sei vielleicht doch noch 'zu schwer', gewann ich allmählich den Eindruck, es müsse sich hier um so etwas wie einen echten Zauberberg handeln, dessen Besteigung für eine Halbwüchsige zu anstrengend sei, oder um einen Sesam-öffne-dich, der sich nur der Erwachsenen auftun würde. Als ich das Buch dann endlich aufschlug, also in den vermeintlich schweren und ernsten Zauberberg eintrat, war ich zunächst verblüfft.

When I was a teenager, I would ask my father every year if I could finally read *The Magic Mountain*, but every year my father would give me something else to read instead, something by Adalbert Stifter or Laurence Sterne, because *The Magic Mountain* still seemed to him like it might be 'too difficult'. Eventually I got the impression that it must be a real magic mountain of some kind, too strenuous for a mere teenager to climb, or perhaps some sort of 'open sesame' that would reveal its secrets only to a grown woman. When I finally did open the book, setting foot for the first time in the world of that reputedly serious, difficult magic mountain, I was initially taken aback.[75]

Like Susan Sontag, Alice Munro, and Munro's heroine Vivien Hyde, Erpenbeck grounds the story of her encounter with *The Magic Mountain* in terms of her fascination, as a teenage girl, with the perceived difficulty and inaccessibility of the

[73] Fredric Jameson, *Modernist Papers* (London: Verso, 2007), p. 59.

[74] See Turner, *Marketing Modernism*, p. 107.

[75] Jenny Erpenbeck, 'Dankesrede zum Thomas-Mann-Preis der Hansestadt Lübeck und der Bayrischen Akademie der Schönen Künste', in *Kein Roman: Texte und Reden* (Munich: Penguin, 2018), pp. 274–81, pp. 274–75. Jenny Erpenbeck, '"Will I Come to a Miserable End?": Jenny Erpenbeck on Thomas Mann', trans. Kurt Beals, *Literary Hub*, 3 September 2020 <https://lithub.com/will-i-come-to-a-miserable-end-jenny-erpenbeck-on-thomas-mann/> [accessed 1 May 2021]. I am grateful to Yvette Siegert for drawing my attention to this quote.

book. In a recent collection, *The Critic as Amateur*, Tom Lutz muses: 'how much reading pleasure is like that, aspirational, aloft in the cloud of unknowing, full of the promise of some future self that might read a book like that and understand it [...] I loved thinking of myself as the kind of person who one day could really read the book I was reading.'[76]

Even academic readers sometimes chose to introduce *The Magic Mountain* to non-academic readers by falling back on the metaphor of a mountain ascent. Introducing Claire de Oliveira's new French translation of the novel in 2017, Jacques Le Rider wrote that 'depuis 1931, les lecteurs français faisaient l'ascension du roman dans la traduction de Maurice Betz' ('since 1931, French readers have been making the ascent of the novel in Maurice Betz's translation').[77] Writing about the circulation of Mann's books in China, Yi Zhang commented that *The Magic Mountain* 'bleibt ein Berg mit Zauberkraft, der sich hinter einem undurchdringlichen Nebel verbirgt und ständig eine große zauberhafte Anziehungskraft auf die LeserInnen ausübt und ihnen dennoch unnahbar bleibt' ('remains a mountain with a magical power, a mountain hidden behind impenetrable fog, forever exerting a great magical power of attraction on its readers, and yet remaining inaccessible to them').[78] In a chapter on *The Magic Mountain* in a volume on the landmarks of German literature, Ronald Speirs pointed out that 'the very title suggests [...] a mountain of numinous reputation that stands out from its surroundings, inspiring awe in passing travellers and inviting only the more intrepid to attempt its ascent and exploration', and asked rhetorically: 'how many students of German can have contemplated tackling this mountain of words without feeling that they might not be up to the challenge?'[79] Once again, Mann's *Magic Mountain* is presented as a towering achievement of European culture, an intimidating work of art that requires effort on the part of its reader, who might well prove unequal to the task, or at least feel that way. It is a familiar metaphor used to talk about other books too. When Anna Burns won the 2018 Man Booker Prize for Fiction for her novel *Milkman*, Kwame Anthony Appiah, chair of the judges, called the novel 'challenging [...] but in the way a walk up Snowdon is challenging. It is definitely worth it because the view is terrific when you get to the top'.[80]

[76] Lutz, 'In the Shadow of the Archive', p. 52.

[77] Jacques Le Rider, 'L'Europe malade au sanatorium', *En attendant Nadeau*, 14 March 2017 <https://www.en-attendant-nadeau.fr/2017/03/14/sanatorium-mann-oliveira> [accessed 15 March 2019].

[78] Yi Zhang, *Rezeptionsgeschichte der deutschsprachigen Literatur in China* (Bern: Peter Lang, 2007), p. 241.

[79] Ronald Speirs, 'Mann, *Der Zauberberg*', in *Landmarks in the German Novel (1)*, ed. Peter Hutchinson (Oxford: Peter Lang, 2007), pp. 117–34, p. 117.

[80] Quoted in Alison Flood, 'Booker Winner *Milkman* Defies "Challenging" Reputation to Become Bestseller', *The Guardian*, 23 October 2018 <https://www.theguardian.com/books/2018/oct/23/booker-winner-milkman-defies-challenging-bestseller-anna-burns> [accessed 1 May 2021]. I am indebted to Conor Brennan for this reference.

Yet Mann once remarked about the title of his novel, alluding to Wagner's *Tannhäuser und der Sängerkrieg auf Wartburg* (*Tannhäuser and the Minnesingers' Contest at Wartburg*) (1845), that 'es sich eigentlich um Eindringen *in* den Berg [handelt], nicht um eine Gipfel-Forcierung. Das Bild ist dem Tannhäuser oder dieser Sphäre entlehnt. Bergverzauberung. Es wird fast regelmäßig falsch gebraucht' ('it is actually about penetrating *into* the mountain, not forcibly reaching the summit. The image is taken from Tannhäuser or that sphere. Mountain enchantment. It is almost always used incorrectly').[81] This is an interesting dichotomy: 'Eindringung' and 'Verzauberung' point towards the metaphors of immersion and enchantment, like the willing captivity of the Minnesänger Tannhäuser in the 'Venusberg'—the love goddess's grotto; 'Gipfel-Forcierung', on the other hand, implies an intellectual challenge and the critical reflection that is made possible by the view from the top. *The Magic Mountain* furnishes its readers with a metaphor for both the allure and the difficulty of immersion. Climbing a high mountain is going to take a lot of effort—but the magic will be worth it. As I have shown in Chapter 1, Mann was deeply invested in this productive friction between accessibility and exclusivity. But while many non-academic readers embrace this tension, academic readers necessarily find it difficult to navigate: in a true Catch-22 situation, as an academic reader you cannot really admit that you find the novel challenging, since your professional expertise must ensure that you do not; but the novel is designed in such a way that it can only take full effect if the reader succumbs to its difficulty.

There is a moment in George Eliot's *Middlemarch* (1872) when, on her disastrous honeymoon in Rome, Dorothea talks to Ladislaw about her difficulties enjoying art:

> There are comparatively few paintings that I can really enjoy. At first when I enter a room where the walls are covered with frescos, or with rare pictures, I feel a kind of awe—like a child present at great ceremonies where there are grand robes and processions; I feel myself in the presence of some higher life than my own. But when I begin to examine the pictures one by one the life goes out of them, or else is something violent and strange to me. It must be my own dullness. I am seeing so much all at once, and not understanding half of it. That always makes one feel stupid. It is painful to be told that anything is very fine and not be able to feel that it is fine [...].[82]

Dorothea has been trained to feel intimidated by art ('a kind of awe', 'some higher life than my own'), immature ('like a child'), naïve ('stupid'), and incapable of

---

[81] Mann, *Selbstkommentare*, p. 53.
[82] George Eliot, *Middlemarch* (London: Penguin, 2012), pp. 223–24.

properly appreciating it ('it must be my own dullness', 'not understanding half of it'), much like Selin in Elif Batuman's *The Idiot* was made to feel in a seminar on Russian literature. But Ladislaw tries to comfort her:

> Oh, there is a great deal in the feeling for art which must be acquired [...] Art is an old language with a great many artificial affected styles, and sometimes the chief pleasure one gets out of knowing them is the mere sense of knowing. I enjoy the art of all sorts here immensely; but I suppose if I could pick my enjoyment to pieces I should find it made up of many different threads.[83]

Chiefly by virtue of being an educated man, Ladislaw feels much more at ease in the highly regulated world of assorted cultural pleasures. Not quite self-aware enough to be able to reflect on his and Dorothea's respective positions within the cultural system, he nevertheless grasps the fact that what often goes by the name of critical reflection is itself a type of cultural pleasure, a state of pleasant knowingness.

Ladislaw understands that engagement in critical practice—staged by Settembrini and Naphta in *The Magic Mountain*—is not at all dissimilar from other types of engagement with art. 'To detect and savor' allusions to and quotes from Goethe or Nietzsche in Mann's novel 'is the delight of the scholar and educated reader', writes Theodore Ziolkowski; 'but structurally these elements are irrelevant', he adds, not least 'because many of them are cryptic and intended only as tidbits for a few readers'.[84] Mann also 'kept faith with a kind of cultural pleasure that is unmodernist': traditional, expansive storytelling, which was rapidly becoming unfashionable in the first half of the twentieth century.[85] There are many distinct types of pleasure in encountering art, but some are coded as more exclusive or prestigious than others. As I argue throughout this study, the fraught experience of the limits of cultural membership haunts readers' encounters with Mann's novel—and with culture more generally. A closer reading of *The Magic Mountain* in the spirit of world literature can sensitize us to this dimension of the text.

2. Hans Castorp in Danzig

In Section 1, I discussed various readers who struggled with *The Magic Mountain* because of their deeply ingrained assumptions about how one should approach a

---

[83]   Ibid., p. 224.

[84]   Theodore Ziolkowski, *Dimensions of the Modern Novel: German Texts and European Contexts* (Princeton, NJ: Princeton University Press, 1969), pp. 72–73.

[85]   Michael Minden, 'Popularity and the Magic Circle of Culture', *Publications of the English Goethe Society*, 76.2 (2007), 93–101, p. 93.

work like this—armed with critical knowledge rather than immersing oneself in the narrative with abandon. I also showed how some non-academic readers managed to surpass their perceived limitations by diving into the text, then emerging from it having reached a reflective outlook on it in the process. Hans Castorp himself follows a similar trajectory, from contemplating the enormous confusion of everything—he 'grub gesenkten Hauptes mit dem Stocke im Schnee und bedachte die große Konfusion' ('probed the snow with his cane, hung his head, and pondered the great confusion') (p. 705/p. 554)—to plunging himself into an 'ocean of unfamiliar words' and discovering that 'Hermetik' is 'ein Zauberwort mit weitläufigen Assoziationen' ('a magic word with vague, vast associations'). In the present section as well as in Section 3, I discuss a novel and a film that feature Hans Castorp as a character who approaches culture in similar ways—reaching critical reflection through, and not despite or instead of, emotional engagement with it—in the belief that attending to fictional readers can inform our real-life encounters with cultural texts.

These two case studies take me back to the very beginning of this project. I first had the idea for this book when, in the span of a few weeks, I encountered Hans Castorp in two unexpected contexts. Towards the end of the summer vacation before the final year of my undergraduate degree, which I spent with my family in Poland, I was browsing through books in a local library and stumbled across a recent novel by Paweł Huelle, one of the most celebrated contemporary Polish writers. But it was not Huelle's name that captured my attention: it was a different name, the name that constituted the book's title—*Castorp*. Intrigued and impatient, I tore open the book and started reading. It turned out that Huelle had derived an entire novel from a single half-sentence in *The Magic Mountain*, one that most readers are likely to skim over: Hans Castorp 'hatte [. . .] vier Semester Studienzeit am Danziger Polytechnikum hinter sich' ('had four semesters of study at Danzig Polytechnic behind him') (p. 59/p. 41). The Polish author took it upon himself to tell the story of Hans Castorp's time in the Free City of Danzig, nowadays Gdańsk in Poland—Huelle's hometown. With vivid impressions of Castorp taking up his studies in turn-of-the-century Danzig still lingering at the back of my mind, I returned to Oxford.

In the first week of term, my college's film society hosted a screening of *The Wind Rises*, an animated film by Hayao Miyazaki, the great Japanese master of the genre. Looking up the film, which had recently been released to great critical acclaim, I discovered that it was about the Japanese engineer who invented the aircraft used by Japan during the Second World War. It sounded rather improbable as a topic for a film by Miyazaki. (His most famous work, *Spirited Away*, is about a girl whose parents turn into pigs, so she has to go to work in a dystopian bathhouse, where she strikes up an unlikely friendship with a customer called No-Face.) Still, I decided to go see *The Wind Rises*, and am glad I did: halfway through the film, to my utter astonishment, the engineer meets Hans Castorp in a Japanese mountain resort. The two have a conversation about the murky relationship between technological progress and the escalation of violence and, implicitly, about a particularly fatal time in the history of German-Japanese relations, which would culminate in their alliance during the Second World War.

So there I had it: a prequel and a sequel to Mann's book, a Polish novel and a Japanese anime, created by two critically acclaimed artists, paying special attention to Hans's engineering education, and negotiating the troubled and unequal relationship between Polish and Japanese cultures, respectively, and the overshadowing spectre of German economic and cultural influence. On Christmas Eve 1924—roughly a month after the publication of *The Magic Mountain*—Thomas Mann commented in a letter to Hedwig Buller, his family doctor's daughter, on the fact that the novel was now in circulation, in the hands of readers unknown to him: 'Hans Castorp findet Freunde in der Welt' ('Hans Castorp is finding friends in the world').[86] Nearly a century later, Hans's circle of friends includes not just Thomas Mann's readers, but also other fictional characters whom he happens to meet, be it in Eastern Europe or East Asia. Another striking similarity between *Castorp* and *The Wind Rises* is that they both confront head-on the reverence with which critics tend to talk about the originality and uniqueness of canonical culture and pit it against the immense creative potential of imitation, copying, and repetition. Crucially for my argument, the activity of reading and, more broadly, encountering culture is presented in both these texts as hinging on immersive repetition in a specific context—something that they have in common with *The Magic Mountain* itself. All three works portray Hans Castorp as a reader of sorts, an active participant in culture, broadly defined. In what follows, I will focus on two such scenes of reading or reception: in *Castorp*, Hans's rereading of *Effi Briest* in Danzig, and in *The Wind Rises*, Hans's performance of 'Das gibt's nur einmal' ('This Only Happens Once'), a perversely titled, highly repetitive and repeatable German hit from the early 1930s.

Paweł Huelle (b. 1957) is one of the most critically acclaimed contemporary Polish writers. His novels and short stories—starting with his celebrated debut *Weiser Dawidek* (*Who Was David Weiser?*) in 1987—have been awarded or shortlisted for all the most important Polish literary prizes and translated into several languages. All his novels are set in his hometown Gdańsk. Due to its attractive location on the Baltic coast at the mouth of a large river, by the Middle Ages Gdańsk was a rich Hanseatic port city. Over the centuries it was ruled by Poland, Prussia, and later Germany (in which time it was known as Danzig), interspersed with brief periods of autonomy as a Free City. Huelle's prose explores Gdańsk's/Danzig's mixed heritage as a centuries-old melting pot of Polish, German, Jewish, and Kashub cultures.

---

[86] Mann, *Selbstkommentare*, p. 49.

Originally published in 2004 and soon translated into German (Renate Schmidgall, 2005) and English (Antonia Lloyd-Jones, 2007), *Castorp* clearly resonates with Huelle's interests. In the act of filling in a blank in Hans Castorp's biography, Huelle explores Mann's underlying cultural assumptions about Eastern Europe, shaped by Germany's imperial ambitions. *Castorp* is written in elegant imitation of Mann's prose—as it is known to Polish readers from Józef Kramsztyk's and Władysław Tatarkiewicz's only Polish translation of *The Magic Mountain* from 1930—in a move that both celebrates Mann's literary legacy and subverts stereotypes about the inferiority of Slavic cultures that was widespread in Germany in Mann's time. While most reviewers and critics of Huelle's novel, whether writing in Polish, German, or English, view it through the lens of postcolonial critique,[87] my reading will focus on Hans Castorp's emotionally engaged reading experience and the cultural encounters through which he reaches an understanding of German imperialism.

In other words, I will argue that what is really interesting about *Castorp* is not just that it unmasks prejudices in German attitudes towards Eastern Europe, or that it is related to the widely discussed phenomenon of 'the Empire writing back' (former colonial states subverting the colonizing nations' cultural heritage and exposing the inherent racism and xenophobia); in short, the novel's appeal is not exhausted in the critical reflection Hans develops in the course of it, and which it might inspire in its readers. Instead, my reading of *Castorp* focuses on its depiction of the process of reaching critical reflection not as *opposed* to pleasure, or aiming at the *destruction* of pleasure (as in Mulvey's argument about film), but in fact being achieved *through* pleasure. In *Castorp*, Huelle manages to preserve his admiration for Mann's novel *and* move beyond its ideology. He achieves this feat precisely because he is so immersed in the cadences of *The Magic Mountain* and its story-world, and he portrays a similar process; Hans did not reach any critical insight about Germany's presence in Eastern Europe when he first tried to read *Effi Briest*, without enjoyment, but only upon his second, more pleasurable reading. His second encounter with Fontane's novel is conditioned by the entire problematic historical context of which he will ultimately become more critical.

The theme of repetition is explicitly signalled in the epigraph to Huelle's novel, a quote from Søren Kierkegaard's 1843 work *Gentagelsen* (*Repetition*): 'właśnie dlatego że było, powtórzenie staje się nowością'—in Antonia Lloyd-Jones's translation, 'just by happening, a repetition becomes a novelty'. The translation from Kierkegaard's collected works in English reads: 'the very fact that it has been makes repetition into something new'.[88] This enigmatic statement sets the tone for

---

[87] See especially Dariusz Skórczewski, 'Dlaczego Paweł Huelle napisał *Castorpa*?', *Teksty Drugie*, 3 (2006), 148–57, and Ania Spyra, 'Between Theory and Reality: Cosmopolitanism of Nodal Cities in Paweł Huelle's *Castorp*', *Comparative Literature*, 64.3 (2012), 286–99.

[88] Søren Kierkegaard, *Fear and Trembling/Repetition*, trans. Edna H. Hong and Howard V. Hong (Princeton, NJ: Princeton University Press, 1983), p. 149.

the entire novel: Huelle guides the reader into the text by suggesting that every-thing in it is a repetition—of the characters and events in Mann's novel, presumably—but also claiming novelty for his repetitions. The added twist is that, since *Castorp* is a prequel to *The Magic Mountain*, seen purely chronologic-ally, it is the latter that repeats the former. So whenever Huelle describes a certain habit, character, conversation, or situation that reminds the reader of a similar occurrence in Mann's novel, the Polish writer is in fact recording its *first* occur-rence in Hans Castorp's fictional life.

The paradoxical, mysterious novelty of repetition in the encounter with the literary canon is not just a meta-fictional device in Huelle's novel: it is also thematized in its plot when Hans Castorp rereads Theodor Fontane's *Effi Briest* (1895), a landmark of nineteenth-century German realism, in Danzig. (In her short discussion of Huelle and Fontane, Sandra Richter calls this episode a 'sensation', seeing how 'scant' international reception of *Effi Briest* has been.[89]) Halfway through the novel, young Castorp falls in love with Wanda Pilecka, a mysterious woman from Eastern Europe—he first assumes her to be Russian, but she is later revealed to be Polish—whom he observes only from afar. Parallels to Clawdia Chauchat are obvious. In an irrational attempt to get closer to Pilecka, Castorp intercepts a mysterious package from her lover, a Russian officer. The package turns out to contain a copy of *Effi Briest*, and Hans Castorp reacts as follows:

> Bardzo się zdziwił. Gdzieś, podświadomie, podnosząc książkę do kręgu nocnej lampki, liczył bowiem, że będzie to coś egzotycznego, co najmniej z cyrylicą na okładce, jak tajemnicza i niedostępna księga z magicznego Wschodu, tymczasem trzymał w dłoniach wydaną po niemiecku *Effi Briest* Theodora Fontane, powieść, z którą zawarł już swego czasu powierzchowną i niezbyt miłą znajomość. Było to w ostatniej, maturalnej klasie, gdy zaziębiony musiał spędzić kilka dni w łóżku. Szukając czegoś do czytania w bibliotece wuja Tienappela trafił na egzemplarz tej właśnie historii. Nudził go opis dworu w Hohen-Cremmen i ekspozycja bohaterów, z którymi nie czuł nic wspólnego. Jego własne życie, wzrastające w cieniu portowych dźwigów i oceanicznych statków, giełdy, światowych interesów i kolonialnych towarów, nagle wydało mu się pełne blasku w porównaniu z koleinami piaszczystej drogi na Pomorzu czy niedzielnym kazaniem wiejskiego pastora. Odłożył wówczas powieść dokładnie na opisie weselnego przyjęcia u państwa von Briest i nie wrócił do niej więcej, pewien, że niewiele stracił. Jednakże teraz sprawy przedstawiały się inaczej.   (p. 118)

---

[89] Sandra Richter, *Eine Weltgeschichte der deutschsprachigen Literatur* (Munich: Bertelsmann, 2017), p. 247. In German literature, the reception of *Effi Briest* has been incomparably more robust. For example, Günter Grass uses Fontane's novel as a subject of reflection and re-reading in *Ein weites Feld* (1995) in ways not dissimilar to Huelle. I am grateful to an anonymous reviewer of the manuscript for this observation.

He was very surprised. As he raised the book into the circle of light cast by his bedside lamp, somewhere, subconsciously, he was counting on it being something exotic, at least with Cyrillic lettering on the cover, like a mysterious, inaccessible tome from the magical East, but in fact he was holding a German edition of Theodor Fontane's *Effi Briest*, a novel with which he had already struck up a superficial, not too fond acquaintance in the past. It was in his final, graduation year at school, when he had a cold and was obliged to spend a few days in bed. Looking for something to read in his Uncle Tienappel's library, he had come across a copy of this very story. He had found the description of the manor house at Hohen-Cremmen boring, and felt he had nothing in common with the characters depicted. His own life, growing in the shadow of harbour cranes and ocean-going ships, the stock exchange, world business and colonial goods, suddenly seemed to him a blaze of light in comparison with the ruts in a sandy road in Pomerania, or the Sunday sermon of a country pastor. At the time he had put the novel down when he reached the account of the wedding reception at the von Briest family home and had not gone back to it, convinced he was not losing much. But now everything looked different.   (pp. 127–28)

As the description of Hans Castorp's second encounter with *Effi Briest* goes on, we learn that this repeated reading of the novel turns out to be much more fruitful than the first one. Hans imagines that the novel holds a secret key to the life of the beautiful unknown woman he has fallen for; to uncover it, he 'poddaj[e] się niemal hipnotycznie sugestii pisarza' ('surrender[s] almost hypnotically to the author's suggestions'); 'nigdy jeszcze nie czytał żadnej książki w taki sposób' ('he had never read any book this way before') (pp. 119–20/p. 129). Castorp reads the entire novel in one night, drinking burgundy and smoking his favourite Maria Mancini cigars in bed, and its plot and composition appear crystal-clear, logical, and inevitable to him. He is highly receptive to Fontane's vision.

What makes him so receptive to it? There are three factors at play. First, it is his attraction to Wanda Pilecka and the feeling that reading the novel might bring him closer to her. Second, it is his stay in the provinces on the Baltic coast, alone and isolated, that makes him more amenable to Effi's struggle. He is now well positioned to respond to the performance of boredom in Fontane's novel, to use Brian Tucker's phrase.[90] Third, it is the thrill of exoticism. *Effi Briest* is largely set in the fictional coastal town of Kessin, partly modelled on Swinemünde—or Świnoujście, since it is now a Polish city located exactly on the border with Germany. Like real-life Swinemünde/Świnoujście, Fontane's Kessin is a borderline space, controlled by Prussia, but far removed from the urban centre of Berlin and marked by the unsettling presence of Slavs. The allure of the East that, much to

[90] Brian Tucker, 'Performing Boredom in *Effi Briest*: On the Effects of Narrative Speed', *The German Quarterly*, 80.2 (2007), 185–200.

Settembrini's alarm, ensnares Castorp in Davos is already present in Danzig. To understand the attitude of Huelle's Hans towards Eastern Europe, it is first necessary to consider the attitudes towards it of those around him.

The novel begins with a conversation in which Hans's uncle warns Hans about the dangerous chaos and wilderness of the East. Hans responds that Eastern Europe is not an uncharted territory: 'białe plamy dawno już zniknęły z naszych map' ('the blank spaces have long since disappeared from our maps') (p. 10/p. 5). He ostensibly defends Eastern Europe from his uncle's orientalizing narrative, but in fact he confirms it, merely valorizing it as something positive rather than negative. Hans's comment about 'our' maps subtly channels Germany's imperial ambitions in Eastern Europe. Paul Langhans's *Deutscher Kolonial-Atlas* ('German Colonial Atlas') from 1893 included maps of 'broad expanses of territory in Eastern and Southeastern Europe', especially Poland, 'in addition to the maps of German colonial "protectorates" in Africa and the Pacific'.[91] At the turn of the twentieth century, Poland was fully partitioned—a space forcibly erased from the map of Europe since the end of the eighteenth century by Prussian, Austria-Hungarian, and Russian troops. *Effi Briest* is read by Kristin Kopp as a novel of 'inner colonialism' that juxtaposes oriental fantasies of German overseas expansion (encapsulated in the memorable figure of the Chinese ghost) with the very tangible reality of Prussian control over huge swathes of Eastern Europe. When Major von Crampas—a half-Pole—seduces Effi, he threatens the stability of the Prussian social and cultural system in ways that Kopp persuasively links to the German fear of a 'Slavic flood' and 'reverse diffusion' of Prussian colonization.[92]

Hans is soon confronted with a similar interpretation of German imperialism in a conversation with Kiekiernix—a Dutch colonialist who clearly anticipates Peeperkorn in *The Magic Mountain*—and Pastor Gropius. The latter describes German imperialism in Europe in approving tones:

spóźniliśmy się w Azji i Afryce, prawda. Ale na wschodzie Europy? Od setek lat niesiemy prawo, ład, harmonię sztuki i technikę. Gdyby nie my, Słowianie dawno popadliby w anarchię. To dzięki naszym dobrodziejstwom znajdują swoje miejsce w rodzinie, której na imię cywilizacja i kultura.   (p. 23)

we have been late in reaching Asia and Africa, indeed. But in the east of Europe? For hundreds of years we have brought law, order, the harmony of art and technology. If not for us, the Slavs would long since have fallen into anarchy. It is thanks to our benefaction that they have found their place in the family that bears the name of civilization and culture.   (p. 20)

---

[91] Kristin Kopp, *Germany's Wild East: Constructing Poland as Colonial Space* (Ann Arbor, MI: University of Michigan Press, 2012), pp. 1–2.

[92] Ibid., pp. 96–123.

This narrative is entirely consistent with the history classes at Hans's 'Gymnasium': 'anarchia i pijaństwo szlachty doprowadziły do rozbiorów, bo wrzód ten, w środku Europy, trzeba było czym prędzej wyciąć ze względów higienicznych' ('the anarchy and drunkenness of the nobility had led to the partitions, because that cancer in the middle of Europe had to be cut out as soon as possible for reasons of hygiene') (p. 194/p. 211). Even though Hans Castorp, unlike most other German characters in Huelle's novel, is not openly prejudiced against Poles or Russians—he is not like the German man who advises his friend not to hire any Poles because they are dangerous, or the German clerk who bullies a Polish clerk and ultimately drives him to suicide—the exoticizing lens through which he views Eastern Europe is also an insidious form of prejudice. Perceiving Eastern Europe as an exotic and alluring space means recasting the old prejudice against it in a way that absolves the Westerner of moral guilt and assuages his fear of the East.

The illusion of cultural alienation vis-à-vis the 'White Other' of Eastern Europe is symbolically captured in a scene towards the beginning of the novel, when Hans—on the steamship to Danzig—sees from a distance an intimidating Russian battleship whose name seems utterly unfamiliar to him:

pierwszy [...] raz w życiu Hans Castorp nie potrafił odczytać wyrazu, który zapisała ręka współczesnego człowieka. Forma liter, całkowicie obca, nie składała się na żaden znajomy bądź domniemany sens. 'ABPOPA'—brzmiało to na tyle absurdalnie i wesoło, że obserwator zadowolił się przypuszczeniem, iż musi to być imię jakiegoś rosyjskiego bohatera, który ocalił zapewne przed wiekami swój kraj od mongolskiego lub też chińskiego najazdu.   (p. 29)

it was [...] the first time Hans Castorp had ever been unable to decipher a word written by the hand of modern man. Completely foreign to him, the combination of letters did not form any familiar or putative sense. 'ABPOPA'—it sounded so absurd and comical that the observer settled for the conjecture that it must be the name of some Russian hero who had undoubtedly saved his country from a Mongol or Chinese invasion centuries ago.   (p. 27)

Hans fails to realize that the name of the ship, transcribed into the Latin alphabet, reads 'Avrora', that is 'Aurora'—the Roman goddess of dawn. The name of the Russian battleship—which in 1917 would fire the first shot to unleash the attack on the Winter Palace at the beginning of the October Revolution—refers to the shared European heritage of Graeco-Roman mythology rather than an imagined heroic clash on the battlefields of Central Asia. To Hans, the Cyrillic alphabet connotes otherness, difference, and exoticism. Finding *Effi Briest* in Pilecka's package initially disappoints him, since he yearns for a 'mysterious, inaccessible tome from the magical East' written in Cyrillic; and yet, ironically, it was *Effi Briest* that resisted Hans's penetration upon the first reading—he did not find it accessible or relatable. It is only upon a second reading that it becomes meaningful to him. Similarity and otherness, accessibility and alienation, engagement and boredom are not binaries: in Hans Castorp's readerly encounters with *Effi Briest*, both are at play.

The thrill of exoticism that tinges Hans Castorp's encounters with German culture in Danzig allows him to reinterpret his own national culture—not just Fontane, but also Franz Schubert and Arthur Schopenhauer, who was born in Danzig. Mediated through Castorp's new surroundings, Schopenhauer's philosophy takes on a new meaning. Castorp perceives parallels between the death of Schopenhauer's father and his own father. This repetition of fate feels comforting; Hans starts going on long walks around Danzig, looking for different places where Schopenhauer's family used to live, such as the philosopher's birthplace and his grandfather's house: 'wszędzie znajdował student nasz ową przedziwną nitkę czasu, w istocie niewidzialną [. . .] która łączyła go z gorzkim, ale wyzwalającym przesłaniem Artura Filozofa' ('everywhere our student found the uncanny thread of time that although invisible [. . .] linked him with the bitter, but liberating message of Arthur the Philosopher') (p. 224/p. 210). Similarly, as Hans falls asleep at the end of his first day in Danzig (which takes up a third of the novel; later time seems to speed up, just like in *The Magic Mountain*), he hears '[kogoś grającego] impromptu Schuberta. Łagodne, melancholijne dźwięki, które Castorp pamiętał z wczesnego dzieciństwa, teraz wydały mu się szczególnie piękną kompozycją' ('someone [. . .] playing a Schubert Impromptu. The gentle, melancholy tune that Castorp remembered from early childhood, now seemed to him an especially beautiful piece') (p. 78/pp. 81–82). These repeated encounters with canonical German culture 'out of context' become unexpectedly evocative for Hans, and this prompts him to consider the cultural, contextual conditions of immersion.

Studies of readerly immersion are usually conducted using very short passages—in the most advanced studies, it might be a chapter of a novel or a short story—and readers' brain activity, eye movements, or self-reported impressions during or after reading are studied.[93] Some effort is made to differentiate between the responses of individual readers. But the implicit assumption is that the level of absorption in a text relies on the features of the text, or the traits of the reader, or can be plotted as a combination of both. Meanwhile, our everyday experience of reading suggests that literary immersion cannot be predicted like this. A book read at one point in my life can disappoint or enthrall me at another; some days, I get easily engrossed in the same book that I cannot focus on at other

---

[93] See, for example, Frank Hakemulder and others, eds., *Narrative Absorption* (Amsterdam: John Benjamins, 2017) and Natalie M. Phillips, 'Literary Neuroscience and History of Mind: An Interdisciplinary fMRI Study of Attention and Jane Austen', in *The Oxford Handbook of Cognitive Literary Studies*, ed. Lisa Zunshine (Oxford: Oxford University Press, 2015), pp. 55–81.

times. It is one experience to read a book as a set text with a strict deadline and quite another to read it at leisure over the summer. I read differently at a desk in a library; in bed at home; at the recommendation of somebody who means a lot to me; forced by a professor I do not like; having just experienced a terrible loss; at the end of a good day; when I am sick and tired; when I am well rested and comfortable; in an fMRI scanner; in a soft armchair. The context matters. Hans reads *Effi Briest* differently in Hamburg and in Danzig, at home and away from home, as a sick schoolboy and as an infatuated student.

Responding to Rita Felski's work, Stephen Best argued that 'literary criticism thrives on the distinction between first and second reading, on what is often parsed as absorptive reading versus critical reading, belletristic versus analytic reading'.[94] But *The Magic Mountain* and its reception history disturb this neat temporality of the first absorptive reading and the second reading that enables critical reflection. Readers on the Goodreads forum were revisiting Mann's novel to derive more pleasure from it, to immerse themselves in it more fully. In *Castorp*, it is Hans's second reading of *Effi Briest* that becomes both more engaged and more critical—more fruitful on all counts. In *The Wind Rises*, the repetitive song about the uniqueness of immersion is sung by Hans who has just been revealed to the spectators as a keen political observer. In *Castorp*, emotional engagement is the path to critique. Culture—and especially 'highbrow', canonical culture—is predicated on anxiety about its (in)accessibility: confronted with cultural tradition, we anxiously examine how absorbed we feel by it, how much at home, how familiar, how comfortable. It is when culture makes you aware of its conditions of entry, conditions of absorption, that you become critical.

3. Hans Castorp in Japan

Hayao Miyazaki (b. 1941) is a cult manga artist, animator, and director who has almost single-handedly brought anime to the attention of Western film critics. His works have always enjoyed great success in Japan and across East Asia, both commercially and critically; his career in the West took off with his film *Spirited Away* (2001), which won the Oscar for Best Animated Feature. *Kaze tachinu* (*The Wind Rises*), his most recent film, was released in 2013, garnered critical acclaim around the world, won several important prizes, and was also commercially successful. The film is a heavily fictionalized biopic of Jiro Horikoshi, a Japanese engineer who invented the famous Mitsubishi Zero fighters flown in attacks on Pearl Harbor and on kamikaze missions. *The Wind Rises* is set in Japan and Germany during the decade leading up to the Second World War: we witness Horikoshi's dreams of designing beautiful, slender, technologically advanced

---

[94] Stephen Best, '*La Foi Postcritique*, on Second Thought', *PMLA*, 132.2 (2017), 337–43, p. 337.

passenger planes, his struggle to make this dream come true using old-fashioned Japanese technologies and materials, the growing militarization of the Japanese aircraft industry, Jiro's training in the Junkers aircraft factories in Nazi Germany, and his ultimate professional success—the development of a staggering feat of aerial technology, the Zero fighter aircraft, which was the most powerful and advanced in the world at the beginning of the war.

All this is set against the backdrop of Jiro's personal life, in particular his courtship of and marriage with a young Japanese woman suffering from tuberculosis and confined to mountain hotels and sanatoria, where Jiro accompanies her. A train journey across a mountainous landscape; a comfortable hotel in an alpine-style building, with 'Fachwerk' or timber framing decorating the façade; and obligatory balconies in every room—the surroundings set the stage for the entrance of a character straight out of Mann's *Magic Mountain*. Indeed, a little over an hour into the film, Jiro steps onto the hotel terrace and meets none other than Hans Castorp. The two smoke together on the terrace, in an episode that alludes to Hans's predilection for Maria Mancini cigars in Mann's novel. The German man has not yet been identified by name—only much later in the film is he referred to as 'Mr Castorp'. But a viewer familiar with Mann's book will identify him as such through his explicit reference to *The Magic Mountain*—he compares the Japanese hotel to the setting of the novel. The sentence 'hier ist der Zauberberg' ('here is the Magic Mountain') is, strikingly, uttered in German both in the Japanese and the English-language version of the film. In the English version, the character also has a distinctly German accent (the voice is dubbed by Werner Herzog). The scene ends with the first indication that Jiro's love interest suffers from tuberculosis, strengthening the intertextual link with *The Magic Mountain*.

Viewers familiar with Mann's novel are led to surmise that Hans Castorp survived the First World War, went on to become a pacifist and anti-fascist, escaped Nazi Germany, and ended up in a tuberculosis sanatorium in the Japanese mountains. He comments on the rising political tensions in Japan and Germany, and so becomes the only character in the film to explicitly warn about and condemn the impending war—and as a result is later chased by the Japanese thought police. Castorp explicitly compares the Japanese hotel to a 'magic mountain' and calls it 'a good place for forgetting', but then goes on to list all the recent political events that a Japanese engineer like Jiro might wish to forget: the conflict with China, which was escalating throughout the 1930s, the invasion of Manchuria in 1931, and Japan's withdrawal from the League of Nations in 1933. Castorp makes it clear that both Japan and Germany will soon go to war unless they are stopped.[95]

---

[95] On the history of German-Japanese relations at that time, see Ricky W. Law, *Transnational Nazism: Ideology and Culture in German-Japanese Relations, 1919–1936* (Cambridge: Cambridge University Press, 2019).

Hans thus becomes a mouthpiece for a pacifist political message that was hotly debated in Japan upon the release of the film. Right-wing commentators claimed that the film is anti-patriotic because it emphasizes the futility of war, while some left-wing reviewers argued that the film glorifies militarism and the arms trade and creates an apologetic vision of Japan's involvement in the Second World War.[96] Miyazaki has always been fascinated by warplanes and flying more generally, as all of his films demonstrate; his family owned a factory that produced parts for the Zero fighter planes during the war. The director chose to defend Jiro's idealism and ambitions as an engineer, setting them apart from the war effort and big politics, which some reviewers found troublesome. At the same time, however, Miyazaki wrote an essay published to coincide with the film's release, in which he harshly criticized the Japanese government's plans to amend Article 9 of the Japanese Constitution, which states that armed forces with war potential will not be maintained. That clause was added to the Constitution during the Allied occupation of Japan after the Second World War. Shinzo Abe, Japan's prime minister in 2013, wanted to change it so that Japan could grow its Self-Defence Forces into a proper army. (The issue remained unresolved at the time of Abe's retirement in 2020.) Miyazaki's outright critique of the government and his more ambiguous portrayal of civilian war responsibility in *The Wind Rises* fell on fertile ground: the film became Japan's highest-grossing release of 2013 and sparked debates about the militarization of the country, and about the politics of memory.

The Magic Mountain is introduced into the film's texture as a model of thinking about the genesis of war. But *The Wind Rises* also has the potential to retrospectively influence our understanding of Mann's novel. Jiro is the kind of passionate engineer that Castorp never was—but that Settembrini wanted him to be, always extolling the virtues of Hans's profession and relentlessly encouraging him to leave the 'Magic Mountain' and take up his engineering job in the service of 'die völkerverbindende Verkehrstechnik' ('transportation technology, which brought nations closer together') (p. 248/p. 192). 'Technik und Sittlichkeit' ('technology and morality') go hand in hand, says Settembrini (p. 238/p. 184). And yet, Miyazaki reminds us, it is far from obvious that technology is neutral, let alone that it inevitably leads to social progress, as Settembrini claims. If Hans had taken up his job as a marine engineer, he would likely have ended up building war ships: as I discussed in Chapter 1, Hans arrives in Davos with an English textbook on ocean steamships, which associates him with the naval race between Britain and

[96] See Daisuke Akimoto, 'War Memory, War Responsibility, and Anti-war Pacifism in Director Miyazaki's *The Wind Rises (Kaze Tachinu)*', *Soka University Peace Research*, 28 (2014), 45–72; Deborah Breen, 'Designs and Dreams: Questions of Technology in Hayao Miyazaki's *The Wind Rises*', *Technology and Culture*, 57.2 (2016), 457–59; and Alistair Swale, 'Memory and Forgetting: Examining the Treatment of Traumatic Historical Memory in *Grave of the Fireflies* and *The Wind Rises*', *Japan Forum*, 29.4 (2017), 518–36.

Germany in the run-up to the First World War. Miyazaki's Castorp is not only wiser than Mann's Castorp, he is wiser than Mann's Settembrini.

Miyazaki shows that the intricate interweaving of technology and politics is a repetitive pattern. In Mann's novel, Germans learn from and compete with the British; in Miyazaki's film, the Japanese learn from and compete with Germans. A less generous way of approaching this issue is to call the Japanese 'copycats', as the German engineers in the Junkers factory do, in accordance with European intellectuals' centuries-long stereotypical perception of Japanese culture. Michael Lucken's recent book *Imitation and Creativity in Japanese Arts* discusses 'a substantial body of work in English, French, and German that depicts Japanese culture as one based on copying'[97] and demonstrates that this view is an eighteenth-century colonial construct—despite the fact that, in Ika Willis's words, 'the idea that imitation can be creative has a very long history, and was in fact dominant in Western literature before the advent of the Romantic concept of genius'.[98] Commenting on Lucken's argument, Brenda Jordan pointed out: 'the aesthetics of Romanticism eventually led to the characterization of all forms of borrowing as degenerate and contemptible, thereby forgetting (or not realizing to begin with) the crucial role that dissemination of ideas and technologies has in the development of virtually all cultures around the world'.[99]

European modernism inherited the Romantic cult of originality. As Jacob Edmond has recently argued, 'modernism has been told as the story of novelty, strangeness, and singular genius', as captured by Ezra Pound's slogan 'make it new'. But in fact, Edmond argues, '"make it same" might equally serve as the catchphrase of modernism', given that it 'emerged out of a vast increase in copying, to which it responded through repetition, appropriation, and remixing', ranging from Picasso's aesthetics of montage to Joyce's techniques of pastiche, and beyond.[100] Art predicated on the notion of copying serves to 'foreground the technologies of reproduction and the forces of globalism and commodity capital-ism that shape modernity'.[101]

The Wind Rises embodies this double-edged nature of the copy. Jiro internalizes the view that Japan is a nation of 'copycats' to a great extent. But faced with the Germans' hostility, he responds that the two countries have made an agreement, so he and his colleagues have the right to see the German planes up close. Tensions surrounding the issue of imitation and its legitimacy and effectiveness become one of the main topics of the film. Various forms of copying are

[97] Michael Lucken, *Imitation and Creativity in Japanese Arts: From Kishida Ryusei to Miyazaki Hayao*, trans. Francesca Simkin (New York: Columbia University Press, 2016), p. 9.

[98] Ika Willis, *Reception* (Abingdon: Routledge, 2018), p. 42.

[99] Brenda G. Jordan, 'Michael Lucken, *Imitation and Creativity in Japanese Arts: From Kishida Ryūsei to Miyazaki Hayao*', *Japanese Studies*, 37.2 (2017), 272–74, p. 273.

[100] Jacob Edmond, 'Copy', in *A New Vocabulary for Global Modernism*, ed. Eric Hayot and Rebecca Walkowitz (New York: Columbia University Press, 2016), pp. 96–113, p. 96.

[101] Ibid., p. 108.

ubiquitous in the film. Jiro feels that Japanese technology is deeply inferior to German technology, but when he copies their solutions, his plane manages to surpass its German competitors. Planes and flying in Miyazaki's films also symbolize artistic expression and the technical skills that underlie it. Close-ups of Jiro's hands sketching out his designs also stand for Miyazaki's own hands drawing out the film's frames, as seen in *The Kingdom of Dreams and Madness* (2013), Mami Sunada's documentary about Miyazaki's work on the film.[102] The art of animation consists in producing the illusion of motion through a rapid succession of images. Each image is only slightly different than the previous one; producing a sequence in an animated film is a painstaking process of copying one image after another, changing it only ever so slightly each time.

These two instances of copying—in the film's plot, and in the conditions of its production—must be considered alongside Miyazaki's engagement with *The Magic Mountain* and other intertexts that he uses in *The Wind Rises*. Miyazaki copies Mann's protagonist and setting—and the title of his film is a quote from 'Le Cimetière marin' ('The Graveyard by the Sea', 1922), a poem by Paul Valéry, which had already been used as the title of a famous Japanese text, a classic novella from the 1930s by the modernist writer Tatsuo Hori. Like *The Magic Mountain*, Hori's novella is set in a mountain tuberculosis sanatorium and recounts an ill-fated love story. The title of Miyazaki's film quotes another instance of quoting Valéry's poem. Miyazaki spins a thick web of literary allusions and quotes and thus introduces the question of aesthetic imitation into an art form that by its very nature is predicated on copying. Miyazaki's intertextual strategies remind us why the term intertextuality was coined in the first place: to offer 'a new vision of meaning, and thus of authorship and reading: a vision resistant to ingrained notions of originality, uniqueness, singularity and autonomy'.[103] Michał Głowiński, an eminent Polish critic, wrote about Huelle's intertextual strategy in *Castorp* in similar terms: 'originality consists in shaping that which is borrowed, so—at least on the face of it—something that is not one's own'.[104] This nexus of issues is thrown into sharp relief in another scene in *The Wind Rises* that features Hans Castorp—this time playing a German song on the piano.

The song that Castorp plays, with melody by Werner Richard Heymann and lyrics by Robert Gilbert, is taken from the 1931 Ufa musical comedy film *Der Kongreß tanzt* (*The Congress Dances*) directed by Erik Charell, a romance set against the backdrop of the Congress of Vienna. In both this and Miyazaki's film, the song is used as a commentary on the fleeting nature of happiness, particularly happiness in love. That is the immediate context. But a closer look at the few lines picked from the song by Miyazaki reveals something more particular to *The Wind Rises*:

---

[102] *A Kingdom of Dreams and Madness*, dir. by Mami Sunada (StudioCanal, 2014).
[103] Graham Allen, *Intertextuality* (Abingdon: Routledge, 2011), p. 6.
[104] Michał Głowiński, 'Nad "Castorpem"', *Przegląd Polityczny*, 70 (2005), 65–68, p. 68.

> Das gibt's nur einmal, das kommt nicht wieder,
> das ist vielleicht nur Träumerei.
> Das kann das Leben nur einmal geben,
> vielleicht ist's morgen schon vorbei.
> Das kann das Leben nur einmal geben,
> denn jeder Frühling hat nur einen Mai.
>
> This happens only once, this won't happen again,
> Maybe it's just a dream.
> Life can only give this to us once,
> Maybe tomorrow it'll already be gone.
> Life can only give this to us once,
> For in every spring there's only one month of May.

This passage from the song expresses the tension between 'Einmaligkeit', 'singularity' or 'uniqueness', and its opposite—repetition, copying, or imitation. The phrase 'nur einmal', paradoxically, occurs three times, the repetition further amplified by three related phrases—'nicht wieder', 'schon vorbei', and 'nur einen Mai'. On a formal level, these lines are taken from the chorus—the part of a song based on repetition of individual phrases and whole lines—which itself is repeated a few times in the course of the song. The original song had been written to become a 'Schlager', a hit, intended to be endlessly replayed—as it is in Miyazaki's film. This song is therefore about an inimitable moment that cannot be repeated, but its therapeutic function is to offer endless repetition and imitation of that moment. And, as such, the song—and its inclusion in the film as a piano 'Schlager' played by Hans Castorp, a character from another text, in a resort stylized as the 'Magic Mountain' sanatorium—participate in the discourse on repetition and imitation that is so prominent in the film. The historical situation is repeated— the run-up to the First World War in *The Magic Mountain*, and to the Second World War in *The Wind Rises*; the motif of tubercular lovers is copied; and the enchanting atmosphere of the 'Magic Mountain' sanatorium is imitated. But all this is done in a very self-conscious way that raises meta-fictional questions about creativity and imitation in art.

'Das gibt's nur einmal, das kommt nicht wieder': the line from an old German musical comedy inserted into a contemporary Japanese anime, where it is collectively sung by Japanese and German guests in a mountain resort, becomes an emblem of the tension between the myth of originality and uniqueness of canonical culture and the immense creative potential of imitation, copying, and repetition. 'Das gibt's nur einmal, das kommt nicht wieder'—and yet 'hier ist der Zauberberg', too: Mann's 'Magic Mountain' soars up into the sky outside of his German book; with this sweeping gesture, Miyazaki's film reclaims both the German language and Thomas Mann's novel as cultural resources that resist ownership. An immersive re-enactment of interwar German culture—in which *The Magic Mountain*, a novel usually perceived to be 'highbrow', and a popular musical usually seen as 'lowbrow' can happily coexist—could be seen as an escapist moment in the film. This is how some viewers of the film have seen it. But a different reading is also possible, and it is one that I ultimately find more convincing: the song about repetition, strategically placed in a film that addresses this theme on several different levels, prompts reflection on the repetition of history and the debates about the value of culture. It is impossible to classify different elements of Miyazaki's film as either immersive escapism or detached reflection—these two aspects are intertwined and depend on each other.

4. Hans Castorp in Old Age

In the last section of this chapter I present my final case study of *The Magic Mountain*'s reception, which opens up my discussion to a whole new dimension of cultural uses of Mann's novel. I leave the safe ground of direct references to Mann and enter the speculative territory of what Terence Cave calls 'family resemblances' or 'collective memory'.[105] The impact of a novel like *The Magic Mountain* makes itself felt in culture far beyond what we would usually call its readership: it becomes part of the living tissue of culture, it is 'in the air', much like Freud was for Mann for years before he actually read him. Paolo Sorrentino's *Youth*, upon its release in 2015, was widely perceived to have been inspired by Mann's novel, despite the protestations of the director. Sorrentino's denial of Mann's influence, however, coupled with the film's plot—where the issue of intertextual influences is shown to be a source of cultural anxiety and inferiority complex—raises questions that are strikingly similar to those that have been discussed throughout this book. Perhaps this is the very definition of culture: a text that has ceased to be just a text and has become an instrument of thought which influences the production, reception, and circulation of later texts.[106] In the context of this chapter specifically, *Youth* is interesting because it stages the tension between the pleasure of emotional engagement and the ambition of critical reflection. In the language of the film itself, it sets 'levity' against 'intellectualism' in art and asks which of the two is the true source of cultural value. As my reading of the film will demonstrate, in *Youth* emotional engagement becomes the path to reflection, and in this way, Sorrentino becomes a true heir of Mann.

[105] See Terence Cave, *Mignon's Afterlives: Crossing Cultures from Goethe to the Twenty-First Century* (Oxford: Oxford University Press, 2011), pp. 1–41.
[106] For a recent discussion of literature as an instrument of thought—although not written from the perspective of reception in the sense that I propose—see Terence Cave, *Thinking with Literature: Towards a Cognitive Criticism* (Oxford: Oxford University Press, 2016).

Youth, by Paolo Sorrentino (b. 1970), the most internationally acclaimed of contemporary Italian directors, followed his masterpiece *La grande bellezza* (*The Great Beauty*), which won the Oscar for Best Foreign Language Film in 2013. It was his second film to be shot in English rather than Italian, with British and American actors, including Michael Caine, Harvey Keitel, and Rachel Weisz. The film premiered at the 2015 Cannes Film Festival, where it unsuccessfully competed for the Palme d'Or, and met with a mixed critical response. Many reviewers praised its cinematography, acting, use of music, and the sheer scope of Sorrentino's vision. The film has been described as 'a voluptuary's feast, a full-body immersion in the sensory pleasures of the cinema',[107] 'a perfect example of Sorrentino's ironic art—still further refined, more delicate, studied and beautifully cinematic',[108] and 'a beautiful ode to music and cinema'.[109]

But the film was also described as a diluted and vacuous variation on the themes already developed in Sorrentino's earlier films, especially *The Great Beauty*. Some critics found the film 'insufferable' due to its 'pretentious dialogue, skin-deep psychology, hollow philosophizing, and forced emotion',[110] chided it for 'the kind of stylishness that risks depleting substance',[111] and diagnosed it with 'la ricerca onanistica dell'eccesso, del frame assoluto, [...] giustificata solo dall'ubriacatura post-Oscar che ha fatto perdere di vista all'autore la necessità di dominare il talento, anziché esserne succube' ('an onanistic search for excess, for the absolute frame, [...] justified only by the post-Oscar intoxication that made the author lose sight of the need to dominate his talent, rather than being dominated by it').[112] A similar kind of critique was present in the reception of *The Great Beauty*, which for one critic was a 'document of aesthetic incapacity, a tribute to cinema's ability to move through spaces of grandeur while offering no sense of their coherence, providing no ground for material engagement'.[113] Despite this mixed critical reception, *Youth* went on to win three European Film Awards (Best Film, Best Director, and Best Actor for Caine), among other prizes.

[107] Todd McCarthy, '*Youth*: Cannes Review', *The Hollywood Reporter*, 20 May 2015 <http://www.hollywoodreporter.com/review/youth-cannes-review-797046> [accessed 20 May 2016].

[108] Adrian Wootton, 'Blithe spirit: Paolo Sorrentino on *Youth*', *Sight and Sound*, 26 January 2016 <http://www.bfi.org.uk/news-opinion/sight-sound-magazine/interviews/paolo-sorrentino-youth> [accessed 20 May 2016].

[109] Kaleem Aftab, '*Youth*, Cannes Film Review', *The Independent*, 20 May 2015 <http://www.independent.co.uk/arts-entertainment/films/reviews/youth-cannes-film-review-michael-caine-stakes-his-claim-to-an-oscar-with-the-best-film-so-far-at-the-10265206.html> [accessed 20 May 2016].

[110] David Sterritt, 'The Best (and Worst) Films of 2015', *Quarterly Review of Film and Video*, 33 (2016), 277–83, p. 283.

[111] Peter Bradshaw, '*Youth* review – Life and Death as Seen from a Luxury Hot Tub', *The Guardian*, 28 January 2016 <https://www.theguardian.com/film/2016/jan/28/youth-review-life-and-death-as-seen-from-a-luxury-hot-tub> [accessed 20 May 2016].

[112] Francesca d'Ettorre, 'Recensione: *Youth* – *La giovinezza*', *OndaCinema*, 23 May 2015 <http://www.ondacinema.it/film/recensione/youth_giovinezza.html> [accessed 20 May 2016].

[113] Michael Sicinski, 'Paolo Sorrentino: A Medium Talent', *Cinema Scope*, 58 (2014), 17–21, p. 19.

Youth is set in a luxury spa hotel in the Swiss Alps, which reviewers were quick to identify as strongly reminiscent of the sanatorium in *The Magic Mountain*. The hotel indeed functions very much like a luxury sanatorium: its guests are predominantly sick and elderly, and its staff consists of doctors, nurses, and physiotherapists. The interiors of the hotel were shot in Flims, and the exteriors in Davos, including the façade of Hotel Schatzalp, formerly a sanatorium—the only one mentioned by its real name in *The Magic Mountain*. This is the Mann connection that was drawn in numerous reviews in Germany, Italy, the USA, and beyond. Unsurprisingly, German reviewers were particularly keen to establish a connection between *Youth* and *The Magic Mountain*, for instance by erroneously suggesting that *Youth* is set in the exact same sanatorium in which Mann wrote *The Magic Mountain*.[114] One critic entitled his review 'Die Überlebenden des Zauberbergs lassen grüßen' ('Survivors of the Magic Mountain Say Hello'),[115] while another called *Youth* a more consistent version of *The Magic Mountain*, and, again erroneously, suggested that Mann's novel is set in the Schatzalp sanatorium.[116]

Several Italian reviewers made the connection between Mann and Sorrentino too, with some claiming that the film is set in the same building where Mann wrote *The Magic Mountain*[117] or that the film is set in the same building as Mann's novel.[118] In the USA, the link between Mann and Sorrentino was also made in several reviews: for instance, *Youth*'s setting was described as 'the inspiration for Thomas Mann's *The Magic Mountain*'[119] and a 'hotel for purgation and purification [that] has clearly tumbled down from the Magic Mountain'.[120] However, Sorrentino said in a number of interviews that *Youth* was not inspired by *The*

[114] See e.g. Wenke Husmann, 'Zwei großartige alte Männer', *Die Zeit*, 20 May 2015 <http://www.zeit.de/kultur/film/2015-05/youth-cannes-caine-keitel> [accessed 20 May 2016].

[115] Andreas Kilb, 'Die Überlebenden des Zauberbergs lassen grüßen', *FAZ*, 27 November 2015 <http://www.faz.net/aktuell/feuilleton/kino/ewige-jugend-im-kino-die-ueberlebenden-des-zauberbergs-lassen-gruessen-13931931.html> [accessed 20 May 2016].

[116] See Hanns-Georg Rodek, 'In diesem Film wird Europas Kultur beerdigt', *Die Welt*, 20 May 2015 <http://www.welt.de/kultur/kino/article141227236/In-diesem-Film-wird-Europas-Kultur-beerdigt.html> [accessed 20 May 2016].

[117] See e.g. Stefania Ulivi, 'Cannes, nuovo film di Sorrentino: Successo per *Youth-Giovinezza*', *Corriere della Sera*, 20 May 2015 <http://cinema-tv.corriere.it/cinema/15_maggio_20/cannes-nuovo-film-sorrentino-applausi-buu-giovinezza-97db51a4-fee3-11e4-ab35-8ecb73a305fb.shtml> [accessed 20 May 2016].

[118] See e.g. Eugenio Scalfari, 'Guardando la Giovinezza dalla montagna incantata', *La Repubblica*, 20 May 2015 <http://www.repubblica.it/spettacoli/cinema/2015/05/20/news/guardando_la_giovinezza_dalla_montagna_incantata-114789588/> [accessed 20 May 2016].

[119] Kenneth Turan, 'In *Youth*, Life Is a Boisterous, Wide-Ranging Musical Composition', *Los Angeles Times*, 3 December 2015 <http://www.latimes.com/entertainment/movies/la-et-mn-youth-review-20151204-column.html> [accessed 20 May 2016].

[120] Nigel Andrews, '*Youth* — Film Review: "Rambling"', *Financial Times*, 28 January 2016 <http://www.ft.com/cms/s/2/cf6254d6-c5be-11e5-b3b1-7b2481276e45.html#axzz4A8jKUKvI> [accessed 20 May 2016]. Interestingly, no British reviewers made this connection. This is probably because *The Magic Mountain* has been strongly canonized in continental Europe and the USA, but not so much in the UK.

Magic Mountain, and that he only found out about the Davos/Schatzalp link after he had already decided to set his film there—'un vero puro caso' ('really by sheer chance'), as he emphatically stated.[121] But he did add that the design of the Schatzalp had never been modernized because the owners wanted to preserve its link to Mann's novel, and it was precisely this older aesthetic that appealed to the director when he was looking for a setting for *Youth*.

Rather than concentrating on the Schatzalp connection and Sorrentino's intention to make an intertextual reference to Mann, or lack thereof, it is more useful to go beyond this superficial link and see if a comparison between the film and the novel can reveal something new about these texts. The comparison is warranted by the several general similarities between *The Magic Mountain* and *Youth*. Both focus on the decay of the body (tuberculosis in the former, and old age in the latter); they portray a diverse group of international upper-class guests or patients; and they emphasize boredom and daily routines (meals, performances for the guests, flirtation, walks, check-ups with the doctors), which also form the basis of the narrative structure of both texts. Crucially for my argument, similarly to Mann, Sorrentino is also interested in debates about the value of culture and the tension between the serious and light-hearted tone, the intellectualizing and playful impulse, and emotions and critique in art.

Youth tells the story of a retired British composer, Fred (Michael Caine), who undergoes medical treatment in a luxury spa hotel. He is accompanied by his daughter Lena (Rachel Weisz), his friend Mick (Harvey Keitel)—a Hollywood director struggling to finish his last film—and Jimmy (Paul Dano), a young actor preparing for his breakthrough role of an ageing Hitler. The overall story is framed by Fred's refusal to conduct *Simple Songs*, his most famous piece, before the British Queen, and his subsequent change of heart: the film ends with a performance of *Simple Song #3*. Between these two endpoints Fred undergoes considerable emotional development, as he discusses the nature of art with Jimmy, tries to comfort his daughter Lena after a break-up with her husband, witnesses Mick's suicide, and visits his paralysed wife—a former opera singer—in a care home. However, rather than being organized around a tight plot, *Youth* is structured as a series of relatively self-contained episodes, punctuated by a handful of leitmotifs: the tune of *Simple Songs*; recurrent conversation topics; and the morning health routines and evening performances at the hotel.

While each episode does seem to contribute to the emotional development of several characters, most importantly Fred, Mick, Jimmy, and Lena, the apparent incongruity or superficiality of *Youth*'s plot bothered some critics, who did not

[121] Festival de Cannes, Youth Conference Cannes 2015, online video recording, YouTube, 20 May 2015 <https://www.youtube.com/watch?v=LX_gai9PmJA> [accessed 20 May 2016]. See also [Anon.], 'Intervista a Paolo Sorrentino', *Youth—La giovinezza*, dir. by Paolo Sorrentino (Warner Brothers, 2015).

appreciate the emotional arc running from Fred's initial refusal to perform *Simple Songs* to the final concert. One reviewer, for instance, likened the film to 'a collection of vignettes straining to coalesce into a satisfactory resolution', adding that 'plot rarely [... matters] in a Sorrentino film, which tends to be about the human comedy/tragedy that is life, expressed visually rather than through prosaic exposition'.[122] However, the structure of *Youth* may also be considered as being motivated by the film's overall concern with the value of art. I propose to take this concern more seriously than the critics who have suggested that the film is pleasant to look at, but vacuous—an endless repetition of Sorrentino's old cine-matographic tricks. *Youth* addresses this critique and questions widespread assumptions about artistic value and aesthetic pleasure. In my analysis of the film's closing sequence—Fred's visit to Venice and the performance of *Simple Songs* in London—I argue that it simultaneously shows Fred coming to terms with his music's artistic value and Sorrentino laying bare his own cinematic aesthetic.

Fred Ballinger is a retired composer and conductor, known almost exclusively for his early work entitled *Simple Songs*. Fred feels uneasy about its popularity, partly because, as is gradually revealed, this composition has a special emotional significance for him. He wrote it for his wife Melanie, an operatic soprano, and the only person to perform the work. Melanie is absent for the better part of the film: we are led to believe that she is dead. Through Fred's conversations with his daughter Lena, we find out some details about his relationship with Melanie. Fred was always cold, distant, and focused on his work, and had several affairs, including a period of homosexual experimentation, while Melanie sacrificed her own career to take care of the household and the children. At the end of the film, however, it emerges that Melanie is not dead, but lives in a care home in Venice, suffering from dementia and paralysis, and Fred's monologue at her sickbed suggests that their relationship is much stronger than Lena thinks. Fred's emo-tional development is framed by two formulaic expressions about the role of emotions: 'emotions are overrated' (says Fred towards the beginning of the film)—and 'emotions are all we've got' (the last thing Mick says to Fred before he dies by suicide).

It is in this context that I want to consider the emotional climax of *Youth*. A cut takes us from the graves of Igor and Vera Stravinsky (who are indeed buried at the cemetery of Isola di San Michele near Venice) to Melanie's room. This is unex-pected, as the viewer had been led to expect to see her grave. The camera slowly zooms out, and we first hear, then see Fred entering the room. What ensues is an exchange between Fred and the silent Melanie, Fred giving an emotional speech

[122] Michael O'Sullivan, 'Movie Review: *Youth* Cloys, Despite Gorgeous Visuals', *The Washington Post*, 9 December 2015 <https://www.washingtonpost.com/goingoutguide/movies/movie-review-youth-cloys-despite-gorgeous-visuals/2015/12/08/ad82655a-9aac-11e5-94f0-9eeaff906ef3_story.html> [accessed 20 May 2016].

about how children do not know their parents and their parents' relationship. Melanie is seated by the window, in an uncomfortable position that reveals her physical disability. She is almost entirely motionless. Finally, Fred finishes by saying that their children must never know that despite all the hardship, he and Melanie like to think of themselves as a 'simple song'. At this point the camera zooms in on Melanie, while in the background the orchestra is heard tuning for a concert. We begin to suspect that this will be the performance for the Queen that Fred declined to conduct earlier in the film. Both Fred's speech and the sound bridge that will ultimately take us to the London performance suggest that we are witnessing an important moment in Fred's journey to come to terms with his artistic creation. The scene's emotional impact is clear: *Simple Songs* was not created by a cold and distanced artist, but is a record of a deeply personal and painful experience.

When the camera zooms in, Melanie's parted lips are revealed—and then a sudden cut lets us see her from the other side of the window. This striking shot takes less than five seconds, but it is undoubtedly the emotional pinnacle of the film, underscored by the swift increase in volume of the sound of the musicians tuning their instruments. In a powerful contrast to the hotel guests, who subject themselves to endless medical examinations and health treatments but are well enough to live a normal life outside of the doctor's office, Melanie is portrayed as the embodiment of physical and psychological suffering. Her opened mouth suggests that she is mute, and she looks as though frozen mid-scream. We return to this shot during the performance of *Simple Songs*, and the passage from Sumi Jo's open mouth, singing, and Melanie's open mouth, mute, reminds us that it was Melanie who used to perform *Simple Songs*. The juxtaposition of these two shots underscores the sacrifice Melanie had to make for the sake of Fred's career.

But the next cut takes us to a close-up of Fred's face, and his sorrowful expression reminds us of his own emotional distress connected to conducting this piece. Before moving from Melanie's room to the Philharmonic Hall in London, however, we see Fred on a bridge in Venice, and the camera moves towards it, finally fading to black under the bridge. The tuning of the orchestra can still be heard: it is the sound bridge that will take us to Fred's performance in the next shot. The pun (sound bridge—bridge in Venice) acts as a subtle self-reflexive trope, reminding anyone who notices it that the high emotional impact of this scene is produced by artistic means—the sound bridge, the camera's movements, the cuts in decisive moments, and the plot's structure that places this scene at the apex of Fred's emotional development. Even in the moving shot of Melanie, the inevitable presence of the camera eye is gently emphasized by the fact that Melanie is additionally framed by the window frame. The exploration of Fred's emotional struggle is accompanied by a meta-commentary on Sorrentino's filmic strategies to emotionally involve the spectators in his protagonist's plight.

Seen in this light, the performance of *Simple Songs* in the last scene of the film is highly significant. Viewers are divided in whether they like the last scene or not. Those who dislike it argue that the performance of *Simple Song #3* is disappointing, since it does not meet the high expectations set up earlier in the film, when *Simple Songs* was introduced to the viewers as a legendary masterpiece. But in fact the only thing that one can have against this piece is that it is 'simple'—likeable and uncomplicated. In the economy of the film, the assessment of *Simple Songs* as a piece of art is very ambiguous. We repeatedly hear this tune played badly by a small boy throughout the film, but the final performance elevates the status of this melody from a badly exercised student assignment to a piece performed in front of the British Queen (and it was, after all, composed by David Lang, a prominent US composer). Moreover, Fred's reference to his relationship with Melanie as a 'simple song' recontextualizes the whole debate about the quality of *Simple Songs*: the work might be pleasurable for the audience, but it is also deeply painful and personal to the artist.

Sorrentino used a similar mechanism in *The Great Beauty*, where the protagonist Jep Gambardella is presented as the author of a masterpiece, a book called *L'apparato umano*. But here we never get to know this supposed masterpiece— meaning that it remains an ideal that cannot be attacked or criticized. The film posits the existence of a masterpiece that supposedly reveals the most profound truths about the human condition (its title means 'the human apparatus'); but because we cannot read it, the film does not have to engage in a discussion of those truths. The fact, therefore, that *Simple Song #3* is performed in *Youth* is striking. The comparison between the two films shows that the main premise of *The Great Beauty* was the absence of the artwork, which allowed Sorrentino to sustain the impression that the protagonist's art is aesthetically valuable and intellectually mature. In *Youth*, this pretension to beauty and sophistication is eventually confronted with the actual qualities of the artwork, so that the viewers themselves can judge the protagonist's artistic merits. Sorrentino's decision confronts the viewers with their expectations, with the imperfection and inevitable finitude of art, and with the question of what makes an artwork a masterpiece.

This approach to *Simple Songs* helps explain Fred's worry about the artistic value of his composition. Various conversations in the film paint a gloomy picture of Fred's self-esteem: when he was a young musician, everyone considered him to be 'presumptuous and inelegant'; he was friends with Igor Stravinsky, to whom he always felt inferior; all of his works beyond *Simple Songs* have been largely forgotten. When we meet Fred, he seems to be happily retired, but he is seen in various intimate moments when he secretly tries to keep composing—repeating the same tune by rumpling a candy wrapper, or 'conducting' an orchestra of cows in a meadow. This suggests that Fred still hopes to create a masterpiece that would surpass his *Simple Songs*. In Fred's conversations with Jimmy, the theme of artistic value is a recurrent one. Towards the beginning of the film they talk about levity—as 'an irresistible temptation' to which both Fred and Jimmy have given in just once, only to be associated with it at the expense of their other, more serious work. In a later dialogue Fred argues that levity is a perversion, which reveals his anxiety about the artistic value of *Simple Songs*. In a different conversation, Fred relates to Jimmy what Stravinsky once said to him—'intellectuals have no taste'— and so, Fred proudly declares, he decided never to become an intellectual. And yet Fred's underlying anxiety about intellectualism is promptly revealed when Jimmy responds with a quote from Novalis, to which Fred's knee-jerk response is that Jimmy—a Hollywood star—is not the right person to be reading Novalis. This obsession with intellectualism, the compulsion to judge what is good and what is bad art, and who should be allowed to appreciate it, forms a latent theme of the whole film. On one occasion Fred remarks that to be a pop star is 'the most obscene job in the world'; another time he and Jimmy complain about the quality of the evening shows at the hotel; in his interaction with Miss Universe, Jimmy tries (but fails) to belittle her for her film tastes; and so on.

The tension between intellectualism and levity as two contrasting sources of artistic value is a version of the opposition between critical reflection and emotional engagement that I have been tracing in *The Magic Mountain* and its reception throughout this chapter. Intellectualism is an attitude towards an artwork that treats it as a depository of ideas—a series of philosophical statements acted out through narrative or imagery. But is artistic value about creating a repository of abstract ideas? Or does it lie in the artist's ability to immerse the spectator or reader in the sensual specificity of the artwork? The notion of levity implies suspension in mid-air, weightless, a sensation similar to immersion in water. This feeling of weightlessness contrasts with the weightiness of philosophical ideas. How to perform a balancing act that creates an artwork that perfectly combines both? Who gets to decide when the result is satisfactory?

In this context, Mick is a particularly interesting character. He is a famous director attempting to create his cinematic testament, a project to which he gives a grandiose title, *Life's Last Day*. The theme of a famous filmmaker unsuccessfully trying to make a film in a sanatorium unmistakably echoes Federico Fellini's legendary *Otto e mezzo* (8½, 1963); interestingly, various motifs from Fellini's earlier masterpiece, *La dolce vita* (1960), were also reworked in Sorrentino's *The Great Beauty*. By creating a parallel between Mick and Fellini's protagonist, Sorrentino is emphasizing and contextualizing his character's struggle with writer's block, but is also consciously drawing a parallel between himself and Fellini—two celebrated filmmakers, each making a film about a celebrated film-maker failing to make another film.

A parallel is also being drawn between Mick's unrealized film and *Youth* itself: Mick's film about the reconciliation between a wife and a husband at his death bed resembles Fred's and Melanie's storyline in *Youth*; Mick and his screenwriters cannot come up with a good ending for their film, but in a gruesome turn of events the project to make *Life's Last Day* comes to an end with the last day of Mick's life, when he dies by suicide; and the last shot of *Youth* is a close-up of Mick, who keeps his hands in front of his face, folded to resemble the eye of the camera, and then slowly releases them, upon which the film ends. We can read this shot as a suggestion that everything we have just seen took place only in Mick's imagin-ation, or, less radically, as a product of Fred's imagination—a subtle indication that Fred sees Mick's influence as a shaping force in his life. Establishing a parallel between *Youth* and *8½* creates three levels of anxiety about artistic production: there are two fictional filmmakers anxious about their films; there are two real-life filmmakers addressing this anxiety in their respective films; and there is Sorrentino, inscribing himself into the legend of Fellini, placing himself in a position famously described by Harold Bloom as the anxiety of influence.

Moreover, the character of Mick was allegedly inspired by another celebrated Italian director, Francesco Rosi, to whom Sorrentino's film is dedicated; and another legend of Italian cinema, Luchino Visconti, is also evoked in *Youth* when Fred travels to Venice on a boat, in a shot that clearly alludes to Visconti's *Morte a Venezia* (1971), an adaptation of Mann's *Death in Venice*. This is, then, yet another instance of Thomas Mann's subtle presence in the film, beyond the Davos setting—and another reference to him seems to be made when Fred is presented at the beginning of the film as the composer of a piece called *The Life of Hadrian*, which makes one think of Mann's *Doktor Faustus*, subtitled *Das Leben des deutschen Tonsetzers Adrian Leverkühn, erzählt von einem Freunde* (*The Life of the German Composer Adrian Leverkühn, Told by a Friend*). And to return to Stravinsky, his most famous composition, *The Rite of Spring* (1913), centres on the theme of youth and old age, and the perverse relations between the two, which connects to the overall theme of Sorrentino's film. (In *The Rite of Spring*, the tribal tradition, embodied in the figure of the Sage and the elders, requires a young woman to be sacrificed to the spirits of the ancestors.) All these references to canonical texts of European high art serve a curious function. They locate Sorrentino's film in the sphere of comfortable erudition, at the same time raising the question of how *Youth* itself belongs to this tradition—once again corres-ponding to Bloom's concept of the anxiety of influence.

A shadow of this anxiety falls upon virtually every character in the film: Mick, trying to make a cinematic masterpiece, and failing; Fred, coming to terms with the fact that his best composition is all about the power of emotions; and Jimmy, aiming to live down his role as a robot in a blockbuster movie by taking on the part of old Hitler. If we understand the film's final sequence as Fred being reconciled with his art and what it stands for, we must also read it as Sorrentino admitting to the simple attraction of his cinematic style. From the sound/Venetian bridge pun, and through the orchestra performance which parallels the production and consumption of a film (the conductor directing, the audience watching, the spectacle unfolding), we get to two odd vignettes inserted into the final sequence.

The first is a puzzling scene in the mountains—a surreal and exaggeratedly artificial shot of Lena and Luca, a mountaineer, dangling on a rope in mid-air. Perhaps a clue as to how we are supposed to read this scene is offered by the only words uttered in it: 'look at me', said by Luca to Lena. However, if the whole final sequence of *Youth* is read as a comment on Sorrentino's cinematic aesthetic, the simple line 'look at me'—spoken against the background of a stunning but clearly artificial mountain vista, the characters levitating in mid-air like the Buddhist monk earlier in the film—can be understood as the film's message to the spectator about the value of 'levity', of weightlessness and aesthetic abandon.

The second vignette inserted into the final sequence in *Youth* shows a masseuse working at the hotel dancing in front of a TV screen. She is playing an immersive rhythm game—a type of video game which requires the player to closely imitate dance movements shown on the screen to score points. This is a typical Sorrentino scene—shot in slow motion, combining classical music (*Simple Song #3* still plays in the background) with a thoroughly modern type of entertainment, turning a very popular cultural practice into a pure visual spectacle, and featuring an attractive young woman.[123] This is exactly the kind of Sorrentino signature scene that the 'Generatore automatico di scene del prossimo film di Sorrentino', a mocking generator of Sorrentino-type film scenes on an Italian cultural blog LiberNazione, could spit out.[124]

But Sorrentino seems to be fully aware of this. The dancing masseuse is framed twice, as it were—the inevitable presence of framing in the medium of film is emphasized by the masseuse appearing on screen between two window frames—and she is being watched by a few other women. This visual device, already seen in Sorrentino's portrayal of Melanie, subtly draws viewers' attention to the con-structedness of the filmic image, which is so crucial to Sorrentino's visual poetics. The scene with the masseuse can be also read as a reference to another feature of Sorrentino's style—the sensual and emotional impact of his filmmaking, which often seems to get the better of the plot itself. The only piece of dialogue that the masseuse engages in over the course of the film is her conversation with Fred, when she argues that 'touching' gives pleasure, and is better than 'talking', especially when you 'do not have anything to say'. This short dialogue can be read as a reflection on Sorrentino's aesthetics, too: his films' emotional impact ('touching') goes beyond an articulation of ideas ('talking')—and yet the paradox

[123] For an interesting critique of the portrayal of women in Sorrentino's earlier films, see Alex Marlow-Mann, 'Character Engagement and Alienation in the Cinema of Paolo Sorrentino', in *Italian Film Directors in the New Millennium*, ed. William Hope (Newcastle upon Tyne: Cambridge Scholars, 2010), pp. 161–73.

[124] Alessandro Capriccioli, 'Generatore automatico di scene del prossimo film di Sorrentino', *LiberNazione*, 26 May 2015 <http://libernazione.it/generatore-automatico-di-scene-del-prossimo-film-di-sorrentino/> [accessed 20 May 2016].

of the masseuse's speech is that in fact she *does* have something to say—she ends up articulating Sorrentino's aesthetic manifesto.

Once again—as when Hans thought about hermetically sealed jars to get to grips with Naphta's esoteric philosophy, Goodreads users enjoyed the discussions between Settembrini and Naphta as a game of 'intellectual table tennis', and Hans reread *Effi Briest* and sang a song from an old German musical—in *Youth*, the pleasure of emotional engagement ultimately also leads to critical reflection. Sensual and emotional immersion in the power of the filmic image leads to an exploration of pervasive cultural anxieties about the value of 'levity' and 'intellectualism'—a topic which, as I have been arguing throughout this study, is crucial to *The Magic Mountain* and the novel's impact on its readers.

5. Conclusion: Coming up for Air

Immersion in *The Magic Mountain* can become a source of clarity rather than just muddy the waters. In this chapter I discussed how various readers—real-life as well as fictional—reach a deeper insight into their relationship with culture through an engaged reading of Mann's novel. Section 1 focused on different readers' approaches to the conversations between Settembrini and Naphta, as I argued that the implications of 'the erudition effect' staged by Mann in *The Magic Mountain* can only be fully appreciated if viewed through the lens of the novel's non-academic rather than academic readers. Drawing on reading records from the Goodreads forum, various reviews of the novel, and memories of famous readers, including Susan Sontag, Carlos Fuentes, Jenny Erpenbeck, and Karl Ove Knausgaard, I suggested that one of the most powerful and influential themes in Mann's novel is the question of the terms by which we encounter and interact with culture. *The Magic Mountain* is about subtle gradations in what counts as cultural sophistication, and a recurring trope in the novel's reception is a feeling of inadequacy—and yet, paradoxically, this feeling might be the only adequate reaction to the novel's design. As my three chapters taken together show, this critical insight can only be reached through immersion in the economical, emotional, and rhetorical structures of the novel.

In Sections 2 and 3, I extended my analysis of real-life readers' encounters with *The Magic Mountain* to discuss two fictional characters inspired by Mann's novel whose interactions with cultural texts follow a similar logic. I discussed Huelle's *Castorp* and Miyazaki's *The Wind Rises*, a prequel and a sequel to *The Magic Mountain*, respectively—two texts which bear striking similarities despite their superficial differences, and which, as far as I am aware, have never before been discussed alongside each other. In both texts, Hans Castorp is a character whose trajectory shows emotional engagement and critical reflection as two elements of the same process rather than as conflicting forces. Hans's repeated, absorbing reading of *Effi Briest* in Danzig and his performance of a German song about absorption and repetition in Japan lead to a deeper understanding of historical forces at work in Eastern Europe and East Asia, and the role of Germany and German culture in both these contexts.

The last case study of the chapter marked a move beyond direct references to *The Magic Mountain* in later cultural texts to examine its broader influence on debates about art and culture. Despite the director's protestations, Paolo Sorrentino's award-winning film *Youth* was widely received as an heir to *The Magic Mountain*. In my reading of the film I argued that, in a setting strikingly similar to Mann's, it registers a strikingly similar dilemma to that which I have been exploring throughout this final chapter—the relative role of emotions and critique in art, or 'levity' and 'intellectualism' in the film's own idiom. My own desire to read *Youth* via *The Magic Mountain*, shared by many other viewers of the film, testifies to the lasting impact of Mann's novel—and illustrates the workings of culture: an addictive search for connections and correspondences, in the hope that they can make our lives more meaningful—as Elif Batuman would say, 'as meaningful as our favourite books'.

Conclusion

This book has performed a closer reading of *The Magic Mountain* as a work of world literature. Unlike in the study of national literatures, a critic viewing a text through the lens of world literature tends to be much less preoccupied with overfamiliar categories, such as nation, language, period, even genre: they will not be seen as neutral containers into which texts naturally fall. Mann's novel has circulated around the world, far beyond its point of origin in early twentieth-century Germany, which makes it into a work of twentieth- and twenty-first-century world literature as well as a classic of German modernism. To surrender the certainties of national literary history and, even briefly, restore a text like *The Magic Mountain* to the vast, chaotic, largely unfamiliar ocean of culture around the world is to create scope—and give permission—to construct a new, original, different, unexpected corpus, one among many possibilities, alongside other, more familiar groupings, such as 'German literary canon', 'novels of Western European modernism', or 'Thomas Mann's oeuvre'.

Theories of world literature put emphasis on the circulation of texts: this field is usually understood as the study of how texts move around the world. More recently, however, scholars have begun to highlight another dimension of this definition. To study world literature can also mean to study how texts move *in* the world, that is, what they do to their readers, and what readers do with them. This, to me, is one of the most exciting if still relatively underdeveloped strands of research today. To bring it into focus and gain a better purchase on this practice, I have referred to it as 'closer reading'. In a discipline that has tended to favour critical distance and detachment over any intimations of proximity or intimacy with the object of study, it might give one pause to note that its central methodo-logical tool—close reading—does in fact advocate closeness: readers are meant to remain close to the text, if not to their personal experience (one type of closeness traded for another, if you will); however, all this rigorous attention and analysis cannot but engender emotional attachment, the kind of experience that close reading in theory sets out to dispel. The term 'closer reading', therefore, is intended as an invitation to extend our attention to the question of why and how readers form attachments to books—through close reading, but also in many other ways.

The term is both a nod to a favoured technique of many literary scholars, which I wish to complement rather than displace, and a reaction to the rise of certain types of digital humanities work, which practise distant reading—again, not as an

Mann's Magic Mountain: World Literature and Closer Reading Karolina Watroba, Oxford University Press.
© Karolina Watroba 2022. DOI: 10.1093/oso/9780192871794.003.0005

attempt to replace it (doomed to failure and not at all useful) but rather to indicate another possible path to those who see the methods of the digital humanities as the last word in literary scholarship. Closer reading is an invitation to close read readers' attachments to books. It is a way to marry a traditional, specialized, philological approach to texts with emotional investments that matter to non-academic readers. To go back to the evocative scene from Batuman's *The Idiot* that I discussed in the Introduction, it is an idea for bridging the disconnect between readers like Selin and her mother, on the one hand, and literary professors, on the other.

My hope for this study was to capture something of the exciting, multifaceted, and complex nature of reading by attending to written records and various other traces left behind by all sorts of different readers of *The Magic Mountain*, academic and non-academic, German and global, famous and ordinary, old and young, sick and healthy, admiring and sceptical. These sources have so far been almost entirely ignored in the scholarship on Thomas Mann, partly because of their serendipitous nature and partly—in Rita Felski's words—out of 'nervousness about literature's awkward proximity to imagination, emotion, and other soft, fuzzy ideas'.[1] But all these 'soft, fuzzy ideas' are part and parcel of how we move through and interact with culture, including prestigious, 'highbrow' literature such as *The Magic Mountain*. The profound, personal, emotional investments that diverse readers have made into Mann's novel over the past century do not trivialize more scholarly modes of engagement with it, but can complement, deepen, develop, sometimes challenge, and even correct them.

As I hope to have demonstrated, such a closer reading of *The Magic Mountain* need not be a mere footnote to the 'serious' study of the novel. As the passage from *The Idiot* quoted at the beginning of this book articulates so clearly, non-academic readers are keenly interested in the meaning of books too. ('I wanted to know what books really meant. That was how my mother and I had always talked about literature. "I need you to read this, too", she would say, handing me a *New Yorker* story in which an unhappily married man had to get a rabies shot, "so you can tell me what it really means".') But meaning is, as Jane Tompkins says, 'what happens to a reader as he negotiates the text and not something that was already in place before he experienced it'.[2] In this study I have chronicled various instances of such negotiation of meaning. In Chapter 1, I focused on readers who put more pressure on the terms of access to Mann's enchanted story-world. In these readers' encounters with the novel, what *The Magic Mountain* might 'mean' changes from the realm of bourgeois cultivation of the self—'verboten' to the uninitiated—to an easily accessible attraction visited by enthusiasts of 'intellectual

---

[1] Rita Felski, *Uses of Literature* (Oxford: Blackwell, 2008), p. 59.
[2] Jane P. Tompkins, ed., *Reader-Response Criticism: From Formalism to Post-Structuralism* (Baltimore, MD: Johns Hopkins University Press, 1980), p. xxii.

tourism'. In Chapter 2, I discussed readers who visited *The Magic Mountain* not as tourists, but as patients—figuratively or quite literally, having been to a tuberculosis sanatorium in Davos. These readers tend to respond to the novel with an emotional intensity that can barely be contained within the conventions of literary analysis, which often writes it off as distasteful melodrama. And yet these readers' encounters with the novel show that management of melodrama is part and parcel of the novel's meaning. In Chapter 3, I looked at yet another group of readers whose approach to *The Magic Mountain* diverges from academic reading habits and yet can cast new light on those very habits—readers for whom erudition and specialized knowledge are not a given, but a thorny subject surrounded by various anxieties and tensions. Looking closely at these readers' responses to Mann's novel reveals that they might in fact be uniquely attuned to its meaning.

To borrow two titles from Grayson Perry's fabulous art project on the layers of cultural capital in contemporary Britain, *The Magic Mountain* is about 'the vanity of small differences' and the anxiety to be 'all in the best possible taste'. To draw on Tompkins's definition of meaning in literature once more, all these issues are 'already in place' before readers open up *The Magic Mountain*, but it is only those individual readers, in all their cultural specificity and individuality, who can and do make these issues readable. My case studies of various readerly encounters with *The Magic Mountain* show how the text comes alive when it enters the lives of its diverse readers. It is the connections between life and literature, provisionally and contingently established in each individual meeting between a reader and a text, that constitute culture. These connections must be the central object of study for literary scholarship, which can and should attend more seriously to the question of its own value—in practice, not just in theory.

The Magic Mountain is an excellent case study for exploring the tensions between academic and non-academic reading practices because it is a novel about a young engineer with very little expertise in the humanities who is confronted with the intimidating edifice of European culture. In Russell A. Berman's words, 'that Castorp is an aspiring engineer collides with the aesthetic predilections of the genre [the "Bildungsroman"] and draws the reader's attention to the question of the fate of traditional culture in the technological twentieth century'.[3] Mann depicts both the pleasures and dangers of immersing oneself in culture, and Hans's position as an 'Everyman' who can do so is called into question, with the result that *The Magic Mountain* can be read as a discussion of the value of the humanities and the unequal and unjust distribution of cultural capital—two topics that are at the heart of most contemporary debates about the future of academic literary studies.

---

[3] Russell A. Berman, 'Modernism and the Bildungsroman: Thomas Mann's *Magic Mountain*', in *The Cambridge Companion to the Modern German Novel*, ed. Graham Bartram (Cambridge: Cambridge University Press, 2004), pp. 77–92, p. 78.

In Mann's lecture on *The Magic Mountain* delivered at Princeton in 1939, which used to be included as an introduction in many German and English editions of the novel, he advised the students interested in his book to read it twice—unless they did not enjoy it the first time round: 'diese Forderung wird natürlich sofort zurückgezogen für den Fall, daß man sich das erste Mal dabei gelangweilt hat' ('a request not to be heeded, of course, if one has been bored at the first reading').[4] In a copy of *The Magic Mountain* in the Taylorian Library in Oxford I found a note left in the margin next to this sentence by an earlier reader. It read: 'Phew!' Most academic readers of Mann would not see fit to discuss this marginal note in their studies of the novel, and for two reasons: first, they tend to write off such records of reading as trivial and unimportant; second, they consider the questions of pleasure, interest, and boredom—and more generally the emotional stakes of reading—as peripheral to the business of literary scholarship. For me, both these areas are absolutely central.

In the process of writing this book I identified several avenues of research that can be opened up thanks to this type of analysis. First of all, more archival work is needed—this time not on Thomas Mann himself, but his readers. An impressive project recently completed at the Thomas-Mann-Archiv der ETH-Bibliothek in Zurich aimed to identify, categorize, and digitize all instances of 'Lesespuren' ('reading traces') in Mann's 'Nachlassbibliothek' ('personal library'), including marginal notes, underlines, and even fingerprints. It is remarkable that we are so invested in Mann's library and almost indifferent to libraries that lend Mann's books; in what Mann read, but not in who reads him; in fingerprints that suggest Mann touched a certain book, but not at all in how his writing touches his readers. How about flipping the script, turning the tables, and tracking down as many of Thomas Mann's diverse readers as possible—readers who owned or borrowed his books? As the 'Nachlassbibliothek' project clearly implies, culture only exists in its uses. But we are all users of culture: not just great writers like Thomas Mann, but also the readers of these great writers.

Studies of canonical works tend to focus on their 'pre-histories' rather than 'afterlives'—assuming, often tacitly, that the value of literature rests on how successfully it responds to earlier tradition, rather than how vigorously it is taken up in later cultural production. Or rather: that to understand the work, it is crucial to understand where it comes from, but less important to know how it redirects cultural energies. The perspective of closer reading challenges this assumption and urges us to consider how the uses to which readers put texts also matter. In other words, Goethe, Schopenhauer, Nietzsche, and Wagner are important German predecessors of Mann, and his work in relation to theirs has

---

[4] Thomas Mann, 'Einführung in *Den Zauberberg* für Studenten der Universität Princeton', in *Der Zauberberg* (Frankfurt am Main, 1962), pp. ii–xiv, p. xxii. Thomas Mann, 'The Making of *The Magic Mountain*', in *The Magic Mountain*, trans. H. T. Lowe-Porter (London: Vintage, 1999), p. 724.

been studied exhaustively. But Mann himself has now become an important predecessor to a host of other global artists and thinkers—Susan Sontag, Roland Barthes, Alice Munro, and Haruki Murakami, to mention just a few—and these connections are not being taken seriously enough. Even less attention is paid to less famous readers, whose traces can be found, among other places, in libraries and archives around the world.

The insights afforded by physical archives and libraries can be developed by harnessing the power of the internet. I found many of my case studies of Mann's readers either quite literally on the internet—as with the Goodreads forum—or through internet searches, as with the literary afterlives of *The Magic Mountain* that have not been recorded in the academic scholarship on the novel. Andrew M. Stauffer recently described how 'the synthesis of two types of searching—one among the books in the stacks and another among massive databases online'— enabled him and his students to uncover the hitherto hidden history of nineteenth-century readers of Felicia Hemans.[5] I am sure that we could make similarly thrilling discoveries about Mann's readers, and not just in Germany. My project illustrates the constant refrain of world literature—that most if not all national literatures are also global, in circulation around the world, and German literature is no exception. More archival work coupled with more language expertise would likely uncover fascinating material, especially in the severely understudied Global South. In 1954, Mann wrote a letter to Rolf Italiaander, a writer who had just returned from one of his many journeys to Africa. Presumably in response to Italiaander's reports of African readers of his novel, Mann commented: 'daß man dort unten an den N[. . .]universitäten etwas vom *Magic Mountain* weiß, ist ja erstaunlich' ('it is astonishing that people have some knowledge of *The Magic Mountain* down there at the n[. . .] universities').[6] As this unashamedly racist comment suggests, Mann himself did not fully appreciate the cultural reach of his novel.

This was not Mann's only mediated encounter with those he deemed to be unlikely readers of his work. A few months earlier, in 1953, Peter Huchel wrote a letter to Mann asking him to contribute an essay to *Sinn und Form*, an East German literary journal of which he was the general editor. Engaging in 'shameless flattery',[7] as one critic put it, he recounted an anecdote from his recent trip to Russia, on which he allegedly discovered that Mann was considered to be the most famous contemporary German writer there, celebrated by Russian literati all around the Soviet Union, as well as 'in den breitesten Schichten des sowjetischen

---

[5] Stauffer, 'An Image in Lava', p. 82.

[6] Thomas Mann, *Selbstkommentare: 'Der Zauberberg'*, ed. Hans Wysling and Marianne Eich-Fischer (Frankfurt am Main: Fischer, 1993), p. 175, my ellipsis.

[7] Stephen R. Parker, *Peter Huchel: A Literary Life in 20th-Century Germany* (Bern: Peter Lang, 1998), p. 341.

Volkes' ('across all the social classes of the Soviet people').[8] On a steamship on the River Don, Huchel met a machinist in his fifties; because of the language barrier they were not able to have a long conversation, but when Huchel named a famous Russian author who had written about the Don, the machinist supposedly responded as follows:

> dann legte er die rechte Hand aufs Herz und verneigte sich etwas, eine Geste, die ich nie vergessen werde, denn sie wirkte ausgesprochen russisch schön, und sagte: 'Thomas Mann sehr großer Schriftsteller!' [...] Vielleicht war ihm nur Ihr Name ins Bewußtsein gedrungen, vielleicht aber hatte er Bücher von Ihnen oder Essays über Sie gelesen.

> then he laid his right hand on his heart and bowed a little, a gesture that I will never forget because it seemed so very Russian and beautiful, and said: 'Thomas Mann very great writer!' [...] Perhaps he had only happened to hear your name somewhere, but perhaps he had read your books or essays about you.[9]

Huchel's anecdote 'behrührt[e]' ('touched') Mann 'sehr tief und merkwürdig' ('in a very deep and peculiar way'): 'von fern meinen Namen aus dem Munde des Maschinisten eines Don-Dampfers zu hören—wie eigentümlich traumhaft!' ('to hear my name from afar, spoken by a steamship machinist on the Don—how curiously dreamlike!'), he wrote back.[10] He went on to add that it was certainly highly unlikely that the machinist had read his books—he must have merely heard his name.

By a happy coincidence, none other than Konstantin Fedin happened to read Mann's letter to Huchel a few years later.[11] His take on Huchel's anecdote was very different to Mann's. *Of course* the machinist had read Mann's novels, Fedin responded—the working masses in Soviet Russia are cultured and well read, to the extent that 'das in unserem Volk vorhandene Bedürfnis, die Klassiker zu lesen, selbst durch die produktivste Arbeit der Verlage nicht befriedigt werden [kann]!' ('our people's desire to read the classics cannot be satisfied even by the most efficient work of the publishing houses!').[12] Admittedly, this might be hard to imagine for Mann, Fedin continued, given that the Western intelligentsia is entirely separated from the working masses—but all it means for Western writers like Mann is that 'es eben die Zeit gekommen [ist], einen neuen Leser heranzubilden, die Zahl der Leser zu erhöhen, ihren Kreis zu erweitern, seine eigenen "Dampfermaschinisten" in ihn einzuführen' ('the time has come to train new

---

[8] The letter exchange was published as 'Briefwechsel mit Thomas Mann', *Sinn und Form*, 7.5 (1955), 669–76, p. 673.
[9] Ibid., p. 674.   [10] Ibid.
[11] Konstantin Fedin, 'Thomas Mann: Zu seinem achtzigsten Geburtstag', in *Dichter, Kunst, Zeit*, trans. Georg Schwarz (Berlin: Aufbau, 1959), pp. 212–21, p. 220.
[12] Ibid., p. 221.

readers, to increase their numbers, to broaden the reading public, to introduce its own "steamship machinists" into it').[13]

We will probably never know if this little scene on the steamship 'Pravda' (Russian for 'truth') *really* took place. We can have our doubts about Huchel's intentions in recounting it and his exoticization of Soviet workers, as well as about Fedin's glorification of the cultural resources available to them. But in the exchange between the machinist, Huchel, Mann, and Fedin a familiar question comes back like a boomerang: who should read Mann? Who can read Mann? Who does actually read him? It is not hard to believe that this small glimpse of an unlikely foreign reader really did deeply touch Mann. This is because it matters when books matter to readers. And even if we cannot hear from the machinist on the Don anymore, we can still listen to many other readers of Mann—which is exactly what I wanted to do in this study of world literature and closer reading.

[13] Ibid.

Bibliography

'100 Jahre Faszination Zauberberg und Thomas Mann' <http://www.davos.ch/fileadmin/user_upload/medien/texte_und_themen/Medientext_100JahreZauberberg_d.pdf> [accessed 30 May 2017]

Adam, Christian, '"Nach zwei Jahren spricht von diesem Buch kein Mensch mehr". Kurzer Ruhm und langes Leben zwischen Bestsellerliste und Longsellerdasein', in *Text und Kritik: Sonderband Gelesene Literatur: Populäre Lektüre im Zeichen des Medienwandels*, ed. Steffen Martus and Carlos Spoerhase (Munich: Edition Text + Kritik, 2018), pp. 21–30

Aftab, Kaleem, '*Youth*, Cannes Film Review', *The Independent*, 20 May 2015 <http://www.independent.co.uk/arts-entertainment/films/reviews/youth-cannes-film-review-michael-caine-stakes-his-claim-to-an-oscar-with-the-best-film-so-far-at-the-10265206.html> [accessed 20 May 2016]

Akimoto, Daisuke, 'War Memory, War Responsibility, and Anti-war Pacifism in Director Miyazaki's *The Wind Rises* (*Kaze Tachinu*)', *Soka University Peace Research*, 28 (2014), 45–72

Allen, Graham, *Intertextuality* (Abingdon: Routledge, 2011)

Andrews, Nigel, '*Youth* — Film Review: "Rambling"', *Financial Times*, 28 January 2016 <http://www.ft.com/cms/s/2/cf6254d6-c5be-11e5-b3b1-7b2481276e45.html#axzz4A8jKUKvI> [accessed 20 May 2016]

Anker, Elizabeth S., and Rita Felski, eds., *Critique and Postcritique* (Durham, NC: Duke University Press, 2017)

Apter, Emily, *Against World Literature* (London: Verso, 2013)

Arnold, Heinz L., ed., *Text und Kritik: Sonderband Thomas Mann* (Munich: Edition Text + Kritik, 1976)

'Arts Programme at New Cancer Centre at Guy's Wins Design Award', 22 June 2017 <https://futurecity.co.uk/arts-programme-at-new-cancer-centre-at-guys-wins-design-award/> [accessed 10 June 2019]

Balmes, Hans Jürgen, Jörg Bong, and Helmut Mayer, eds., 'Thomas Mann' [special issue], *Neue Rundschau*, 116.2 (2005)

Bałżewska, Katarzyna, '*Czarodziejska góra*' *w literaturze polskiej: ślady/interpretacje/nawiązania* (Katowice: Śląsk, 2018)

Barthes, Roland, 'L'effet de réel', *Communications*, 11 (1968), 84–89

Batuman, Elif, 'From the Critical Impulse, the Growth of Literature', *The New York Times*, 31 December 2010 <https://www.nytimes.com/2011/01/02/books/review/Batuman-t-web.html> [accessed 10 May 2019]

Batuman, Elif, *The Possessed: Adventures with Russian Books and the People Who Read Them* (New York: Farrar, Straus and Giroux, 2010)

Batuman, Elif, *The Idiot* (New York: Penguin, 2018)

Baudot, Laura, 'Closer Reading', *The Point*, 19 (2019) <https://thepointmag.com/examined-life/closer-reading/> [accessed 1 May 2021]

Bayard, Pierre, *How to Talk about Books You Haven't Read*, trans. Jeffrey Mehlman (New York: Bloomsbury, 2007)

Beddow, Michael, *The Fiction of Humanity* (Cambridge: Cambridge University Press, 1982)

Bennett, Andrew, ed., *Readers and Reading* (Abingdon: Routledge, 2013)

Benson, Renate, *Erich Kästner: Studien zu seinem Werk* (Bonn: Bouvier, 1973)

Berman, Russell A., 'Modernism and the Bildungsroman: Thomas Mann's *Magic Mountain*', in *The Cambridge Companion to the Modern German Novel*, ed. Graham Bartram (Cambridge: Cambridge University Press, 2004), pp. 77–92

Bernofsky, Susan, 'Fresh Air', *The Berlin Journal*, 34 (2020), 58–59

Best, Stephen, '*La Foi Postcritique*, on Second Thought', *PMLA*, 132.2 (2017), 337–43

Bloom, Harold, *The Western Canon* (London: Macmillan, 1995)

Boes, Tobias, 'Thomas Mann, World Author: Representation and Autonomy in the World Republic of Letters', *Seminar: A Journal of Germanic Studies*, 51 (2015), 132–47

Boes, Tobias, *Thomas Mann's War: Literature, Politics, and the World Republic of Letters* (Ithaca, NY: Cornell University Press, 2019)

Bollnow, Otto Friedrich, 'Gespräche in Davos', in *Erinnerung an Martin Heidegger*, ed. Günther Neske (Pfullingen: Neske, 1977), pp. 25–29

Bonifazio, Massimo, '"Non si leggeva poco…"'. Considerazioni su Hans Castorp lettore', *Bollettino dell'Associazione italiana di germanistica*, iv (2011), 83–95

Booth, Stephen, *'King Lear', 'Macbeth', Indefinition, and Tragedy* (New Haven, CT: Yale University Press, 1983

Booth, Wayne, *The Company We Keep* (Berkeley, CA: University of California Press, 1988)

Bradshaw, Peter, '*Youth* review—Life and Death as Seen from a Luxury Hot Tub', *The Guardian*, 28 January 2016 <https://www.theguardian.com/film/2016/jan/28/youth-review-life-and-death-as-seen-from-a-luxury-hot-tub> [accessed 20 May 2016]

Bradshaw, Peter, 'And the 2018 Braddies Go To…Peter Bradshaw's Films of the Year', *The Guardian*, 10 December 2018 <https://www.theguardian.com/film/2018/dec/10/braddies-peter-bradshaw-films-of-the-year> [accessed 10 June 2019]

Braun, Rebecca, 'Cultural Impact and the Power of Myth in Popular Public Constructions of Authorship', in *Cultural Impact in the German Context*, ed. Rebecca Braun and Lyn Marven (Rochester, NY: Camden House, 2010), pp. 78–96

Brecht, Bertolt, 'Anmerkungen zur Oper *Aufstieg und Fall der Stadt Mahagonny*', in *Werke: Große Kommentierte Berliner und Frankfurter Ausgabe*, ed. Werner Hecht and others (Frankfurt am Main: Suhrkamp, 1988–98), xxiv: *Schriften 4: Texte zu Stücken*, ed. Peter Kraft (1991), pp. 74–86

Brecht, Bertolt, 'Thomas Mann im Börsensaal', in *Werke*, ed. Werner Hecht and others, xxi: *Schriften 1: 1914–1933* (Frankfurt am Main: Suhrkamp, 1992), pp. 61–62

Breen, Deborah, 'Designs and Dreams: Questions of Technology in Hayao Miyazaki's *The Wind Rises*', *Technology and Culture*, 57.2 (2016), 457–59

Briggs, Kate, *This Little Art* (London: Fitzcarraldo, 2017)

Brody, Richard, 'The Tasteless Intricacies of *A Cure for Wellness*', *The New Yorker*, 16 February 2017 <https://www.newyorker.com/culture/richard-brody/the-tasteless-intricacies-of-a-cure-for-wellness> [accessed 10 March 2019]

Brooks, Peter, *The Melodramatic Imagination: Balzac, Henry James, Melodrama, and the Mode of Excess* (New Haven, CT: Yale University Press, 1995)

Bruford, W. H., *The German Tradition of Self-Cultivation: 'Bildung' from Humboldt to Thomas Mann* (Cambridge: Cambridge University Press, 1975)

Buchanan, Ian, *Oxford Dictionary of Critical Theory* (Oxford: Oxford University Press, 2018)

Byatt, A. S., 'Introduction', in Thomas Mann, *The Magic Mountain* (New York: A. A. Knopf, 2005), trans. John E. Woods, pp. vii–xxi

Bynum, Helen, *Spitting Blood: The History of Tuberculosis* (Oxford: Oxford University Press, 2012)

Byrne, Katherine, *Tuberculosis and the Victorian Literary Imagination* (Cambridge: Cambridge University Press, 2011)

Byron, Mark, 'Close Reading', in *Oxford Research Encyclopedia of Literature*, 25 March 2011 <https://doi.org/10.1093/acrefore/9780190201098.013.1014> [accessed 1 May 2021]

Calvino, Italo, *Six Memos for the Next Millennium*, trans. Patrick Creagh (Cambridge, MA: Harvard University Press, 1988)

Capriccioli, Alessandro, 'Generatore automatico di scene del prossimo film di Sorrentino', *LiberNazione*, 26 May 2015 <http://libernazione.it/generatore-automatico-di-scene-del-prossimo-film-di-sorrentino/> [accessed 20 May 2016]

Cassirer, Toni, 'Cassirer und Heidegger in Davos', in *Nachlese zu Heidegger*, ed. Guido Schneeberger (Bern: [n. pub.], 1962), pp. 7–9

Cave, Terence, *Mignon's Afterlives: Crossing Cultures from Goethe to the Twenty-First Century* (Oxford: Oxford University Press, 2011)

Cave, Terence, *Thinking with Literature: Towards a Cognitive Criticism* (Oxford: Oxford University Press, 2016)

Chow, Rey, *Writing Diaspora: Tactics of Intervention in Contemporary Cultural Studies* (Bloomington, IN: Indiana University Press, 1993)

Claeys, Gregory, *Marx and Marxism* (London: Penguin, 2018)

Clark, Suzanne, *Sentimental Modernism: Women Writers and the Revolution of the Word* (Bloomington, IN: Indiana University Press, 1991)

Cocks, Geoffrey, 'Death by Typewriter: Stanley Kubrick, the Holocaust, and *The Shining*', in *Depth of Field: Stanley Kubrick, Film, and the Uses of History*, ed. Geoffrey Cocks, James Diedrick, and Glenn W. Perusek (Madison, WI: University of Wisconsin Press, 2006), pp. 185–217

Cohen, Ralph, 'The First Decade: Some Editorial Remarks', *New Literary History*, 10 (1979), 417–21

Colman, Andrew M., *Oxford Dictionary of Psychology* (Oxford: Oxford University Press, 2015)

Cooke, Paul, 'Abnormal Consensus? The New Internationalism of German Cinema', in *German Culture, Politics, and Literature Into the Twenty-first Century: Beyond Normalization*, ed. Stuart Taberner and Paul Cooke (Rochester, NY: Camden House, 2006), pp. 223–36

Cox, Ailsa, ' "Almost Like a Ghost": Spectral Figures in Alice Munro's Short Fiction', in *Liminality and the Short Story: Boundary Crossings in American, Canadian, and British Writing*, ed. Jochen Achilles and Ina Bergmann (Abingdon: Routledge, 2014), pp. 238–50

Cusack, Andrew, *The Wanderer in Nineteenth-Century German Literature: Intellectual History and Cultural Criticism* (Rochester, NY: Camden House, 2008)

Damrosch, David, *What Is World Literature?* (Princeton, NJ: Princeton University Press, 2003)

Damrosch, David, *Comparing the Literatures: Literary Studies in a Global World* (Princeton, NJ: Princeton University Press, 2020)

Danius, Sara, *The Senses of Modernism: Technology, Perception, and Aesthetics* (Ithaca, NY: Cornell University Press, 2002)

Darnton, Robert, 'First Steps Toward a History of Reading', *Australian Journal of French Studies*, 23 (1986), 5–30

Davis, Philip, *Reading and the Reader* (Oxford: Oxford University Press, 2013)

De Mendelssohn, Peter, *Nachbemerkungen zu Thomas Mann* (Frankfurt am Main: Fischer, 1982)

De Montherlant, Henry, *Selected Essays*, trans. John Weightman (London: Weidenfeld & Nicholson, 1960)

Detering, Heinrich, and Stephan Stachorski, eds., *Thomas Mann: Neue Wege der Forschung* (Darmstadt: WBG, 2008)

D'Ettorre, Francesca, 'Recensione: *Youth—La giovinezza*', *OndaCinema*, 23 May 2015 <http://www.ondacinema.it/film/recensione/youth_giovinezza.html> [accessed 20 May 2016]

Dimock, Wai-Chee, 'Genre as World System: Epic and Novel on Four Continents', *Narrative*, 14.1 (2006), 85–101

Eagleton, Terry, 'Not Just Anybody', *London Review of Books*, 39.1 (2017), 35–37

Edmond, Jacob, 'Copy', in *A New Vocabulary for Global Modernism*, ed. Eric Hayot and Rebecca Walkowitz (New York: Columbia University Press, 2016), pp. 96–113

Eliot, George, *Middlemarch* (London: Penguin, 2012)

Ellis, A. E., *The Rack* (London: Heinemann, 1958)

Ellis, Markman, *The Politics of Sensibility: Race, Gender and Commerce in the Sentimental Novel* (Cambridge: Cambridge University Press, 2004)

Elsaesser, Thomas, *Weimar Cinema and After: Germany's Historical Imaginary* (New York: Routledge, 2000)

Elstun, Esther N., 'Two Views of the Mountain: Thomas Mann's *Zauberberg* and Konstantin Fedin's *Sanatorium Arktur*', *Germano-Slavica*, 3 (1974), 55–71

Ender, Evelyne, and Deidre Shauna Lynch, eds., 'Cultures of Reading' [special issue], *PMLA*, 134.1 (2019)

Englert, Ludwig, 'Als Student bei den Zweiten Davoser Hochschulkursen März 1929', in *Nachlese zu Heidegger*, ed. Guido Schneeberger (Bern: [n. pub.], 1962), pp. 1–6

Erpenbeck, Jenny, 'Dankesrede zum Thomas-Mann-Preis der Hansestadt Lübeck und der Bayrischen Akademie der Schönen Künste', in *Kein Roman: Texte und Reden* (Munich: Penguin, 2018), pp. 274–81

Erpenbeck, Jenny, '"Will I Come to a Miserable End?": Jenny Erpenbeck on Thomas Mann', trans. Kurt Beals, *Literary Hub*, 3 September 2020 <https://lithub.com/will-i-come-to-a-miserable-end-jenny-erpenbeck-on-thomas-mann/> [accessed 1 May 2021]

Ette, Ottmar, *WeltFraktale. Wege durch die Literaturen der Welt* (Stuttgart: Metzler, 2017)

Fedin, Konstantin, *Sanatorium Arktur*, trans. Olga Shartse (Moscow: Foreign Languages Publishing House, 1957)

Fedin, Konstantin, 'Thomas Mann: Zu seinem achtzigsten Geburtstag', in *Dichter, Kunst, Zeit*, trans. Georg Schwarz (Berlin: Aufbau, 1959), pp. 212–21

Fedin, Konstantin, *Sanatorii Arktur*, in *Sobranie sochinenii* (Moscow: Khudozh. lit-ra, 1969–73), v: *Sanatorii Arktur—Pervye radosti* (1971), pp. 7–134

Felski, Rita, *Uses of Literature* (Oxford: Blackwell, 2008)

Felski, Rita, *The Limits of Critique* (Chicago: The University of Chicago Press, 2015)

Felski, Rita, 'Response', *PMLA*, 132.2 (2017), 384–91

Felski, Rita, *Hooked: Art and Attachment* (Chicago: The University of Chicago Press, 2020)

Festival de Cannes, Youth Conference Cannes 2015, online video recording, YouTube, 20 May 2015 <https://www.youtube.com/watch?v=LX_gai9PmJA> [accessed 20 May 2016]

Fish, Stanley, *Is There a Text In This Class? The Authority of Interpretive Communities* (Cambridge, MA: Harvard University Press, 1980)

Flood, Alison, 'Booker Winner *Milkman* Defies "Challenging" Reputation to Become Bestseller', *The Guardian*, 23 October 2018 <https://www.theguardian.com/books/2018/oct/23/booker-winner-milkman-defies-challenging-bestseller-anna-burns> [accessed 1 May 2021]

Frank, Alison F., 'The Air Cure Town: Commodifying Mountain Air in Alpine Central Europe', *Central European History*, 45 (2012), 185–207

Friedländer, Salomo [Mynona], 'Zauberpredigt eines ungläubigen Thomas an Mannbare: Rezept zum Kitsch allerersten Ranges', *Die neue Bücherschau*, 4 (1926), 186–87

Fuechtner, Veronika, 'The Magician's Mother: A Story of Coffee, Race, and German Culture', presented at The American Academy in Berlin, 14 February 2020 <https://www.american academy.de/videoaudio/the-magicians-mother-a-story-of-coffee-race-and-german-culture/> [accessed 1 May 2021]

Fuentes, Carlos, 'How Zurich Invented the Modern World', *Salon*, 30 September 1997 <https://www.salon.com/1997/09/30/zurich> [accessed 10 May 2019]

Fuller, David, 'A Kind of Loving: Hans Castorp as Model Critic', in *Thomas Mann and Shakespeare: Something Rich and Strange*, ed. Tobias Döring and Ewan Fernie (New York: Bloomsbury, 2015), pp. 207–28

Głowiński, Michał, 'Nad "Castorpem"', *Przegląd Polityczny*, 70 (2005), 65–68

Gooderham, W. B., 'Winter Reads: *The Magic Mountain* by Thomas Mann', *The Guardian*, 14 December 2011 <http://www.theguardian.com/books/2011/dec/14/winter-reads-thomas-mann-magic-mountain> [accessed 10 May 2019]

Gordon, Peter E., *Continental Divide: Heidegger, Cassirer, Davos* (Cambridge, MA: Harvard University Press, 2010)

Goßens, Peter, *Weltliteratur. Modelle transnationaler Literaturwahrnehmung im 19. Jahrhundert* (Stuttgart: Metzler, 2011)

Gutmann, Helmut, 'Das Musikkapitel in Thomas Manns *Zauberberg*', *The German Quarterly*, 47 (1974), 415–31

Haefs, Wilhelm, 'Geist, Geld und Buch. Thomas Manns Aufstieg zum Erfolgsautor im S. Fischer Verlag in der Weimarer Republik', in *Die Erfindung des Schriftstellers Thomas Mann*, ed. Michael Ansel, Hans-Edwin Friedrich, and Gerhard Lauer (Berlin: De Gruyter, 2009), pp. 123–59

Hakemulder, Frank, and others, eds., *Narrative Absorption* (Amsterdam: John Benjamins, 2017)

Hamsun, Knut, *Chapter the Last*, trans. Arthur G. Chater (London: A. A. Knopf, 1930)

Han, Angie, 'Interview with Gore Verbinski on Returning to Horror with *A Cure for Wellness*', 21 December 2016 <https://www.slashfilm.com/a-cure-for-wellness-gore-verbinski-interview/> [accessed 10 March 2018]

Hanuschek, Sven, *Keiner blickt dir hinter das Gesicht* (Munich: Hanser, 1999)

Hardach, Gerd, '1929: Wirtschaft im Umbruch', in *Die Welt spielt Roulette. Zur Kultur der Moderne in der Krise 1927 bis 1932*, ed. Werner Möller (Frankfurt am Main: Campus, 2002)

Hawes, James, *The Shortest History of Germany* (London: Old Street Publishing, 2017)

Heftrich, Eckhard, 'Der gehaßte Kollege: Deutsche Schriftsteller über Thomas Mann', *Thomas-Mann-Studien*, 7 (1987), 351–69

Heftrich, Eckhard, 'Der *Homo oeconomicus* im Werk von Thomas Mann', in *Der litera-rische Homo oeconomicus*, ed. Werner Wunderlich (Bern: Haupt, 1989), pp. 153–69

Heilbut, Anthony, *Thomas Mann: Eros & Literature* (London: Macmillan, 1996)

Heller, Erich, *Thomas Mann: The Ironic German* (London: Secker & Warburg, 1958)

Herlth, Jens, 'Słodko-gorzkie heterotopie. Bruno Schulz i "tekst sanatoryjny" w europejskiej literaturze okresu międzywojennego', *Wielogłos: Pismo Wydziału Polonistyki UJ*, 2 (16) 2013, 25–37

Hermand, Jost, *Die Toten schweigen nicht: Brecht-Aufsätze* (Frankfurt am Main: Peter Lang, 2010)

Herrnstein Smith, Barbara, 'Contingencies of Value', *Critical Inquiry*, 10 (1983), 1–35

Herrnstein Smith, Barbara, 'What Was "Close Reading"? A Century of Method in Literary Studies', *the minnesota review*, 87 (2016), 57–75

Herwig, Malte, 'The "Magic Mountain Malady": *The Magic Mountain* and the Medical Community, 1924–2006', in *Thomas Mann's 'The Magic Mountain': A Casebook*, ed. Hans Rudolf Vaget (Oxford: Oxford University Press, 2008), pp. 245–64

Hildebrandt, Wolfgang, 'Zauberberg und Kriegsgefangenschaft: Offener Brief an Thomas Mann', *Der Ruf*, 1 October 1945, 4

Hillesheim, Jürgen, *Augsburger Brecht-Lexikon* (Würzburg: Königshausen & Neumann, 2000)

Hofmannsthal, Hugo von, 'Der Ersatz für die Träume', in *Gesammelte Werke*, ed. Bernd Schoeller (Frankfurt am Main: Fischer, 1979–80), ix: *Reden und Aufsätze II: 1914–1924* (1979), pp. 141–45

Hölter, Achim, '*Doppelte Optik* und *lange Ohren*—Notes on Aesthetic Compromise', in *Quote, Double Quote: Aesthetics between High and Popular Culture*, ed. Paul Ferstl and Keyvan Sarkhosh (Amsterdam: Rodopi, 2014), pp. 43–63

Horton, David, *Thomas Mann in English: A Study in Literary Translation* (New York: Bloomsbury, 2016)

Howard, June, 'What Is Sentimentality?', *American Literary History*, 11.1 (1999), 63–81

Howard, Maureen, 'This Long Disease, My Life', *The Kenyon Review*, 22.1 (1960), 156–59

Huelle, Paweł, *Castorp*, trans. Antonia Lloyd-Jones (London: Serpent's Tail, 2007)

Huelle, Paweł, *Castorp* (Cracow: Znak, 2009)

Husmann, Wenke, 'Zwei großartige alte Männer', *Die Zeit*, 20 May 2015 <http://www.zeit.de/kultur/film/2015-05/youth-cannes-caine-keitel> [accessed 20 May 2016]

'In Praise of…The Magic Mountain', *The Guardian*, 27 January 2011 <https://www.theguardian.com/commentisfree/2011/jan/27/the-magic-mountain-thomas-mann> [accessed 10 June 2019]

'Intervista a Paolo Sorrentino', *Youth—La giovinezza*, dir. by Paolo Sorrentino (Warner Brothers, 2015)

Iser, Wolfgang, *Die Appellstruktur der Texte: Unbestimmtheit als Wirkungsbedingung literarischer Prosa* (Konstanz: Universitätsverlag, 1970)

Jameson, Fredric, *Modernist Papers* (London: Verso, 2007)

Janssens-Knorsch, U., and L.R. Leavis, '"Buddenbrook & Son": Thomas Mann and Literary Influence', *English Studies*, 82.6 (2001), 521–38

Jauss, Hans Robert, *Literaturgeschichte als Provokation* (Frankfurt am Main: Suhrkamp, 1970)

Jonas, Klaus, and Holger R. Stunz, eds., *Die Internationalität der Brüder Mann: 100 Jahre Rezeption auf fünf Kontinenten (1907–2008)* (Frankfurt am Main: Klostermann, 2011)

Jordan, Brenda G., 'Michael Lucken, *Imitation and Creativity in Japanese Arts: From Kishida Ryūsei to Miyazaki Hayao*', *Japanese Studies*, 37.2 (2017), 272–74

Joseph, Erkme, 'Hans Castorps biologische Phantasie in der Frostnacht', *Wirkendes Wort*, 46 (1996), 393–411

'Journal articles about The Magic Mountain' <https://www.goodreads.com/topic/show/1404552-journal-articles-about-the-magic-mountain> [accessed 15 March 2019]

Kästner, Erich, *Der Zauberlehrling*, in *Kästner für Erwachsene: Ausgewählte Schriften*, ed. Luiselotte Enderle (Stuttgart: Deutscher Bücherbund, 1984), iii: *Fabian—Der Zauberlehrling—Die Schule der Diktatoren*, pp. 203–97

Kästner, Erich, *Kästner im Schnee*, ed. Sylvia List (Zurich: Atrium, 2011)

Kessler, Frank, '"Spellbound in Darkness": Narrative Absorption Discussed by Film Theory', *Narrative Absorption*, ed. Frank Hakemulder and others (Amsterdam: John Benjamins, 2017), pp. 119–32

Kierkegaard, Søren, *Fear and Trembling/Repetition*, trans. Edna H. Hong and Howard V. Hong (Princeton, NJ: Princeton University Press, 1983)

Kilb, Andreas, 'Die Überlebenden des Zauberbergs lassen grüßen', *FAZ*, 27 November 2015 <http://www.faz.net/aktuell/feuilleton/kino/ewige-jugend-im-kino-die-ueberlebenden-des-zauberbergs-lassen-gruessen-13931931. html> [accessed 20 May 2016]

Kim, Young-Ok, 'Übernahme, Anverwandlung, Umgestaltung. Thomas Mann in der koreanischen Literatur', *Zeitschrift für Germanistik*, 7 (1997), 9–24

Kinder, Anna, *Geldströme: Ökonomie im Romanwerk Thomas Manns* (Berlin: De Gruyter, 2013)

Kitcher, Philip, *Deaths in Venice: The Cases of Gustav von Aschenbach* (New York: Columbia University Press, 2016)

Knausgaard, Karl Ove, *Dancing in the Dark*, trans. Don Bartlett (London: Vintage, 2015)

Knausgaard, Karl Ove, *Some Rain Must Fall*, trans. Don Bartlett (London: Vintage, 2016)

Kontje, Todd, *Thomas Mann's World: Empire, Race, and the Jewish Question* (Ann Arbor, MI: University of Michigan Press, 2011)

Koopmann, Helmut, *Die Entwicklung des 'intellektuellen Romans' bei Thomas Mann* (Bonn: Bouvier, 1980)

Koopmann, Helmut, ed., *Thomas-Mann-Handbuch* (Stuttgart: A. Kröner, 2001)

Kopp, Kristin, *Germany's Wild East: Constructing Poland as Colonial Space* (Ann Arbor, MI: University of Michigan Press, 2012)

Kornienko, N. V., and I. E. Kabanova, eds., *Konstantin Fedin i ego sovremenniki: iz literaturnogo naslediia XX veka* (Moscow: Institut mirovoi literatury im. A. M. Gor'kogo RAN, 2016)

Kurzke, Hermann, *Thomas-Mann-Forschung, 1969–1976: Ein kritischer Bericht* (Frankfurt am Main: Fischer, 1977)

Kurzke, Hermann, ed., *Stationen der Thomas-Mann-Forschung: Aufsätze seit 1970* (Würzburg: Königshausen & Neumann, 1985)

Kurzke, Hermann, 'Der mit den Wölfen heulte', *FAZ*, 3 January 2001 <http://www.faz.net/aktuell/feuilleton/buecher/rezension-sachbuch-der-mit-den-woelfen-heulte-11267861. html> [accessed 30 May 2017]

Kurzke, Hermann, *Thomas Mann: Epoche, Werk, Wirkung* (Munich: Beck, 2010)

Lämmert, Eberhard, 'Doppelte Optik. Über die Erzählkunst des frühen Thomas Mann', in *Literatur, Sprache, Gesellschaft*, ed. Karl Rüdinger (Munich: Bayerischer Schulbuch-Verlag, 1970), pp. 50–72

Lane, David, *Leninism: A Sociological Interpretation* (Cambridge: Cambridge University Press, 1981)

Last, Rex William, *Erich Kästner* (London: Wolff, 1974)

Law, Ricky W., *Transnational Nazism: Ideology and Culture in German-Japanese Relations, 1919–1936* (Cambridge: Cambridge University Press, 2019)

Lawlor, Clark, *Consumption and Literature: The Making of the Romantic Disease* (Basingstoke: Palgrave Macmillan, 2006)

Lee, D. C., 'On the Marxian View of the Relationship between Man and Nature', in *Karl Marx's Social and Political Thought*, ed. Bob Jessop and Russell Wheatley (London: Routledge, 1999), viii: *Nature, Culture, Moral, Ethics*, pp. 1–15

Lehnert, Herbert, *Thomas-Mann-Forschung: Ein Bericht* (Stuttgart: Metzler, 1969)

Le Rider, Jacques, 'L'Europe malade au sanatorium', *En attendant Nadeau*, 14 March 2017 <https://www.en-attendant-nadeau.fr/2017/03/14/sanatorium-mann-oliveira> [accessed 15 March 2019]

Lodge, David, *Changing Places* (London: Vintage, 2011)

Lodge, David, *Small World* (London: Vintage, 2011)

Love, Heather, 'Critique Is Ordinary', *PMLA*, 132.2 (2017), 364–70

Lucken, Michael, *Imitation and Creativity in Japanese Arts: From Kishida Ryusei to Miyazaki Hayao*, trans. Francesca Simkin (New York: Columbia University Press, 2016)

Lukács, Georg, *Thomas Mann* (Berlin: Aufbau, 1949)

Lutz, Tom, 'In the Shadow of the Archive', in *The Critic as Amateur*, ed. Saikat Majumdar and Aarthi Vadde (New York: Bloomsbury, 2020), pp. 49–61

Mani, B. Venkat, *Recoding World Literature: Libraries, Print Culture, and Germany's Pact with Books* (New York: Fordham University Press, 2017)

Mank, Dieter, *Erich Kästner im nationalsozialistischen Deutschland: 1933–1945, Zeit ohne Werk?* (Frankfurt am Main: Peter Lang, 1981)

Mann, Thomas, 'Briefwechsel mit Thomas Mann', *Sinn und Form*, 7.5 (1955), 669–76

Mann, Thomas, 'Richard Wagner und *Der Ring des Nibelungen*', in *Gesammelte Werke*, ed. Hans Bürgin (Frankfurt am Main: Fischer, 1960–1974), ix: *Reden und Aufsätze 1* (1960), pp. 505–27

Mann, Thomas, 'Einführung in *Den Zauberberg* für Studenten der Universität Princeton', in *Der Zauberberg* (Frankfurt am Main, 1962), pp. ii–xiv

Mann, Thomas, 'Romane der Welt: Ein Geleitwort', in *Weimarer Republik: Manifeste und Dokumente zur deutschen Literatur 1918–1933*, ed. Anton Kaes (Stuttgart: Metzler, 1983), pp. 287–89

Mann, Thomas, *Briefwechsel mit Autoren*, ed. Hans Wysling (Frankfurt am Main: Fischer, 1988)

Mann, Thomas, *Selbstkommentare: 'Der Zauberberg'*, ed. Hans Wysling and Marianne Eich-Fischer (Frankfurt am Main: Fischer, 1993)

Mann, Thomas, *Death in Venice and Other Stories*, trans. David Luke (London: Vintage, 1998)

Mann, Thomas, 'The Making of *The Magic Mountain*', in *The Magic Mountain*, trans. H. T. Lowe-Porter (London: Vintage, 1999)

Mann, Thomas, *Der Zauberberg*, ed. Michael Neumann, GKFA (Frankfurt am Main: Fischer, 2002)

Mann, Thomas, *Frühe Erzählungen: 1983–1912*, ed. T. J. Reed, GKFA (Frankfurt am Main, 2004)

Mann, Thomas, *The Magic Mountain*, trans. John E. Woods (London: Everyman, 2005).

Marche, Stephen, 'The "Debate of the Century": What Happened When Jordan Peterson Debated Slavoj Žižek', 20 April 2019 <https://www.theguardian.com/world/2019/apr/20/jordan-peterson-slavoj-zizek-happiness-capitalism-marxism> [accessed 20 June 2019]

Marcus, Judith, *Georg Lukács and Thomas Mann: A Study in the Sociology of Literature* (Amherst, MA: University of Massachusetts Press, 1987)

Marling, William, *Gatekeepers: The Emergence of World Literature and the 1960s* (Oxford: Oxford University Press, 2016)

Marlow-Mann, Alex, 'Character Engagement and Alienation in the Cinema of Paolo Sorrentino', in *Italian Film Directors in the New Millennium*, ed. William Hope (Newcastle upon Tyne: Cambridge Scholars, 2010), pp. 161–73

Marx, Karl, *The Grundrisse*, trans. and ed. David McLellan (New York: Harper Torchbooks, 1971)

Marx, Karl, *Grundrisse der Kritik der politischen Ökonomie* (Berlin: Dietz, 1974)

Marx, Karl, and Friedrich Engels, 'Manifest der Kommunistischen Partei', in *Ausgewählte Werke in sechs Bänden* (Berlin: Dietz, 1972), i, pp. 383–451

Marx, Karl, and Friedrich Engels, *The Communist Manifesto*, trans. David McLellan (Oxford: Oxford University Press, 2008)

Mayer, Hans, and Jack Zipes, 'Thomas Mann and Bertolt Brecht: Anatomy of an Antagonism', *New German Critique*, 6 (1975), 101–15

McCarthy, Todd, '*Youth*: Cannes Review', *The Hollywood Reporter*, 20 May 2015 <http://www.hollywoodreporter.com/review/youth-cannes-review-797046> [accessed 20 May 2016]

McDonald, John, 'Movie Review: *A Cure for Wellness* (2016) Offers a Nightmarish View of Wall St', *Australian Financial Review*, 24 March 2017 <https://www.afr.com/lifestyle/arts-and-entertainment/film-and-tv/movie-review-a-cure-for-wellness-2016-20170322-gv3fhj> [accessed 10 May 2019]

McGrane, Sally, 'To the Magic Mountain!', *The New Yorker*, 17 February 2014 <http://www.newyorker.com/books/page-turner/to-the-magic-mountain> [accessed 30 May 2017]

Mews, Siegfried, 'The Professor's Novel: David Lodge's *Small World*', *MLN*, 104 (1989), 713–26

Meyers, Jeffrey, *Disease and the Novel 1880–1960* (London: Macmillan, 1985)

Meyers, Jeffrey, 'Comedy in *The Magic Mountain*', *The New Criterion*, 30.2 (2011), 1–6

Minden, Michael, ed., *Thomas Mann* (London: Longman, 1995)

Minden, Michael, *The German Bildungsroman. Incest and Inheritance* (Cambridge: Cambridge University Press, 1997)

Minden, Michael, 'Popularity and the Magic Circle of Culture', *Publications of the English Goethe Society*, 76.2 (2007), 93–101

Miyazaki, Hayao, dir., *The Wind Rises* (StudioCanal, 2014)

Moretti, Franco, 'Conjectures on World Literature', *New Left Review*, 1 (2000), 54–68

'"Mountain" at Guy's and St Thomas' Hospital' <https://www.pentagram.com/work/mountain-at-guys-and-st-thomas-hospital/story> [accessed 10 June 2019]

Muir, Edwin, 'Endurance Point: *The Rack* by A. E. Ellis', *The Observer*, 9 November 1958, 21

Mukhopadhyay, Priyasha, 'On Not Reading *The Soldier's Pocket-book for Field Service*', *Journal of Victorian Culture*, 22.1 (2017), 40–56

Mulvey, Laura, 'Visual Pleasure and Narrative Cinema', *Screen*, 16.3 (1975), 6–18

Munro, Alice, 'Amundsen', in *Dear Life* (London: Chatto & Windus, 2012), pp. 31–66

Munro, Alice, 'Amundsen', *The New Yorker*, 20 August 2012 <https://www.newyorker.com/magazine/2012/08/27/amundsen> [accessed 5 February 2018]

Munro, Alice, 'Dear Life', in *Dear Life* (London: Chatto & Windus, 2012), pp. 299–319

Murakami, Haruki, *Norwegian Wood*, trans. Jay Rubin (London: Vintage, 2003)

Murata, Tsunekazu, 'Thomas Mann in Japan', in *Thomas Mann 1875–1975: Vorträge in München—Zürich—Lübeck*, ed. Beatrix Bludau, Eckhard Heftrich, and Helmut Koopmann (Frankfurt am Main: Fischer, 1977)

Nabokov, Vladimir, 'An Affair of Honor', in *Nabokov's Quartet*, trans. Dmitri Nabokov (London: Panther, 1969), pp. 11–49

Neider, Charles, ed., *The Stature of Thomas Mann* (New York: New Directions, 1947)

Neuhaus, Stefan, *Das verschwiegene Werk: Erich Kästners Mitarbeit an Theaterstücken unter Pseudonym* (Würzburg: Königshausen & Neumann, 2000)

Neumann, Michael, *Thomas Mann, 'Der Zauberberg': Kommentar*, GKFA (Frankfurt am Main: Fischer, 2002)

Newman, Kim, '*A Cure for Wellness*', *Sight and Sound*, 27.4 (2017), 76

Newton, Maud, 'Pulling Thomas Mann's *The Magic Mountain* Off the Shelf', 28 June 2009 <http://maudnewton.com/blog/pulling-thomas-manns-the-magic-mountain-off-the-shelf/> [accessed 10 June 2019]

Nicholson, Geoffrey, 'Back to the Mountain', *The Spectator*, 31 October 1958, 592

Nirenberg, David, 'When Philosophy Mattered', *The New Republic*, 13 January 2011 <https://newrepublic.com/article/81380/heidegger-cassirer-davos-kant> [accessed 10 June 2019]

Oatley, Keith, *Such Stuff as Dreams: The Psychology of Fiction* (Chichester: Wiley-Blackwell, 2011)

Oguro, Yasumasa, 'Die Brechungen der modernen japanischen Literatur: Thomas Mann bei Yukio Mishima, Kunio Tsuji und Haruki Murakami', *Neue Beiträge zur Germanistik*, 2.4 (2003), 107–21

Oklianskii, Iurii, *Fedin* (Moscow: Molodaia gvardiia, 1986)

O'Sullivan, Michael, 'Movie Review: *Youth* Cloys, Despite Gorgeous Visuals', *The Washington Post*, 9 December 2015 <https://www.washingtonpost.com/goingoutguide/movies/movie-review-youth-cloys-despite-gorgeous-visuals/2015/12/08/ad82655a-9aac-11e5-94f0-9eeaff906ef3_story.html> [accessed 20 May 2016]

Panizzo, Paolo, 'Ambiguität und Doppelte Optik', in *Thomas Mann Handbuch: Leben, Werk, Wirkung*, ed. Andreas Blödorn and Friedhelm Marx (Stuttgart: Metzler, 2015), pp. 281–83

Parker, Ceri, 'Everything You Need to Know About Davos 2017', 10 January 2017 <https://www.weforum.org/agenda/2017/01/everything-you-need-to-know-about-davos-2017> [accessed 10 June 2019]

Parker, Stephen R., *Peter Huchel: A Literary Life in 20th-Century Germany* (Bern: Peter Lang, 1998)

Passage, Charles E., 'Hans Castorp's Musical Incantation', *Germanic Review*, 38 (1963), 238–56

Peel, Robin, *Writing Back: Sylvia Plath and Cold War Politics* (London: Associated University Presses, 2002)

Phillips, Natalie M., 'Literary Neuroscience and History of Mind: An Interdisciplinary fMRI Study of Attention and Jane Austen', in *The Oxford Handbook of Cognitive Literary Studies*, ed. Lisa Zunshine (Oxford: Oxford University Press, 2015), pp. 55–81

Piatti, Barbara, 'Erich Kästners Davos' <http://www.literatur-karten.ch/de/schauplatz/erich-kaestners-davos> [accessed 10 May 2019]

Pils, Holger, *Thomas Manns 'geneigte Leser': die Publikationsgeschichte und populäre Rezeption der 'Bekenntnisse des Hochstaplers Felix Krull', 1911–1955* (Heidelberg: Universitätsverlag Winter, 2012)

Poe, Edgar Allan, *Poetry and Tales* (New York: Literary Classics of the US, 1984)

Pohland, Vera, *Das Sanatorium als literarischer Ort* (Frankfurt am Main: Peter Lang, 1984)

Potempa, Georg, ed., *Thomas Mann-Bibliographie: Übersetzungen/Interviews* (Morsum/Sylt: Cicero Presse, 1997)

Prager, Debra N., *Orienting the Self: The German Literary Encounter with the Eastern Other* (Rochester, NY: Camden House, 2014)

Pugliese, Cristiana, 'Dangerous Appetites: Food and Deception in "Amundsen"', in *Alice Munro and the Anatomy of the Short Story*, ed. Oriana Palusci (Newcastle upon Tyne: Cambridge Scholars Publishing, 2017), pp. 129–38

Radway, Janice, *Reading the Romance* (Chapel Hill, NC: University of North Carolina Press, 1991)

Radway, Janice, *A Feeling for Books* (Chapel Hill, NC: University of North Carolina Press, 1997)

Reed, T. J., *Thomas Mann: The Uses of Tradition* (Oxford: Clarendon Press, 1996)

Rehm, Stefan, '"Könnte das Massenhafte, das Massengerechte nicht einmal gut sein?" Thomas Mann und die Massenkultur des Literaturmarktes der Weimarer Republik', *Düsseldorfer Beiträge zur Thomas Mann-Forschung*, 2 (2013), 199–209

Reich-Ranicki, Marcel, ed., *Was halten Sie von Thomas Mann?* (Frankfurt am Main: Fischer, 1988)

Reisiger, Hans, '*Der Zauberberg*', *Die Weltbühne*, 21 (1925), 810–15

Reynolds, Matthew, 'Prismatic Translation' <http://www.occt.ox.ac.uk/research/prismatic-translation> [accessed 22 March 2019]

Reynolds, Matthew, Mohamed-Salah Omri, and Ben Morgan, 'Guest Editors' Introduction', *Comparative Critical Studies*, 12 (2015), 147–59

Richards, Donald Ray, *The German Bestseller in the 20th Century: A Complete Bibliography and Analysis 1915–1940* (Bern: H. Lang, 1968)

Richter, Sandra, *Eine Weltgeschichte der deutschsprachigen Literatur* (Munich: Bertelsmann, 2017)

Ridley, Hugh, *The Problematic Bourgeois: Twentieth-Century Criticism on Thomas Mann's 'Buddenbrooks' and 'The Magic Mountain'* (Columbia, SC: Camden House, 1994)

Robbins, Bruce, 'Not So Well Attached', *PMLA*, 132.2 (2017), 371–76

Rodek, Hanns-Georg, 'In diesem Film wird Europas Kultur beerdigt', *Die Welt*, 20 May 2015 <http://www.welt.de/kultur/kino/article141227236/In-diesem-Film-wird-Europas-Kultur-beerdigt.html> [accessed 20 May 2016]

Rose, Jonathan, 'Rereading the English Common Reader: A Preface to a History of Audiences', *Journal of the History of Ideas*, 53.1 (1992), 47–70

Roskothen, Johannes, '"Der Stehkragen sprach": Die unproduktive Spannung zwischen Thomas Mann und Bertolt Brecht—eine Rekonstruktion', *Düsseldorfer Beiträge zur Thomas Mann-Forschung*, 2 (2013), 61–78

Rubin, Jay, *Haruki Murakami and the Music of Words* (London: Vintage, 2005)

Ryan, Marie-Laure, *Narrative as Virtual Reality 2: Revisiting Immersion and Interactivity in Literature and Electronic Media* (Baltimore, MD: Johns Hopkins University Press, 2015)

Scalfari, Eugenio, 'Guardando la Giovinezza dalla montagna incantata', *La Repubblica*, 20 May 2015 <http://www.repubblica.it/spettacoli/cinema/2015/05/20/news/guardando_la_giovinezza_dalla_montagna_incantata-114789588/> [accessed 20 May 2016]

Schaeffer, Jean-Marie, and Ioana Vultur, 'Immersion', in *Routledge Handbook of Narrative Theory*, ed. David Herman, Manfred Jahn, and Marie-Laure Ryan (Abingdon: Routledge, 2010), pp. 237–39

Scharfschwerdt, Jürgen, *Thomas Mann und der deutsche Bildungsroman: Eine Untersuchung zu den Problemen einer literarischen Tradition* (Stuttgart: Kohlhammer, 1967)

Scheuren, Franz Josef, 'Ernst Bertrams Lesespuren im Widmungsexemplar von Thomas Manns *Der Zauberberg*', *Thomas Mann Jahrbuch*, 16 (2003), 55–65

Schlegel, Friedrich, *Kritische Ausgabe seiner Werke*, ed. Ernst Behler and others (Padeborn: F. Schöningh, 1958-), ii: *Charakteristiken und Kritiken I: 1796–1801*, ed. Hans Eichner (1967)

Schlegel, Friedrich, 'From "Athanaeum Fragments" (1798)', trans. P. Firchow, in *Classic and Romantic German Aesthetics*, ed. J. M. Bernstein (Cambridge: Cambridge University Press, 2018), pp. 246–60

Schlutt, Meike, *Der repräsentative Außenseiter: Thomas Mann und sein Werk im Spiegel der deutschen Presse 1898 bis 1933* (Frankfurt am Main: Peter Lang, 2002)

Schröter, Klaus, ed., *Thomas Mann im Urteil seiner Zeit: Dokumente 1891–1955* (Frankfurt am Main: Klostermann, 2000)

Seidlin, Oskar, 'The Lofty Game of Numbers: The Mynheer Peeperkorn Episode in Thomas Mann's *Der Zauberberg*', *PMLA*, 86 (1971), 924–39

Shakespeare, William, *King Lear*, in *The New Oxford Shakespeare: The Complete Works*, ed. Gary Taylor and others (Oxford: Oxford University Press, 2016), pp. 2347–433

Shu, Changshan, *Die Rezeption Thomas Manns in China* (Frankfurt am Main: Peter Lang, 1995)

Sicinski, Michael, 'Paolo Sorrentino: A Medium Talent', *Cinema Scope*, 58 (2014), 17–21

Simmons, Ernest J., *Russian Fiction and Soviet Ideology: Introduction to Fedin, Leonov, and Sholokhov* (New York: Columbia University Press, 1958)

Sina, Kai, 'Reading *The Magic Mountain* in Arizona: Susan Sontag's Reflections on Thomas Mann', *Naharaim*, 9 (2015), 89–107

Skórczewski, Dariusz, 'Dlaczego Paweł Huelle napisał *Castorpa*?', *Teksty Drugie*, 3 (2006), 148–57

Slattery, J. F., 'Thomas Mann und die B.B.C.: Die Bedingungen ihrer Zusammenarbeit 1940-1945', *Thomas Mann Jahrbuch*, 5 (1992), 142–70

Small, Helen, *The Value of the Humanities* (Oxford: Oxford University Press, 2013)

Smith, David Woodruff, 'Phenomenology', in *The Stanford Encyclopedia of Philosophy*, ed. Edward N. Zalta <https://plato.stanford.edu/archives/sum2018/entries/phenomenology> [accessed 18 March 2019]

Söldenwagner, Ronja, 'Love, Gender and Social Pressure in "Amundsen"', in *For (Dear) Life: Close Readings of Alice Munro's Ultimate Fiction*, ed. Eva-Sabine Zehelein (Münster: LIT, 2014), pp. 13–19

Solomon, Robert C., 'On Kitsch and Sentimentality', *The Journal of Aesthetics and Art Criticism*, 49.1 (1991), 1–14

Sontag, Susan, 'Pilgrimage', in *A Companion to Thomas Mann's 'The Magic Mountain'*, ed. Stephen D. Dowden (Columbia, SC: Camden House, 1999), pp. 221–39

Sorrentino, Paolo, dir., *Youth* (StudioCanal, 2016)

Speirs, Ronald, 'Mann, *Der Zauberberg*', *Landmarks in the German Novel (1)*, ed. Peter Hutchinson (Oxford: Peter Lang, 2007), pp. 117–34

Spivak, Gayatri Chakravorty, *Death of a Discipline* (New York: Columbia University Press, 2003)

Sprecher, Thomas, '"Ich glaube an den Fortschritt, gewiß". Quellenkritische Untersuchungen zu Thomas Manns Settembrini-Figur', *Thomas-Mann-Studien*, 11 (1995), 79–116

Sprecher, Thomas, *Davos im 'Zauberberg': Thomas Manns Roman und sein Schauplatz* (Munich: Fink, 1996)

Sprecher, Thomas, 'Kur-, Kultur- und Kapitalismuskritik im *Zauberberg*', *Thomas-Mann-Studien*, 16 (1997), 187–249

Sprecher, Thomas, ed., *Im Geiste der Genauigkeit. Das Thomas-Mann-Archiv der ETH Zürich 1956–2006* (Frankfurt am Main: Klostermann, 2006)

Spyra, Ania, 'Between Theory and Reality: Cosmopolitanism of Nodal Cities in Paweł Huelle's *Castorp*', *Comparative Literature*, 64.3 (2012), 286–99

Stauffer, Andrew M., 'An Image in Lava: Annotation, Sentiment, and the Traces of Nineteenth-Century Reading', *PMLA*, 134.1 (2019), 81–98

Stern, Guy, 'Exile Honoris Causa: The Image of Erich Kästner among Writers in Exile', in *Flight of Fantasy: New Perspectives on Inner Emigration in German Literature 1933–1945*, ed. Neil H. Donahue and Doris Kirchner (New York: Berghahn, 2003), pp. 223–34

Sternburg, Wilhelm von, *Als wäre alles das letzte Mal: Erich Remarque* (Cologne: Kiepenheuer & Witsch, 2010)

Sterritt, David, 'The Best (and Worst) Films of 2015', *Quarterly Review of Film and Video*, 33 (2016), 277–83

Stinson, Emmett, and Beth Driscoll, 'Difficult Literature on Goodreads: Reading Alexis Wright's *The Swan Book*', *Textual Practice*, 26 June 2020 [pre-print] <https://doi.org/10.1080/0950236X.2020.1786718> [accessed 1 May 2021], 1–22

Strecher, Matthew Carl, 'At the Critical Stage: A Report on the State of Murakami Haruki Studies', *Literature Compass*, 8.11 (2011), 856–69

Sunada, Mami, dir., *A Kingdom of Dreams and Madness* (StudioCanal, 2014)

Swale, Alistair, 'Memory and Forgetting: Examining the Treatment of Traumatic Historical Memory in *Grave of the Fireflies* and *The Wind Rises*', *Japan Forum*, 29.4 (2017), 518–36

Swales, Martin, *The German Bildungsroman from Wieland to Hesse* (Princeton, NJ: Princeton University Press, 1978)

Swales, Martin, *Mann: 'Der Zauberberg'* (London: Grant & Cutler, 2000)

Symington, Rodney, 'Music on Mann's Magic Mountain: "Fülle des Wohllauts" and Hans Castorp's "Selbstüberwindung"', in *Echoes and Influences of German Romanticism: Essays in Honour of Hans Eichner*, ed. Michael S. Batts, Anthony W. Riley, and Heinz Wetzel (New York: Peter Lang, 1987), pp. 155–82

Taylor, Ronald, *Kurt Weill: Composer in a Divided World* (London: Simon & Schuster, 1991)

Thomas, Daniel M., *Captain of Death: The Story of Tuberculosis* (Rochester, NY: University of Rochester Press, 1997)

'The Thomas Mann Group Discussion, Week 7—September 23–29' <https://www.goodreads.com/topic/show/1410475-week-7——september-23-29-read-from-the-city-of-god-an-evil-delive> [accessed 15 March 2019]

'Thomas Mann's *The Magic Mountain* Discussion, Chapter VI [October 7 to 27]' <https://www.goodreads.com/topic/show/1406735-4-chapter-vi-october-7-to-27> [accessed 15 March 2019]

'Thomas Mann & The Magic Mountain' <https://www.davos.ch/en/davos-klosters/portrait-image/storytelling/thomas-mann-the-magic-mountain/> [accessed 20 May 2016]

Tompkins, Jane P., ed., *Reader-Response Criticism: From Formalism to Post-Structuralism* (Baltimore, MD: Johns Hopkins University Press, 1980)

Tucker, Brian, 'Performing Boredom in *Effi Briest*: On the Effects of Narrative Speed', *The German Quarterly*, 80.2 (2007), 185–200

Turan, Kenneth, 'In *Youth*, Life Is a Boisterous, Wide-Ranging Musical Composition', *Los Angeles Times*, 3 December 2015 <http://www.latimes.com/entertainment/movies/la-et-mn-youth-review-20151204-column.html> [accessed 20 May 2016]

Turner, Catherine, *Marketing Modernism Between the Two World Wars* (Amherst, MA: University of Massachusetts Press, 2003)

Ulivi, Stefania, 'Cannes, nuovo film di Sorrentino: Successo per *Youth-Giovinezza*', *Corriere della Sera*, 20 May 2015 <http://cinema-tv.corriere.it/cinema/15_maggio_20/cannes-nuovo-film-sorrentino-applausi-buu-giovinezza-97db51a4-fee3-11e4-ab35-8ecb73a305fb.shtml> [accessed 20 May 2016]

Vaget, Hans Rudolf, *Seelenzauber. Thomas Mann und die Musik* (Frankfurt am Main: Fischer, 2006)

Vaget, Hans Rudolf, 'The Making of *The Magic Mountain*', in *Thomas Mann's* The Magic Mountain: *A Casebook*, ed. Hans Rudolf Vaget (Oxford: Oxford University Press, 2008), pp. 13–30

Vaget, Hans Rudolf, '"Politically Suspect": Music on the Magic Mountain', in *Thomas Mann's* The Magic Mountain: *A Casebook*, ed. Hans Rudolf Vaget (Oxford: Oxford University Press, 2008), pp. 123–41

Van Arsdale, Sarah, 'Hobbling Up the Magic Mountain', *Fiction Writers Review*, 20 September 2009 <https://fictionwritersreview.com/essay/hobbling-up-the-magic-mountain-with-illustrations-by-the-author/> [accessed 10 June 2019]

Verbinski, Gore, dir., *A Cure for Wellness* (20th Century Fox, 2017)

Vogt-Praclik, Kornelia, *Bestseller in der Weimarer Republik 1925–1930* (Herzberg: Bautz, 1987)

Völker, Klaus, *Bertolt Brecht. Eine Biographie* (Munich: Hanser, 1976)

Völker, Ludwig, 'Ein Mißverständnis und seine Folgen: "placet experiri" als Wahlspruch Petrarcas in Thomas Manns Roman *Der Zauberberg*', *Euphorion*, 67 (1973), 383–85

Walkowitz, Rebecca, *Born Translated: The Contemporary Novel in an Age of World Literature* (New York: Columbia University Press, 2015)

Wallach, Ruth, 'Konstantin Aleksandrovich Fedin (12 February 1892–15 July 1977)', in *Russian Prose Writers Between the World Wars*, ed. Christine Rydel (Detroit, IL: Thomson Gale, 2003), pp. 88–100

Wasihun, Betiel, 'The Name "Kafka": Evocation and Resistance in Haruki Murakami's *Kafka on the Shore*', *MLN*, 129.5 (2014), 1199–216

Watroba, Karolina, 'World Literature and Literary Value: Is "Global" the New "Lowbrow"?', *The Cambridge Journal of Postcolonial Literary Inquiry*, 5 (2018), 53–68

Watroba, Karolina, 'Blind Spots on the Magic Mountain: Zofia Nałkowska's *Choucas* (1926)', *The Slavonic and East European Review*, 99.4 (2021), 676–98

Watroba, Karolina, 'Reluctant Readers on Mann's *Magic Mountain* (Ida Herz Lecture 2020)', *Publications of the English Goethe Society*, 90.2 (2021), 146–62

Watroba, Karolina, 'The Anxiety of Difficulty: Trying to Read Thomas Mann', *The Point*, 27 (2022) <https://thepointmag.com/criticism/the-anxiety-of-difficulty/> [accessed 25 May 2022]

Webber, Andrew J., 'Mann's Man's World' in *The Cambridge Companion to Thomas Mann*, ed. Ritchie Robertson (Cambridge: Cambridge University Press, 2001), pp. 64–83

Weigand, Hermann J., *'The Magic Mountain': A Study of Thomas Mann's Novel 'Der Zauberberg'* (Chapel Hill, NC: University of North Carolina Press, 1964)

Weisinger, Kenneth, 'Distant Oil Rigs and Other Erections', in *A Companion to Thomas Mann's Magic Mountain*, ed. Stephen Dowden (Columbia, SC: Camden House, 1999), pp. 177–220

Wenzel, Georg, *Gab es das überhaupt? Thomas Mann in der Kultur der DDR* (Gransee: Schwarzdruck, 2011)

Weyand, Björn, *Poetik der Marke: Konsumkultur und literarische Verfahren 1900–2000* (Berlin: De Gruyter, 2013)

Willett, John, *Brecht in Context: Comparative Approaches* (London: Methuen, 1984)

Williams, Seán M., 'Home Truths and Uncomfortable Spaces: Swiss Hotels and Literature of the 1920s', *Forum for Modern Language Studies*, 55.4 (2019), 444–65

Willis, Ika, *Reception* (Abingdon: Routledge, 2018)

Winthrop-Young, Geoffrey, 'Magic Media Mountain: Technology and the Umbildungsroman', in *Reading Matters: Narrative in the New Media Ecology*, ed. Joseph Tabbi and Michael Wutz (Ithaca, NY: Cornell University Press, 1997), pp. 29–52

Wootton, Adrian, 'Blithe Spirit: Paolo Sorrentino on *Youth*', *Sight and Sound*, 26 January 2016 <http://www.bfi.org.uk/news-opinion/sight-sound-magazine/interviews/paolo-sorrentino-youth> [accessed 20 May 2016]

World Economic Forum, 'The Beginning' <https://widgets.weforum.org/history/1971.html> [accessed 10 May 2019]

'The World Economic Forum: A Partner in Shaping History. The First 40 Years, 1971–2010' <http://www3.weforum.org/docs/WEF_First40Years_Book_2010.pdf> [accessed 10 June 2019]

Wysling, Hans, 'Der Zauberberg', in *Thomas-Mann-Handbuch*, ed. Helmut Koopmann, (Stuttgart: A. Kröner, 2001), pp. 397–422

Zander, Peter, *Thomas Mann im Kino* (Berlin: Bertz + Fischer, 2005)

'*Der Zauberberg* (*The Magic Mountain*) by Thomas Mann (Review)', 1 August 2013 <https://tonysreadinglist.wordpress.com/2013/08/01/der-zauberberg-the-magic-mountain-by-thomas-mann-review > [accessed 15 March 2019]

Zhang, Yi, *Rezeptionsgeschichte der deutschsprachigen Literatur in China* (Bern: Peter Lang, 2007)

Zielińska, Monika, *Twórczość Konstantego Fiedina w okresie międzywojennym* (Wrocław: Zakład Narodowy im. Ossolińskich, 1983)

Ziolkowski, Theodore, *Dimensions of the Modern Novel: German Texts and European Contexts* (Princeton, NJ: Princeton University Press, 1969)

Index

For the benefit of digital users, indexed terms that span two pages (e.g., 52–53) may, on occasion, appear on only one of those pages.